MAKING

SCIENCE

MENTORS

MAKING

SCIENCE

MENTORS

A 10-Session Guide for Middle Grades

Bernie Zubrowski, Vivian Troen, and Marian Pasquale

 Education Development Center, Inc.

National Science Teachers Association

National Science Teachers Association

Claire Reinburg, Director
Judy Cusick, Senior Editor
Andrew Cocke, Associate Editor
Betty Smith, Associate Editor
Robin Allan, Book Acquisitions Coordinator

ART AND DESIGN
Will Thomas, Director, Cover and Inside Design

PRINTING AND PRODUCTION
Catherine Lorrain, Director
Nguyet Tran, Assistant Production Manager
Jack Parker, Electronic Prepress Technician

NATIONAL SCIENCE TEACHERS ASSOCIATION
Gerald F. Wheeler, Executive Director
David Beacom, Publisher

Library of Congress Cataloging-in-Publication Data

Zubrowski, Bernie.
  Making science mentors : a 10-session guide for middle grades / Bernie Zubrowski, Vivian Troen, and Marian
Pasquale. -- 1st ed.
     p. cm.
  Includes bibliographical references.
  ISBN-13: 978-1-933531-14-4
  ISBN-10: 1-933531-14-2
  1. Science teachers--Training of--United States. 2. Middle school teachers--Training of--United States. 3. Mentoring in
education--United States. 4. Teachers--In-service training--United States. 5. Science--Study and teaching (Continuing
education)--United States. I. Troen, Vivian, 1940- II. Pasquale, Marian. III. Title.
Q149.U5Z78 2007
510.71'2--dc22
                        2007030152

CONTENTS

Contents

Handouts and Overheads

ACKNOWLEDGMENTS

T his book was a team effort, and the authors extend their gratitude to the many people who contributed in ways large and small both to the work upon which this book is based and to the creation of the manuscript.

First, we must thank the National Science Foundation for its support of the Center for Science Education at Education Development Center, Inc. (EDC) in Newton, Massachusetts, to develop a science-focused mentoring model at a time when many in the field seemed satisfied with generic mentoring programs.

To develop an effective pilot program, we looked for the advice and wisdom of those with expertise in mentoring and those with middle-grades science expertise. Among the best counsel came from experienced science teachers who were "volunteered" by their school districts to be part of the first EDC Middle-Grades Science Mentoring Program. We owe profound thanks to the mentors, the teachers they mentored, and the administrators who supported their participation. The mentors included Mary Archambault, Brenda Busta, Michael Chace, Robert Correia, Susan Dost, Maria Drobiak, Ellen Forman, John Hodsdon, Nancy Hsu, Denise Kochanski, Laura Krich, Roseanne Kurposka, Tammi LaFleur, Priscille LeBlanc, Carol Mardeusz, Pegeen Moreau, Cynthia Quaratiello, Patricia Shattuck, June Thall, Michele Torkomian, Nancy Voght, and Cindy Wrobel.

We also thank our advisers, in particular those who were with us for several years: Sarah Davis, Sharon Feiman-Nemser, Sandy Mayrand, Harold Pratt, and Pam Tickle. In addition, we appreciate the expertise offered by Nancy Ames and Gary Bloom, as well as rotating sets of advisers from Learning Innovations at WestEd, the Massachusetts Department of Education, and the Massachusetts Teachers Association. Together with our evaluators, Ann Brackett and Nancy Hurley of Learning Innovations at WestEd, they challenged us to think hard, think smart, and balance what we knew about adult learning with what we knew about the realities of school life.

Most of all, we thank our colleagues at EDC's Center for Science Education and the team who lived with this program and guide for days, months, and years. Barbara Brauner Berns and Catherine McCulloch worked expertly and tirelessly on both the pilot program and the guide. Millicent Lawton oversaw the writing and editing of the manuscript. Silvia LaVita, Matt Maguire, and Kerry Ouellet provided support in manuscript production. Martha Davis and Karen Worth gave us feedback on early drafts of the manuscript. Beyond EDC, we also thank Peter Sasowsky for his work on the CD-ROM and DVD and Kim Elliott for her production assistance.

As science becomes a higher priority in schools across the country, we hope that attention will be paid to preparing teachers new to teaching middle-grades science. They should all have mentors, and professional development for those mentors is critical. We hope this guide provides a framework for this very important work.

Bernie Zubrowski, Vivian Troen, and Marian Pasquale

A DIFFERENT APPROACH TO MENTORING

This mentoring program is different from others with which you may be familiar. Some mentoring programs cast mentors in social and emotional support roles. Others focus solely on science content. As important as those things are, we chose to create a different kind of mentoring program for middle-grades science teachers.

The National Science Education Standards place significant emphasis on inquiry in teaching and learning (NRC 1996). Just as the field has advocated inquiry-based science teaching, so, too, must we think in terms of an inquiry-based approach to mentoring. Our program uses inquiry as a common thread interwoven among science content, science pedagogy, and mentoring skills. We call this unique fusion inquiry-based mentoring.

Experience has taught us that good science mentors aren't born; they need to be prepared to be good science mentors. We also believe mentors need to have a strong background in science content and science pedagogy before they begin to support other teachers. Finally, mentors need to learn to communicate in a certain way about teaching in order to be effective in guiding their mentees.

Using this guide, you will master inquiry-based mentoring and share it with mentors, who, in turn, will share it with their mentees, all in the name of improving the classroom experiences—and achievement—of students.

Overview

This guide will enable you, as a facilitator, to prepare science mentor teachers from a wide range of backgrounds to support teachers new to middle-grades science. In your work with these mentors, you will model an inquiry-based approach to teaching and learning. The mentors you prepare will, in turn, share this approach with their mentees—who may be recent college graduates, career changers, or new to teaching at the middle grades—and support them in using it with their students.

The program presented in this guide is an adaptation of one designed and facilitated by our team at the Center for Science Education at Education Development Center, Inc. (EDC) in Newton, Massachusetts. EDC's Middle-Grades Science Mentoring Program was a three-year project funded by the National Science Foundation from 2001 to 2004. We piloted the program with more than 50 experienced and new teachers in nine diverse Massachusetts school districts. After we completed the pilot, we adapted the model, by request, for use in several other locations around the country, and we have further adapted it for your use.

In this guide, we describe a one-year program. Although our original pilot project in Massachusetts took place over three years, we realize that most districts and schools cannot allocate such a long period to preparing and sustaining mentors. Thus, we have modified our original mentoring preparation program to fit within one year.

We expect that this guide will be used by facilitators, who, like you, might be a teacher leader or coach, a curriculum coordinator, a department chairperson, a science specialist, a college or university faculty member, or a consultant. You can offer this mentor program as part of a larger project or as a stand-alone initiative of a school, school district, consortia, intermediate agency, or state.

This guide offers some tips for getting a program started ("Getting the Program Started," p. xxxiv), but we cannot anticipate every kind of situation in which this mentoring program might be put to use. It is not within the scope of this book, for instance, to address local policies, politics, or funding issues that may be particular to your situation. We hope you will adapt the guide to fit your specific needs.

Parts of the Guide: What You'll Find Inside

"About The Program, starting on p. xviii, describes the mentoring program. We present the introductory description of the mentoring program in three formats: at a glance, in brief, and in detail. The introduction moves on to describe topics related to getting the program started and to program evaluation.

The introductory section is followed by the lesson plans. These plans guide the facilitator step-by-step through each of the 10 day-long sessions of the training institute that make up the program for creating middle-grades science mentors. For ease of use, each session is self-contained, so that everything the facilitator needs to run that day's session is described in that session's pages.

The lesson plan for each session contains the following features:

1. **A Session Overview.** The Session Overview provides a brief description of the topic and purpose of the session and its intended outcomes.

2. **A Session Snapshot.** The Session Snapshot includes the Agenda for the session. It tells you what you need to do to prepare in advance for the session, and it lists the materials and equipment you will need. (All materials and equipment are inexpensive and commonly available.) Each Snapshot also includes a media list, which details all of the session's overheads, handouts, and video clips, if any. The video clips may be found on the DVD accompanying this guide. The handouts for each of the institute sessions appear both in paper form in Appendix C and in electronic form on the CD-ROM that also comes with this guide.

3. **Descriptions of Activities.** For each session, following the overview and snapshot, we provide a highly detailed description of each day's lesson, starting with a welcome period. These descriptions include *training tips* to help you guide mentors' explorations and reflections, *discussion points* that you can refer to as you introduce concepts and activities, and *science background facts* to help you inform mentors' science investigations. The activity descriptions also contain information on how to use the video clips in the context of the sessions, oversee reflection about the day, guide mentors' preparation for the next session, and conduct a brief session evaluation.

This guide wraps up with three appendixes—The Planning and Observation Protocol, which is unique to this program; a list of resources; and Handouts and Overheads.

On the DVD accompanying this guide are video segments we have produced. They provide examples of standards-based science teaching and allow mentors to develop a common understanding of, and language for, describing high-quality classroom teaching. On the CD-ROM, read the "User's Guide" first. As mentioned, the CD-ROM contains printable electronic copies of all of the handouts and overhead transparencies that are to be used in the sessions. It also contains more information on the mentoring program, an "Inquiry Framework," credits and acknowledgment, and transcripts of the material on the DVD.

The Venn Diagram

The graphic, reproduced in slightly changed form at the beginning of each chapter, (see Figure 1, p. xvi) provides a visual guide to our model of mentoring. It is a modified Venn diagram, showing the components of and relationship between the two major parts of the EDC Middle Grades Science Mentoring Program: science teaching and mentoring. The Venn diagram sits inside a larger oval representing the basic principles and practices underlying the professional development model.

The Outer Oval

In the model, all teaching and learning is grounded in four basic principles and practices:

1. **Questions.** Forming and asking questions and investigating answers to those questions drives learning. Helping someone improve his or her ability to form, ask, and investigate worthwhile questions in a focused area of study is the work of teaching and mentoring.

2. **Collaborative Learning.** Learning is a dynamic and fundamentally collaborative activity. Collaborating with another person allows learners to add the skills, knowledge, understandings, and labor of that other person to their own sets of learning resources and abilities. Together, learners can develop understandings they would not be able to develop alone.

3. **Standards.** Standards can provide a unifying framework within which to focus our teaching and learning efforts. We can refer to specific standards when deciding what to do and how to do it, as well as when we want to assess how well we are doing something. To be truly effective, standards must be understood and accepted.

4. **Formative Assessment.** Formative assessment supports our efforts to evaluate our relationship to a goal, adapt our strategies and practices in an effort to progress toward that goal, and even refine or change the goal. We continually assess our progress in teaching and learning through an iterative process of formulating questions, investigating data in the search for answers, evaluating results, and forming new questions based on those results, all within a set of standards.

The Left Circle

Science Teaching Content and Pedagogical Content Knowledge

The left circle represents the science knowledge, skills, and processes that teachers need to know to help students improve their science knowledge. For example, students need to understand the concepts of heat transfer. For teachers to help students gain that understanding, teachers must understand the concepts themselves and know how to create experiences that help all students learn the concepts, assess whether any particular experience is effective in this regard, and adjust or move forward accordingly.

The Right Circle

Science Mentoring Content and Pedagogical Content Knowledge

This circle represents the science mentoring knowledge, skills and processes that teacher mentors need to know to help teachers improve their science teaching. For mentors to help teachers gain the understanding of how to best teach their students particular science understandings, knowledge, skills, and processes, the mentors must understand these things themselves and know how to create experiences that help teachers learn to assess whether any particular experience has resulted in the lesson goals and adjust their teaching or move forward accordingly. For example, a teacher working on a heat transfer unit may want to investigate whether or not his or her questions are eliciting the type of thinking he or she believes will help the students move to the next level of understanding about the concepts involved. A mentor will need to assess the teacher's background knowledge of questioning, work with the teacher to develop effective experiences to provide knowledge, collect data on the teacher's current questioning practices and student responses, provide feedback to the teacher in a way that supports the teacher to gain an understanding about what is involved in effective questioning, assess whether the teacher has been effective based on the teacher's goals and the students' responses, and plan how to proceed. The mentor needs to keep in mind the goals for student learning and teacher learning at the same time, while also assessing the mentor's own effectiveness in helping the teacher, and, ultimately, the students.

The Center

The Overlap of the Science Teaching and Science Mentoring Circles

The overlapping area in the center represents the ways in which teaching and mentoring practices overlap in our model. As described above, students, teachers, and mentors are engaged in a process of learning. Each group is forming and investigating a question, collecting data, and evaluating and making sense of the data—the steps of inquiry. In mentoring, the steps of this inquiry process are labeled preobservation conference, observation, postobservation conference. Each group is simultaneously involved in the content members are learning and in the processes by and through which they learn. The teacher and the mentor first evaluate the background knowledge of the respective learner—student or teacher—and provide some information or experience to ready the learner for the next step. The teacher or mentor then helps the learner investigate and collect information about some aspect of the content or problem under consideration, such as heat transfer or effective questioning. The teacher or mentor then helps the learner make sense of the information the learner has collected. The processes of learning are parallel; the content differs, though both teacher and mentor need to keep all the learners in mind. A mentor must consider the students' and the teacher's needs for learning, as well as the mentor's own.

Figure 1. The Venn Diagram

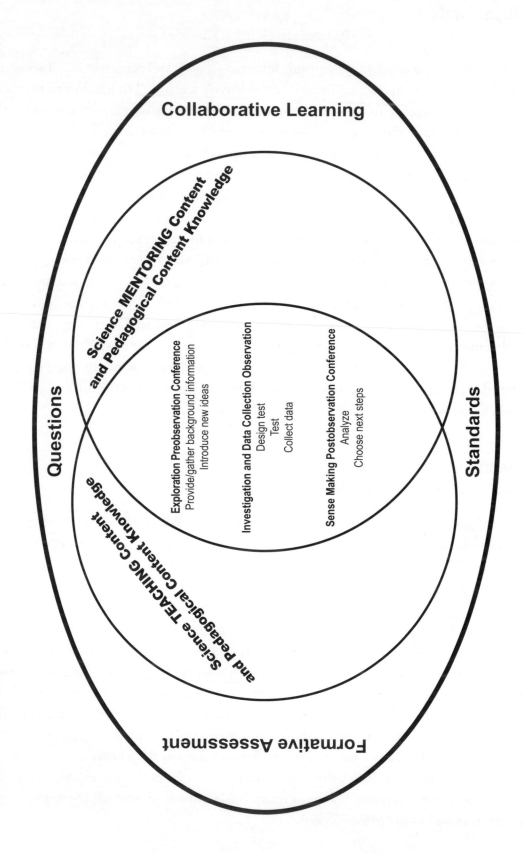

Collaborative Learning

Science MENTORING Content
and Pedagogical Content Knowledge

Science TEACHING Content
and Pedagogical Content Knowledge

Questions

Standards

Formative Assessment

Exploration Preobservation Conference
Provide/gather background information
Introduce new ideas

Investigation and Data Collection Observation
Design test
Test
Collect data

Sense Making Postobservation Conference
Analyze
Choose next steps

The Program at a Glance

Who?	Mentees: New to teaching and/or new to middle grades and/or new to science. Mentors: Five years of science teaching experience; experience in inquiry instruction in middle grades; solid content knowledge; experience doing professional development or working with adult learners.
What?	Inquiry-based Mentoring. Program interweaves science content, science pedagogy, and mentoring skills, using inquiry as a common thread. Follows National Science Education Standards emphasis on inquiry.
When and How Long?	Minimum of one year (with follow-up sessions thereafter). A. Four-day summer mentor preparation institute, followed by a school year of monthly or bimonthly institute sessions and time in school with mentees. B. If the above plan is not possible, mentors can attend program institutes during one school year, practice mentoring with peers, and take on mentees the next year. After the end of either yearlong formal program, mentors continue to meet monthly as a group.
Where?	On- or off-site training sessions and in-school mentoring.

The Program in Brief

Philosophy

Our mentoring program aims to create a professional development experience rich in content, guided by *National Science Education Standards* (NRC 1996) and the *Benchmarks for Science Literacy* (AAAS 1993), and focused on enhancing both teachers' science content knowledge and their practice. The program uses inquiry as an explicit common ground between science teaching and mentoring methods. In other words, it is based on the idea that deep examination of practice by mentors and mentees is inquiry.

Components

You will facilitate the following parts of the program:

- **Training institute sessions.** Each of the 10 sessions lasts a full day, five to seven hours, for a total of approximately 60 hours of preparation. The sessions are built around the hands-on use of published science curricula that target concepts recommended by the National Science Education Standards for grades 5–8. We have selected those institute sessions from our pilot program that we believe are the most critical in terms of developing mentors' familiarity with science content, pedagogical content knowledge, and mentoring skills and strategies. The institute sessions are intended for mentors, but mentees may join in the later sessions.

- **Study groups.** These small discussion groups for mentors, held monthly or biweekly, supplement and complement the training sessions. Study groups enable mentors to reflect on their own practice and that of others in an informal setting.

- **Mentoring activities.** These include both the skill-building activities contained in the institutes and the real-world, in-school mentoring. Guided by the protocol (see Appendix A, The Planning and Observation Protocol), mentors may begin working with mentees as soon as Session 5 and continue doing so throughout the school year. Mentors and mentees should meet formally at least once every two weeks. One meeting a month is acceptable, as long as it is supplemented by informal communication such as e-mails, phone calls, and drop-ins.

Recommended Timetable

We advise that you carry out the sessions and activities on the following timetable:

1. Begin the mentor training during the summer, and offer the first four mentor training sessions (four days) together in a block. By completing these sessions, mentors experience one complete science unit as adult learners, including the development of key science concepts and the inquiry learning cycle. Mentors also acquire the fundamental mentoring strategies and skills that will enable them to begin mentoring that fall.

2. As the school year starts, mentors should use the same science unit from the summer institute in their own classrooms. This allows them to apply their knowledge of, and experience with, the

inquiry learning cycle before they continue with the rest of the sessions, attend study groups, or work with their own mentees. (We used this approach during the pilot project, and it was invaluable for helping mentor teachers develop a better understanding of the science concepts and inquiry pedagogy. When all of the mentors in training teach the unit at the same time, they share a context that results in rich discussions during training sessions and study groups.) If mentors do not have their own classes, encourage them to borrow a class from someone.

3. Hold Session 5 early in the school year to provide a bridge from the summer session experience to the mentoring work, and begin the study groups at about that time. Mentors' work with mentees may commence after Session 5.

4. Offer sessions 6 through 10 as bimonthly weekend institutes (on a Friday and Saturday, for instance, to limit teachers' time away from the classroom). Or you could present them as one-day sessions each month or use whatever schedule works in your particular context. In any case, alternate the sessions with study groups (held monthly or every two weeks), so that there is some kind of mentoring program activity on a monthly basis to maintain momentum and familiarity. As a forum for examination of practice, the study groups help mentors immediately apply in their classrooms what they are learning in the institute sessions.

Following the first year of institutes and mentoring, mentors should come together once a month to discuss ongoing issues and challenges. The program director or facilitator or a principal or district-level science administrator could run these forums—or the mentors themselves could rotate leadership.

Alternate Program

If you cannot implement the program in the way described, you can use the following option:

1. Begin the mentor preparation program with the start of the school year. Hold sessions every other month (some during weekends), and convene study groups in alternate months until all 10 sessions have been completed.

2. As soon as possible in the school year, but certainly by Session 6, mentors should begin using the science curriculum unit from the earlier training sessions in their own classrooms.

3. After Session 5, have the mentors start to practice mentoring with a peer mentor from the institute sessions.

4. At the beginning of the next school year, assign mentors to take on mentees. We suggest a mentor work with a mentee for at least a year.

5. It is helpful for mentors to continue meeting as a group on a monthly basis to discuss their mentoring experiences and to provide each other support.

The Program in Detail
Program Goals

As a facilitator, you will seek to achieve the following program goals:

1. To use inquiry as an explicit common ground between science teaching and mentoring methods; that is, show mentors and mentees that deep examination of their practice *is* inquiry.

2. To improve the ability of both veteran (mentor) teachers and less-experienced (mentee) teachers to teach science based on the National Science Education Standards and the Benchmarks for Science Literacy (or based on state frameworks that are consistent with the national documents).

3. To enhance practice among mentors and mentees in a way that will help their middle-grades students have a better grasp of science and scientific processes and a more complete understanding of the world around them.

4. To increase the mentors' expertise and to support them as they practice the art of teaching and increase their science content knowledge.

5. To enable mentors to make their own teaching practices explicit for mentees.

Program Concepts

Inquiry as the Common Ground Between Science Teaching and Mentoring

School culture and working conditions often conspire against the support of teachers. Yet, support is what new teachers—or teachers new to a discipline like science—both want and need. "What new teachers want in their induction is experienced colleagues who will take their daily dilemmas seriously, watch them teach and provide feedback, help them develop instructional strategies, model skilled teaching, and share insights about students' work and lives. What new teachers need is sustained, school-based professional development—guided by expert colleagues…." (Johnson and Kardos 2002, p. 13).

We couldn't agree more. Indeed, Sharon Feiman-Nemser recommends that mentors approach mentoring as an educational endeavor focused on the "intellectual and practical challenges of teaching for understanding" (Feiman-Nemser et al. 1999, p. 8). In this type of mentoring, mentors "think about mentoring as a joint inquiry into teaching and learning" (ibid).

In that vein, our program goes beyond an emphasis on science teaching or on generic mentoring and focuses even more on the overlap and synergy between the two. In our program, learning how to teach science and learning how to be a mentor continually reinforce one another because they share the common ground of inquiry.

Allow us to put this in practical terms. Teachers must think and make decisions on their feet.

Because our inquiry-oriented approach to practice has the mentors examine their experience, generate alternatives, and evaluate actions, they are able to develop problem-solving skills that are like bread and butter to teachers who must continually make complex decisions influenced by context.

In our program, mentors approach teaching and their mentoring work as an inquiry into practice. They learn skills and strategies that they use in each of several different interactions with their mentees: coplanning, conferences prior to classroom observations, classroom observations themselves, and postobservation conferences. This process of inquiry into another teacher's teaching involves the same phases as inquiry in the classroom: *exploration* takes place through coplanning and preobservation conferences; *investigation and data collection* take place through classroom observations of teachers and students; and *sense making* occurs in postobservation conferences.

Inquiry Learning Cycle

The inquiry teaching and learning framework we use is one of guided inquiry. On a science inquiry teaching continuum, it lies somewhere in the middle, between open inquiry on one end in which students are the main instigators and designers of an investigation and a teacher-centered, cookbook approach on the other end. As we define it, inquiry has three main phases:

1. In the first phase, *exploration*, students get acquainted with a problem or phenomenon and contribute ideas and questions about it.

2. During the *investigation and data-collection* phase, students carry out investigations, measurements, and observations and record the data gathered.

3. Throughout the *sense-making* phase, teachers and students discuss the usefulness of the data, interpret the data, and develop explanations and understandings.

The First Phase of Inquiry: Exploration

Traditional curriculum books or published programs often give inquiry very little attention at all. Even in many inquiry-based programs, the exploratory phase is often limited or omitted. Students have very few opportunities to get truly acquainted with a scientific or technical phenomenon.

Exploration is, however, a critical phase. It provides students with an opportunity to develop experience with a phenomenon and to begin to sort out what they are witnessing. This phase also gives students and teachers a chance to develop a shared understanding of students' prior knowledge (the accurate and the mistaken).

Sometimes, students experience a phenomenon through direct manipulation of materials. At other times, exploration involves close observation, such as with living organisms. Or, exploration may involve getting acquainted with multiple visual images, such as satellite images of cloud movement, to begin to develop some sense of weather patterns.

Knowing how to structure an exploratory phase is very challenging for new teachers or teachers making the transition from a traditional stand-and-deliver teaching approach to one that is more inquiry-based. What may appear to be too unstructured, open ended, or even chaotic to the teacher actually has a subtle structure that directs the students' attention and exploration. Learning how to work with students during this phase is also challenging. Teachers need to stand back and observe, yet know when to intervene at the right moment, based on student behaviors and actions. So, our mentoring program uses specific investigations within the curriculum-based training sessions. These investigations help mentors gain a better understanding of the exploratory phase and how they—and their mentees—can function in an effective manner.

The Second Phase of Inquiry: Investigation and Data Collection

As students gain more experience with any given phenomenon, they can move into this phase by generating questions, making predictions, and designing and carrying out investigations. Then, they can gather data through measurement or observation, record and represent the results in a useful way, and report findings to others. Teachers guide this process, talking over with students what they can investigate and identifying areas to which students need to pay attention to develop an understanding of targeted concepts.

Engaging students in data gathering and representation are common practices, even in traditional approaches to laboratory science teaching, but deciding how to represent data is often unexamined. Yet, how data are represented can make a difference in how students make sense of those data. The information that students collected through investigation needs to be in a form that helps them draw reasonable conclusions and develop explanations. If experimental results are unclear, students cannot make firm conclusions and their conceptualization is handicapped. Teachers need to work with students to determine how to represent data. Graphs and drawings represent two ways that raw numbers or observations can be put together to help students discover patterns or relationships and confirm or reject an idea.

Too often, students collect data and are not sure why they are doing it. Teachers need to help students understand the need for collecting data, placing it in the larger context of the investigation. In our program's institute sessions, the facilitator guides mentors in explicitly examining pedagogical practices—especially relating to the need for students to obtain clear results and practice good experimental procedures—and helps the mentors relate the practices to their own teaching. As a result, mentors become more effective at this stage of inquiry and can better support their mentees.

The Third Phase of Inquiry: Sense Making

Once students move from the exploratory phase through the investigation and data-collection phase of inquiry, they need to make sense of the results they collect. During the sense-making phase, teachers need to help students make their understandings explicit. This usually takes place through interactive discussion.

Sense making is one of the most challenging parts of inquiry for most teachers and learners. Indeed, a common complaint among those who observe teachers is that teachers spend too little time with follow-up discussions, conduct them at an intellectual level lower than students' capabilities, and tend to deliver "the answers" rather than debate the claims and evidence.

It can be difficult for teachers to know how to guide students to interpretations, explanations, and conceptualizations, rather than taking over and telling students what they are supposed to know. It takes a great deal of skill, and an ability to improvise, to carry guidance out confidently and successfully. It also involves a keen sensitivity to students' current thinking, a good grounding in the science content, and knowing how and when to ask probing questions.

Again, our program's training sessions deal extensively with these issues, giving mentors hands-on opportunities to develop these skills, which will allow them to assist their mentees, in turn. For example, if the collected data show a pattern, it is up to the teacher to spur student discussion beyond statements that a pattern exists and instead ask, "Why?" or "What might happen next?"

The Mentoring Cycle: Incorporating Phases of Inquiry Into Teaching Practice

Our approach—a mentoring cycle that incorporates the phases of inquiry—keeps mentors and mentees focused on assessing and refining teaching practice. Mentors guide their mentees' process of reflection on practice through conversations. That includes prompting mentees to do inquiry about their own teaching—asking questions about their goals, what students are learning, and what evidence there is to support their conclusions. These conversations highlight the relationship between instructional practice and student performance. Simultaneously, mentors peel back the layers of their own practice, permitting insights that benefit their mentees, themselves, and their students.

The phases of inquiry into teaching practice are built into the mentoring cycle:

- *Coplanning,* which represents the exploration phase in inquiry, offers a chance for the mentor and mentee to sit down together and to think about the concepts and skills the mentee's lesson will help students develop and how they fit into an overall science unit.

- Along with coplanning, the *preobservation conference* constitutes inquiry exploration. In it, the mentor asks the mentee a series of questions about the upcoming lesson, and they agree on a focus for the mentor's attention during the observation.

- *Classroom observation*, as the investigation phase of putting inquiry into practice, provides a chance for the mentor to observe an actual class with students, during which the mentee either leads a lesson that the mentor and mentee discussed earlier or, less often, watches the mentor model a lesson.

- In the *postobservation conference,* the mentor and mentee discuss what occurred during the observation; this conference represents the sense-making phase of inquiry into practice.

Now, we'll discuss these mentor-mentee interactions in greater detail.

Coplanning

Coplanning is the most important step in the multistage mentoring cycle. Mentors and mentees can cover many issues in a planning session, such as whole units and individual lessons, the best pedagogical approaches, students' preconceptions and misconceptions, assessing what students know and can do, and how to handle issues around materials. Coplanning also offers mentors a chance to assume a leadership role. For example, a mentor might discuss how the mentee's planned curriculum covers a given lesson and, by contrast, how the mentor would recommend the lesson be done to better address the intent of state standards. In so doing, mentors convey best practices to mentees. Mentors, however, are not evaluating mentees; instead, they are acting as coaches.

> **Given the limited time teachers have to plan and hold conversations with colleagues about their practice, we know that finding common planning time is difficult, but it is absolutely necessary.**

Coplanning can prove useful in predicting opportunities or heading off problems in advance—a great gift to mentees or to any teacher. If planning is done right, mentees are not always playing catch-up—they are not always troubleshooting on the fly. Planning can also be a great way to address classroom management. The better a lesson is, the more engaged the students are and the more likely they are to focus on learning.

We developed our mentor activities in accordance with our belief that teachers should avoid simply implementing a given curriculum in a mechanical way. We urge mentors (and mentees) to think about teaching differently: to prioritize goals and clarify the content that they want students to learn. In a planning conversation, the mentor should guide the mentee in looking at how the lesson's or unit's content aligns with state curriculum frameworks. Next, the pair might look at how conceptual understanding can arise from student investigations and sense-making discussions.

When it comes to lesson planning, we try to impress upon mentors that it is important for teachers to abandon the common practice of planning lesson by lesson. Traditionally, with each lesson planned and taught in isolation, the curriculum becomes full of stand-alone activities. As one of our team likes to put it, "You don't want science to be a series of magic tricks for kids."

Instead, the idea is to plan a whole unit at once, with each lesson having a logical place in the larger framework. In planning conversations, mentors can help mentees keep in mind the targeted concepts that they want to convey, as well as the concepts' places in the unit—even how they fit with what students learn in the preceding and succeeding grade levels. Mentors and mentees should also keep in mind assessments for determining what the students know and can apply from their learning.

Inquiry is central to our approach to mentoring, but even the most well-intentioned teachers can find it challenging to keep it front and center in each lesson. A coplanning session can be one place for a mentor to help the mentee understand and incorporate inquiry.

When it comes to inquiry, a mentor can also help a mentee overcome the limitations of texts selected by the district. It can be tempting for a less-experienced teacher to jump right into an activity, especially if that's what the textbook suggests. In a planning session, however, a mentor can discuss with the mentee the importance of, say, exploration.

For example, a textbook might describe a traditional activity in which students bounce balls on the floor and measure how high they go. But, a standards-based lesson would begin with an exploratory phase. This phase might involve allowing students to explore the materials, trying different balls and bouncing surfaces to generate ideas and questions before beginning a more formal investigation of the phenomenon.

During coplanning sessions, mentors and mentees can also talk about the science content of the curriculum. Teachers need to have the science clear in their heads—especially when they lead students through the sense-making phase of inquiry.

In science, teachers often encounter student misconceptions. For instance, in an investigation around ice cream making, some misconceptions will arise about heat transfer. Does the light from a fluorescent bulb contribute to the melting of ice cubes? In a coplanning session, the mentor might suggest the mentee organize a discussion with students that would allow the mentee to identify such misconceptions and address them by, for example, setting up a controlled investigation to test a prediction.

For science teachers, the materials needed for a hands-on science lesson can be a source of anxiety: How do I set up the materials and prepare for the lesson? Will I lose control of the class? Will students be out of their seats? Will the classroom become messy? In a coplanning session, mentors can share strategies about materials with mentees or discuss how to organize students into cooperative groups. If the mentees have concerns about carrying out lessons, mentors might offer to model the lesson first.

The Preobservation Conference

For the mentor, the preobservation conference represents a chance to express a genuine interest in thinking about another person's practice and, for the mentee, it offers a chance to "get inside" his or her own practice. For reasons discussed earlier, this kind of examination of professional practice can seem foreign, but the mentor should try to convey to the mentee that the two of them are investigating some very complicated intellectual work: student learning and teaching practice.

Mentors and mentees should use the following questions as a starting point for every observation. They can add more, or more detailed, questions if desired:

• What are students supposed to be learning and what critical-thinking skills will you address?

• In which phase of the inquiry cycle is this lesson?

• How do the teaching and learning activities promote the desired learning outcomes?

• How will you check for student understanding during the lesson, and what are the strategies for embedded assessment?

• What kind of data would you like the observer to collect?

Coplanning is about the mentee receiving help with a lesson or unit. In the preobservation conference, the mentor-mentee pair focuses on a particular aspect of a lesson or unit that is troubling the mentee. For instance, the two might discuss how to begin a lesson.

Together, the mentor and mentee can review the lesson to be observed, including its goals, its structure, and what the mentee wants the mentor to look for in terms of teaching and student learning. A mentee might decide to examine the pedagogy in a given lesson, perhaps choosing a particular area, such as "Are my questions open-ended enough?" Or, a mentee might strive to hone his skills at helping students interpret data collected in an earlier investigation. The Planning and Observation Protocol helps provide a framework for discussion in this area: "How does the teacher help the students interpret the data?" Delving further, the protocol asks, "What types of questions does the teacher ask in this phase?"

It is preferable for the mentor to observe a lesson that the mentee and mentor have planned together. After all, there is a difference between a lesson as planned and a lesson as executed. Teaching is a form of live theater, and interactions with students can prompt a midstream change in the plan. Moment-to-moment judgments and decisions made while teaching form a large portion of an experienced teacher's expertise, and that expertise can be shared, to great benefit, with the mentee.

Early in their teaching careers, mentees can feel that discipline and behavior are among the most pressing issues they face. In the mentoring journal kept by one mentor with whom we worked, the mentor recorded the mentee's "despondency over behavior issues" and reflected a plan to schedule an observation of the mentee's difficult class "just to get a feel for the class and why it's a problem [and] possible steps to solving the problem."

The Classroom Observation

For mentors watching a lesson taught by a mentee, the classroom observation is not a time to make judgments but, instead, is an opportunity to record what occurs in the classroom during a lesson—a "just the facts" approach. Mentors should script what they see and hear in the portion of the lesson they were asked to focus on by the mentee. In scripting, mentors create a transcript of conversations and events that includes student learning and behavior as well as teacher behavior. Scripting eliminates generalizations or judgments.

Sticking to the facts can be challenging. But, ideally, mentors can hand over to mentees the notes they took. If mentees can see a page with facts only, it builds trust with mentees, because nothing is being hidden. Then, during the postobservation conference, mentors can discuss interpretations or analysis.

The Postobservation Conference

Within a day or two after the mentor's observation of the mentee's lesson, the pair comes back together to discuss what occurred. This is a potentially powerful conversation, full of valuable feedback for the mentee, and every effort should be made to hold it as soon as possible after the observation.

It is up to the mentor to help the mentee make sense of the data that the mentor recorded during the observation. The mentor has to help the mentee tease out the take-home message.

First, the mentor shares data about the lesson. Next, the pair analyzes that data together, based upon the focus agreed upon in the preobservation conference. Questions for the mentee might include, "Do you think that the students learned what you wanted them to learn?" and "What is the evidence?"

Then, if necessary, the pair addresses any other issues that arose. They also touch on possible changes to the lesson, methods for building on the day's lesson, and next steps in planning, teaching, and observing.

The postobservation conference is also a time for the mentor to celebrate the successes the mentee had in the classroom: what went well or, at least, better than expected. In addition, the mentor and mentee can use the conference to set up an agenda for the next planning session or conference, including homework to be completed by the teachers in the interim.

Mentors and mentees should meet formally at least once every two weeks and should check in with one another informally through phone calls, e-mails, and quick visits more often than that.

Program Components

Participation by mentors and mentees in all components of the program should be required in order to meet the goals of improved expertise and support for teachers.

Institute Sessions

Curriculum Units

We built the 10 institute sessions around the hands-on use of published, standards-based, science curricula (written for grades 6–8) that target concepts recommended by the National Science Education Standards for the span of grades 5–8.

We use standards-based units as a context in which mentors experience the development of these targeted science concepts through carefully sequenced, developmentally appropriate activities and investigations. We have selected those institute sessions from our pilot program that we believe are the most critical in terms of developing mentors' familiarity with science content, pedagogical content knowledge, and mentoring skills and strategies. In each science session, and throughout the use of the curriculum unit, mentors experience the inquiry learning cycle (exploration, investigation and data collection, and sense making) as adult learners. To hone their mentoring techniques, mentors analyze practice by inquiring into their own teaching as well as into the practice of others.

Regardless of the curriculum used in the schools in which your mentors teach, we encourage use of the units presented in this guide. They highlight the inquiry skills and habits of mind students need to develop and practice for success in science now, in high school, and beyond. These units model good development of concepts and sound pedagogy, which you might not find in other curricula, and they can serve as templates that mentors can use to design their own lessons and units.

> You may prefer to use other curriculum units in the sessions. If that's the case, make sure they are standards-based inquiry units, they focus on important concepts, and they can be used without changing the structure of our investigations and sessions.

The first institute (Sessions 1 through 4) uses *Ice Cream Making and Cake Baking,* a physical science unit (Zubrowski 1994). The investigations contained in the unit, in which the mentors engage as adult learners, develop concepts related to heat transfer: conduction, convection, and radiation. Many middle school students find it difficult to understand heat transfer. Thus, that mentors and mentees feel secure in their understanding of these ideas is important, so they can help students develop their thinking about conduction, convection, and radiation.

Session 5 is a transition session. It offers a segue both for mentors beginning their mentoring practice and for the shift into the life sciences curriculum unit. Sessions 6 through 10 allow mentors to investigate life science concepts through the context of a pond. The pond environment lends itself to the development of many different life science concepts relating to populations and ecosystems, structure and function in living systems, and diversity and adaptation of organisms. The focus over these five sessions is on macroinvertebrates and concepts relating to form and function. EDC's *Investigating Pond Organisms* (Neo/Sci 2006) is the source for this unit.

We recommend that mentors keep a science notebook during the institute sessions. The notebook, a blank spiral notebook or school composition book, has several purposes. It allows mentors to take notes on their thinking (such as predictions), the process, and the data of the science investigations. It is a place to record tables, charts, and graphs, and, during subsequent sessions, it provides an example of how student notebooks should look in terms of content and organization.

Mentors also record their Classroom Connections ideas in their notebooks, as is described in the lesson plans for the sessions. As the name implies, the Classroom Connections segments of the sessions provide mentors with opportunities to connect the conceptual focus of each session to the classroom. For example, in Session 2, mentors design their own investigations. In the Classroom Connections section of that session, mentors think about what opportunities they give their students to design their own investigations.

The Planning and Observation Protocol

The Planning and Observation Protocol (see Appendix A) guides mentors' interactions with their mentees—including classroom observations and conferences—and helps mentors and mentees plan and conduct their own lessons. The protocol functions as a framework for thinking. For example, that can mean thinking about which phase of inquiry needs to be addressed in a lesson, what needs to be assessed and how, or how to respond to data collected previously.

The protocol expands each component of the inquiry learning cycle with a list of questions that frame the expected roles and behaviors of teachers and students during each of the three phases of scientific inquiry: exploration, investigation and data collection, and sense making. (As discussed earlier, these are also the phases of inquiry into teaching practice.) The protocol also includes expectations around classroom infrastructure—classroom management and embedded and formal (formative and summative) assessment.

Use of the protocol is, itself, inquiry into teaching practice, and it represents an explicit common ground between the ways educators should teach science to students and the approaches mentors should use to advise mentees on pedagogical practices. In short, we use inquiry to teach inquiry.

The Role of Video

We use video to promote reflection on, and analysis of, practice. The videos we provide show-case real teachers unknown to your mentors; therefore, the mentors can feel comfortable and open about observing, analyzing, and discussing what has occurred in those classrooms. Within this comfort zone, mentors learn how to conduct focused, data-gathering observations, and they develop skills to support data-driven reflection on teaching and student learning.

You will find three sets of video segments on the DVD that we have included. Each set contains three related clips, together representing the "mentoring cycle" of a single science lesson:

1. the preobservation conference between a mentor and mentee,

2. the classroom lesson taught by a mentee, and

3. the postobservation conference, again between a mentor-mentee pair.

The classroom video segments tie in with the preparation sessions because they show teachers teaching lessons from the curriculum units that mentors experience in the sessions. The clips are not meant to show perfect teaching or mentoring; rather, they represent a spectrum of expertise in those endeavors.

The videotaped classroom episodes can also be used as the basis for real-time observations. You can use the pre- and postobservation conferences included on the DVD as examples to discuss and analyze in order to build common understandings, language, and skills for mentoring. The lesson plans that follow in this guide provide all of the necessary steps and structure for taking mentors through these activities.

Eventually, you can encourage mentors to record their own teaching and mentoring interactions, first for their own viewing, and then for group analysis and reflection. And, once they begin mentoring, mentors may help their mentees put their teaching on video, too.

Mentoring Journal and Other Tools

In the lesson plans for the sessions, you will find a variety of written tools and organizers that appear as handouts for your use as well as the use of the mentors and mentees.

One example of these is the mentoring journal. We recommend using a mentoring journal to help organize the thoughts and work of mentors and mentees when they meet—and to preserve a record of their discussions. The journal is a sheet of paper that has space for a description of the focus of the discussion, other comments, the mentor's next steps, and the mentee's next steps in the improvement of their teaching practice. The right side of the sheet has a copy of the The Planning and Observation Protocol to focus the conversation on standards-based teaching. Mentor-mentee pairs can use the mentoring journal for any of the mentoring cycle's steps: coplanning, preobservation conference, classroom observation, and postobservation conference. In essence, the journal is a formative assessment tool for the work of mentors and mentees.

One collaborative journal from a planning session between a mentor-mentee pair we worked with shows that they used their meeting to focus on several pedagogical issues. The mentor's notes read, "Planning assessment of unit on photosynthesis, respiration, and cell cycle processes, based on inquiry style and emphasizing skills needed for standards-based … testing, e.g., interpreting diagrams."

Study Groups

It is critical for the improvement of teaching and learning for teachers to get together to talk as professionals about professional issues. Although such discussions—and the time to have them—are becoming more common than they once were, they are not widespread enough to erase the isolation of teaching. Alone with their students behind closed doors, many teachers have time only to focus on getting through the daily business of school. Intellectual conversations among adults in schools are not a priority; teachers often do not get the chance to sit down and think deeply about their practice.

By contrast, study groups enable mentors to reflect on their own practice and that of others in an informal setting. The study-group discussions are designed to center on the curriculum units the mentors are experiencing as adult learners in the sessions and on professional and research articles about mentoring and science teaching and learning. Study groups provide a bridge between the curriculum units and scientific inquiry the mentors are learning in the institute sessions on the one hand and the real-world experiences in their classrooms on the other. With the study groups as a forum for examination of practice, the mentors can apply right away in the classroom what they are learning in the training sessions.

Even if you do not follow our recommendation to have mentors teach concurrently in their classrooms the same science curriculum units they learn in institute sessions, study groups can still be of value. They represent an additional opportunity for the mentors to talk about a host of issues, including best practices, the research literature, student work, and their mentoring experiences. An added bonus is that the curriculum units create common discussion ground in the study groups—an icebreaker for the mentors, who may not know one another as they come into the program.

Study groups add an invaluable dimension to the mentoring program, greatly enriching mentors' experiences. A study group can be a place to hear about new ideas or techniques and express skepticism—or excitement.

An anecdote from our pilot program provides an example of how productive a study group can be after participants have been meeting together for some time. One mentor was doing a unit on planets, but she was dissatisfied with it. Her study group offered to critique the unit to try to improve it. The discussion bubbled over with suggestions and caveats. The teacher of the unit madly took notes. At the end, she was beaming. "The thinking, the discussion—it was remarkable," our EDC staff facilitator recalled. "They really were a community of learners." The teacher's comment? "This is going to be one helluva unit!"

Managing Study-Group Logistics

We recommend that mentors gather in study groups either monthly or biweekly, alternating with the institute sessions. In our pilot, we offered study groups in each of the months between our bimonthly training institutes (so about four times during the school year). That way, the mentors in the program met every month for either one purpose or the other, maintaining momentum and familiarity.

Our study groups met for two hours at a time after school, and participating mentors hosted the groups in their classrooms on a rotating basis. Certainly, there are other options, and your choice will necessarily take into consideration how your program and schools are structured.

To keep the size of a study group manageable, you might need to divide your total group of mentors. Each of our study groups had about 8 to 10 participants. Yours should be no larger than that.

At first, a program facilitator should run each session, but the idea is to get the mentors to take on the role of initiating topics for discussion. Many teachers are not familiar or comfortable at first with that role, so it can be a challenge to get them to guide the conversation. However, it does happen with time and as mentors develop an increasing sense of comfort and camaraderie.

The facilitator could begin a discussion of assigned readings by asking some open-ended questions. Generally, our study group discussion stayed close to the content of the articles that facilitators assigned in advance, with classroom issues coming up as warranted. During the life of our study groups, topics included what inquiry is, how to ask good questions of students, and the challenges of mentoring other teachers.

In our pilot program, we had mentors participating from a variety of school districts. Although this created some challenges in the training institutes, it turned out to be very helpful when it came to study groups. For one thing, it kept the small-group discussion from turning into sessions devoted to district gossip or complaints about bureaucracy. We have since learned from trying to replicate this mentoring program in a large urban district that gossip and complaints are exactly what happened when all of the teachers in the study group were from the same school district.

In addition, having mentors from different districts—with varying socioeconomic and demographic profiles and a range of levels of achievement on the state tests—gave the mentors insight into communities and experiences that were foreign to them. They learned that, regardless of background, students had some of the same conceptual hurdles to overcome in learning science.

There was also freedom in not knowing everyone initially. The conversation about practice could be more freewheeling, candid, and analytical than if the mentors felt the need to be circumspect or diplomatic in their remarks.

Getting the Program Started

Based on our experience preparing and supporting middle-grades science teacher mentors, we have compiled a few tips to help program directors get programs off to the right start. You may already have a mentoring program or programs in your state, district, or school, so this may help you examine certain program components. If you do not, this section is intended to help you think about getting a program started. (If you are not the program director, please pass this material on to the appropriate person.)

However, this section is *not* meant to be an exhaustive "how to," describing every aspect of program planning, design, or implementation. Instead, we focus on two key areas: (1) selecting mentors and mentees and (2) involving principals and other key administrators. We close this section with a few words about communication. Naturally, you may need to devote time and attention to a host of additional matters, including planning well in advance of the program's recommended summer start, setting aside the necessary fiscal resources; establishing schedules, developing flexible staff assignments, and integrating the science mentoring program with other mentoring and induction programs, professional development opportunities, and reform-based science initiatives. Last, but far from least, you'll need to inform new middle-grades science teachers that support is on the way.

Selecting Mentors and Mentees

Choosing the Mentors

Teachers who become effective mentors possess certain characteristics. They include, but are certainly not limited to, the following:

- A minimum of five years of science teaching experience

- Experience in inquiry instruction at the middle grades or use of research-informed curriculum programs that promote inquiry instruction

- Solid content knowledge

- Outstanding teaching skills and effectiveness in classroom management

- Experience working with colleagues through such means as professional development, analysis of student work, curriculum adoption committees, standards review, and development of assessments

- The ability to communicate well with students and colleagues

- Proven leadership in the profession

- Experience with, and openness to, collaborating with other teachers

- Flexibility, open-mindedness, and empathy

- Experience with diverse learners

We believe the most critical elements are a mentor's knowledge of subject matter and pedagogy as well as proven expertise in working with other adults.

Clarifying the Mentor's Role

Different settings define mentors in a variety of ways. This makes it very important for you to determine early on the experience and knowledge you want the mentors to have and the preparation they need to support new teachers.

You must also define the role you expect mentors to fill. Knowing this early on prevents problems later. For example, in most programs, mentors do not evaluate the mentees; rather, they function as coaches.

The different mentoring activities that emerged for mentors in our program ran the gamut. The list below offers some examples of different topics or activities our mentors reported covering or taking part in with their mentees during one specific year of mentoring:

- *Planning:* serving as a sounding board for ideas, reviewing science curriculum requirements, discussing science concepts, planning lessons, discussing how mentor and mentee can use the The Planning and Observation Protocol, strategizing about classroom management.

- *Student learning:* how students learn through science inquiry, how students can most effectively learn particular concepts.

- *Assessment:* how best to assess student learning of science concepts, developing student assessments, examining state assessment data, reviewing results of student assessments and implications for instruction.

- *Classroom teaching:* observing the mentee and giving feedback, observing the mentor and giving feedback, demonstrating lessons for the mentee, coteaching.

- *Professional development:* referring the mentee to other resources, attending professional development activities together and discussing what was learned.

- *Parent-student issues:* strategizing about needs of specific students, strategizing about communication with parents.

Selecting the Mentees

Responsibility for matching mentors with mentees usually resides at the site level. We urge you to use a transparent process, regardless of the selection method.

Our experience is that matching mentors and mentees by school, grade, and subject taught is most helpful, although not essential. In large schools, this may be possible; in small schools, creativity will be required.

Deciding who will receive mentoring support has implications for the type of preparation mentors need. Will the mentees be first- or second-year teachers, teachers just out of higher education or alternative certification programs, teachers new to a grade level, teachers new to science education, or career changers? Also, you must address whether the new teachers have strong or weak science backgrounds. If they are midcareer teachers, are they just beginning to teach at the middle grades? Our experience demonstrated that mentees' greatest struggles with teaching science were lack of science knowledge, letting go of particular teaching strategies, and feeling overwhelmed.

You should let mentors and mentees know what to expect in the program, including what kind of time commitment is involved. Make clear that the interactions between the mentor and mentee are confidential and that it is not the mentor's role to evaluate the performance of the mentee teacher.

Engaging Principals and Other Key Administrators

In their efforts to improve science education, reformers have often inadvertently left administrators on the sidelines. Yet principals, especially, are crucial to the success of the instruction that goes on in their buildings. A science mentoring program cannot succeed without the engagement of the mentors' and mentees' principals.

Middle school principals often find themselves overburdened and with little preparation for overseeing science instruction. They may have little or no expertise in middle-grades science, yet they must supervise science teachers and oversee the identification and selection of science curricula and assessments.

Such hurdles make it absolutely critical for directors of mentoring programs to be explicit and intentional in reaching out to principals and engaging them in the operations and expectations of the science mentoring program. The importance of their instructional leadership cannot be overstated.

In addition, if your school district is one in which power is concentrated in a central or regional office, then you must reach out to engage those administrators, as well as those on the school level. For mentoring to be successful, administrators on the school and district levels must

1. understand the implications of inquiry-based science education on teaching and learning,

2. support mentors through planning time and other incentives, and

3. support a school culture that has collegiality as a norm.

Building alliances with principals and district administrators is essential if you are to combat the ingrained culture and organization that threaten to block this rigorous mentoring program. Those blocks can include the lack of planning time for mentors and mentees, no or limited release time for mentors, too many new teachers assigned to individual mentors, and overloading new teachers with extra responsibilities and several different classroom preparations. (In our pilot program, incentives for mentors included professional development and graduate credits. Other types of incentives include stipends, full-time release for teachers to serve as mentors, and the release of teachers from certain school duties.)

When we and our outside evaluators asked mentors about their experiences in our pilot mentoring program, their enthusiasm was frequently tempered by what appeared to be their principals' limited understanding of standards-based science instruction and science teacher needs. They also commented about a lack of administrative support or, in more cases than not, a sort of benign neglect from principals. The mentors said their principals viewed them as leaders and thought that the work they were doing with teachers new to science was important. That, however, is where matters frequently ended. This appreciation did not translate into the types of incentives and support that make science mentoring an integral part of a school's intellectual and professional life.

The lack of support from school administrators is the second most frequently given reason for the dissatisfaction-related turnover of math and science teachers (after poor salary), according to a study of federal data by Richard Ingersoll (2003). More recently, teachers from two different states both reported that having a principal with a strong instructional emphasis was the second-most important working condition (behind a collegial atmosphere) when it came to their decisions about whether or not to stay in the school in which they work (Southeast Center for Teaching Quality 2005a and Southeast Center for Teaching Quality 2005b).

Fostering Principals as Promoters and Sustainers

Engagement of the principals of participating mentors must be a clearly articulated expectation when mentors from the individual buildings sign on. There must be twin goals: helping principals understand the mentoring program and what it requires from the mentor, mentee, school, district (or larger, regional entity), and putting in place incentives, school or district policies, and an infrastructure to support this demanding mentoring work.

As the mentoring program takes shape, with specific mentors in specific schools, districts, or consortia, you—as the director of the program—can take some specific steps to convert principals to the role of promoters and sustainers of science mentoring. To help improve principals' understanding of science-based standards and their implications for teaching and learning, you can familiarize them with both the goals of the mentoring and the substance of the science work. We recommend the following activities (further discussion about the first three bulleted items follows):

- a memorandum of understanding (MOU) outlining the activities and expectations of the mentoring program,

- a group orientation meeting for principals and administrators only,

- participation by principals in at least two mentor trainings, and

- ongoing, in-person, and written communication between the mentor program and the principal or administrator and between the mentors and the principal (the mentors may be the best advocates for the mentoring program).

Memorandum of Understanding

The purpose of the memorandum of understanding is to clarify the program's expectations, activities, and any calendar or timetable of events. It formalizes the roles and responsibilities of the principal, mentor, and mentee and holds all parties accountable for participating in activities. It helps ensure that principals support specific activities, such as training days, classroom use of the science curriculum units mentors experience in the institutes, release time for classroom observations and pre- and postconferencing, assignment of substitutes, the relationship of the mentoring program to other schools and the district, and participation in evaluation activities. The MOU can also spell out financial matters related to the program. The principal, the mentor, and the mentee should sign the MOU.

Orientation Meeting for Principals and Administrators

Because of the importance of strong school-district commitment to this program, we recommend inviting district curriculum leaders to accompany principals to the orientation meeting. These leaders could include, but need not be limited to, an assistant superintendent for curriculum and instruction or a professional development coordinator. Use this meeting to focus administrators' attention on the role of standards in middle-grades science instruction and to provide an opportunity for them to examine their own science program to see what changes might be necessary. During the meeting, show the group a video that displays standards-based science instruction. (You could use the DVD that accompanies this guide or one of your choosing.) By watching the video, participants in this meeting can analyze this form of instruction and see how it compares with instruction in their schools.

During this first meeting, you should also provide participants with an overview of the mentoring program. Engage the group in a discussion of assumptions and expectations that leads to a conversation about possible mentoring designs and decisions that administrators will need to make. This meeting sets the stage for principals to identify challenges they need to tackle to get the mentoring program up and running. The facilitator can encourage collective responses to how the administrators will support mentors and mentees in order to attract, nurture, and sustain high-quality science teaching.

Principal Participation in at Least Two Mentor Training Sessions

Taking part in mentor training sessions gives principals an opportunity to observe and learn about science instruction and the mentors' role. Principals could attend any of the sessions described in this guide, and you need not change the sessions to accommodate their presence. The important points are to encourage the principals to attend training sessions and to ensure that, when they attend, they get a sense of the program.

In addition to attending the orientation and two institute sessions, principals should also be invited to take part in two additional meetings, each of which might run about two hours and could be scheduled following one of the institute sessions. The first of these meetings should occur around the time the program starts, and the second could follow later during the program's minimum one-year duration.

The first meeting invites principals and mentors to come together to understand the implications of the mentoring program for teaching and learning in their buildings. It also provides a forum for principals and mentors to discuss the type of support that will be necessary for mentor training and the in-school mentoring cycle. At this meeting, you should distribute a tentative timetable, so principals and mentors can see the time commitments and expectations.

The second meeting contains a more nuts-and-bolts discussion dedicated to how to support the mentoring cycle. Topics could include clarification of the mentor's role, identification of incentives for mentors and mentees, scheduling classroom observations and conferencing between mentors and mentees, organizing biweekly consultations between mentors and mentees, and fiscal support for the ongoing training of mentors.

As a result of the activities described above and others that can be added, the most important outcomes are that schools (or districts with strong advocacy from principals) put in place incentives, school or district policies, and procedures to ensure that the mentor-mentee relationship and process is as strong as it can be.

Recommended Actions for Principals

During the teacher interview process, principals should clarify that the new teacher will have a mentor and explain how the process will work. Principals need to select and match mentors, clarify expectations and time commitments, and determine how this program connects with district staff development and school services, such as site-based staff development and support from the science chairperson. Ideally, principals need to organize the teaching assignments of new teachers, so that they are free of multiple assignments, preparation periods, and extra duties. They also need to explain the mentoring program to all teachers in the building and encourage them to think of ways they can support the initiative.

The principals who participated in our pilot project identified the following actions, also identified as needed by the research literature:

- If it is a large school, arrange room assignments so mentors and new teachers have easy access to each other. (If it is a very small school, finding both a mentor and a mentee science teacher at the middle grades may be difficult. In that case, a mentor could work with a science teacher mentee from the elementary grades or two small schools could join forces.)

- Write schedules so mentors and new teachers have common lunch periods and planning times.

- Create release time for mentor-mentee visits to observe each other's classrooms.

- Free up the mentors' time so they can be effective in their work with new teachers. Full-time release is best; release from a few classes or other assignments is a good alternative. As a last resort, an hour every few days plus duty-free periods will work.

- Explore options for substitute teachers when mentors or mentees need to be out of their own classrooms.

- Include mentor and mentee goals in preparing annual evaluations or professional development plans.

- Schedule opportunities for collaboration among teachers in a school, and offer opportunities for mentors and mentees to network with the larger group of mentors and mentees in the district.

- Respect the program's requirement for confidentiality (i.e., the mentor probably does not have supervisory or evaluative responsibilities over the mentee).

Ensuring Accurate Communication About the Program

It is important for all the right people to know how and when you will prepare mentors. In addition, you must clearly articulate the philosophy and goals of the program. For example, explain that the program will blend content, pedagogy, and mentoring skills; will be standards-based; will emphasize inquiry; and will take place, at least in part, at the school.

Interested parties may include everyone from the participating mentors and mentees to school and district leaders, other teachers not participating, and even parents. You should describe to them both the program's short- and long-term ramifications. Short-term effects include teachers being out of the classroom for a certain number of days during the school year, having visitors in their classrooms, and making changes in their instructional program. Also, mentors might be released from other duties, or the principal might ask them to do some professional development for their colleagues.

You will probably need to tailor communications, such as memos, e-mails, and brochures, to each of the interested groups in your community. If it is not your responsibility to develop the communications plan, try to work with the person doing that (or the project's director). In any communication, make sure you mention whether this mentor program links to any other professional development or induction in the school system, and describe its connection (in terms of teacher quality) to the federal No Child Left Behind act.

MAKING SCIENCE MENTORS

Program Evaluation

Your own program goals for this mentoring work must be explicit, with measures identified along the way. We anticipate that you will customize the program for your individual setting; therefore, designs for evaluation of the program overall will also vary. Nonetheless, our experience may inform your thinking. We designed our overall evaluation with twin goals in mind:

- to provide in-depth, formative evaluation of the program (not of the mentors and mentees) for the project staff and those involved in the program's effectiveness, and

- to promote reflection and sharing of progress, learning, and experiences among all participants within the program (including project staff, mentors, mentees, and school and district staff).

Our methods included qualitative and quantitative data collection, each organized with the above goals in mind. We collected qualitative data through hour-long focus groups at the conclusion of each training institute. This allowed for timely and quick synthesis of information delivered in writing to facilitators who could integrate, as appropriate, suggestions into the next institute's agenda.

In general, there are two kinds of evaluation for a program such as this: (1) session evaluation that is helpful to the facilitator (formative assessment) and (2) evaluation to try to understand the program's effectiveness. In terms of the former, focus group questions, for example, might ask mentors for their perceptions of the institute content, resources, and process; what they would have to do between this and the next institute; and whether they were unclear about any of the institute goals or expectations.

To further program evaluation, you may want to collect data on the mentoring program to determine its impact on teacher retention, teacher pedagogical content knowledge, use of mentoring activities and skills, and, ultimately, student learning. Questions for participants would go beyond the session content and ask about such topics as how the work is going with mentees, how often the mentors are able to meet with mentees, and whether mentors are using the science curriculum units in their classrooms.

Our pilot project had the benefit of an outside evaluator, who not only conducted focus groups but also observed the institute training sessions and some aspects of the in-school mentoring cycle; interviewed principals, mentors, and mentees; and provided feedback to the program staff and participants. Interviews with principals focused on their participation and the usefulness of that participation in mentor activities, how they were supporting the mentors and the in-school mentoring cycle, and what type of communication they had had concerning the mentoring program with other principals, teachers, district administrators, and the parent community. Interviews with mentors took a somewhat different tack. Questions focused on science inquiry in the classroom, changes in instruction due to the program, supports in place in the school or district, challenges to date, and interactions with other teachers in the building. Taken all together, this information allowed for ongoing corrections as needed.

Having an external evaluator was extremely helpful. You and your colleagues can develop evaluation questions to pose orally, or in writing, at the end of each training institute. (If you wish to do this, include additional time at the end of an institute session.) In addition to data about the institutes, facilitators should conduct their own observations of the mentoring cycle, such as preconferences and postconferences and classroom observations. If this is not possible, viewing and analyzing videos of mentors at work might be a good second choice. The challenge is, of course, for facilitators who play this role to stay objective.

The collection of quantitative, as well as qualitative data, about the mentoring cycle and the impact on classroom instruction becomes increasingly important if your program extends beyond one year, or if you plan to replicate it later.

Administering questionnaires to mentors and building principals would be useful for gathering feedback about activities, resources, and tools of the project; learning what mentors (and mentees) did together in the mentoring work; ascertaining perceptions of the mentors on the impact of the mentoring work on their mentee, and of the mentee's ability to conduct inquiry-based science instruction; and learning how mentors believe they have been affected through participating in this project.

The resulting information and tracking of mentoring activities can begin to reveal program effectiveness and raise questions that your program developers and staff school leaders may find valuable for planning, publicity, and accountability purposes.

If funding is not available in your program for a professional evaluator, you can ask a colleague not involved in the sessions to step in.

References

American Association for the Advancement of Science. 1993. *Benchmarks for science literacy*. Washington, DC: Author.

Educational Development Center. 2006. *Investigating Pond Organisms*. Nashua, NH: Neo/Sci.

Feiman-Nemser, S., C. Carver, S. Schwille, and B. Yusko. 1999. Beyond support: Taking new teachers seriously as learners. In *A better beginning: Supporting and mentoring new teachers*, ed. M. Scherer, 3–12. Alexandria, VA.: Association for Supervision and Curriculum Development.

Ingersoll, R. 2003. Turnover and shortages among science and mathematics teachers in the United States. In *Science teacher retention: Mentoring and renewal*, eds. J. Rhoton and P. Bowers, 1–12. Arlington, Va.: NSTA Press.

Johnson, S. M., and S. Kardos. 2002. Keeping new teachers in mind. *Educational Leadership* 59 (6): 12–16.

National Research Council (NRC). 1996. *National Science Education Standards*. Washington, DC: National Academy Press.

Southeast Center for Teaching Quality. 2005a. *Teacher working conditions are student learning conditions: A report to Governor Mike Easley on the 2004 North Carolina working conditions survey*. Hillsborough, NC: Author.

Southeast Center for Teaching Quality. 2005b. *Listening to the experts: A report on the 2004 South Carolina teacher working conditions survey*. Hillsborough, NC: Author.

Zubrowski, B. 1994. *Ice cream making and cake baking*. White Plains, NY: Cuisenaire Company of America.

ABOUT THE AUTHORS

Marian Pasquale

Marian Pasquale is a senior scientist in the Center for Science Education at Education Development Center, Inc. She has been a coprincipal investigator on the Middle-Grades Science Mentoring Program and she has led the middle school team for both the Education Development Center's (EDC) National Science Foundation-funded EDC K-12 Science Curriculum Dissemination Center and the middle grades' science and mathematics mentor training for the Cleveland Math-Science Partnership. She is one of the authors of *Guiding Curriculum Decisions for Middle-Grades Science*. She consulted with public television channel WNET in New York City on the development of the *Learning Science Through Inquiry* series funded by Annenberg/CPB. She has designed and conducted professional development for administrators and teacher leaders throughout the nation. For 20 years prior to her work at EDC, she was a middle school teacher in Haverhill, Massachusetts, where she served as K–6 science coordinator for the district.

Vivian Troen

Vivian Troen has been the mentoring specialist for EDC's Middle-Grades Science Mentoring Program. She is a cofounder, with Katherine Boles, of the Learning/Teaching Collaborative, one of the first professional development schools in the country to link colleges and public schools in partnerships for preservice education of teachers and is currently implementing professional development school initiatives at Brandeis University. She is the coauthor of *Who's Teaching Your Children? Why the Teacher Crisis is Worse than you Think and What Can be Done about It* (Yale University Press) as well as numerous papers and articles on mentoring. Her extensive experience includes coordinator of teacher and principal mentoring programs in Boston (North Zone). She is a veteran teacher, having taught all grades levels in several different types of school districts.

Bernie Zubrowski

Bernie Zubrowski is a senior scientist in the Center for Science Education at Education Development Center, Inc., and has been a lead science specialist for the Middle-Grades Science Mentoring Program. He was a part-time instructor at the Boston University School of Education and has conducted numerous workshops for elementary and middle school teachers. In addition, he has been principal investigator on the *Design It! Engineering in After School Programs, Explore It! Science Investigations in Out-of-School Programs,* and *Video Resources for In-Depth Investigations of Pond Organisms* projects. He has published 17 children's hands-on activity books on science and technology topics. He was principal investigator for the curriculum program *Models in Technology and Science,* which resulted in the development of eight extended investigations, and worked on *A World in Motion II,* which presents three engineering challenges for middle school students. He designed eight exhibits for the Boston Children's Museum that traveled to science centers in the United States through a program of the Association of Science and Technology Centers.

SESSION 1

The beginning is the most important part of the work.

Plato, The Republic

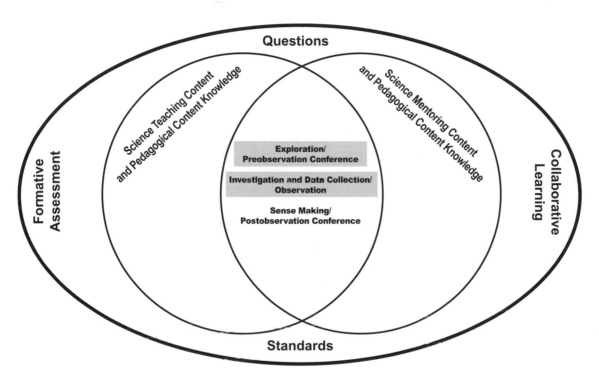

Overview

In this first session participants get to know one another and begin to build a community of learners. They are introduced to two important tools—the inquiry learning cycle and the inquiry protocol—which serve as the foundation for their work as science mentors. They begin preliminary investigations of heat transfer, specifically conduction and convection, and the underlying pedagogy of inquiry.

Outcomes
- Link mentoring to the professionalism of teaching.
- Build a community of mentor teachers.
- Understand the role of a science mentor teacher.
- Develop a vision of high-quality science teaching.
- Become familiar with the inquiry protocol as a planning and observation tool.
- Identify phases of inquiry in classroom practice.
- Experience the exploratory phase of inquiry.

Session Snapshot

Agenda

1¼ hours	**Welcome and Orientation**
	Building a Community of Mentors
	Introducing the Parking Lot
	Putting Mentoring Into a Broader Context
	Establishing Norms
2½ hours	**Science**
	Activity 1: The Inquiry Learning Cycle
	Activity 2: Introduction to the Exploratory Phase
	Activity 3: Investigation and Data Collection
	Activity 4: Classroom Connections and Science Pedagogy
2¼ hours	**Mentoring**
	Activity 1: Qualities and Characteristics of Good Science Teaching
	Activity 2: Introduction to Inquiry Protocol
	Activity 3: Introduction to the Exploratory Phase of Inquiry in the Classroom
30 minutes	**Reflection and Next Steps**
	Reflective Journal
	For Next Time
	Evaluation

How to Prepare for Session 1

What You Need to Do

- Read all introductory and background information with a particular focus on the purpose and use of the inquiry protocol (see Activity 2: Introduction to Inquiry Protocol).
- Scan through the session and review all of the directions and sidebar notes. These include activity descriptions and directions, the science background sections, the training tips, and the discussion points.
- Do the activities, if you haven't done them before as a participant.

What You Need to Make

- Make a sign-in sheet, name tags.
- Make a transparency of the Agenda or write the session's Agenda on chart paper: Hang the Agenda on a wall where participants can see it and you can refer to it throughout the day.
- Write the session's Outcomes on chart paper, and hang the paper on the wall.
- Make all of the overheads.

- Duplicate all of the handouts.
- Prepare the Norms and Parking Lot charts.
- Make a transparency of the science challenge. "Participants investigate ice cubes melting in containers of different materials and sizes to see how these factors influence melting rate."
- Duplicate the article, "Teaching for Conceptual Change: Confronting Children's Experience," by Bruce Watson and Richard Konicek.
- Make the following headings on four pieces of chart paper: Exploratory, Investigation and Data Collection, Sense Making, Infrastructure.

What You Need to Acquire
- Chart paper and markers
- Sticky notes
- Spiral-bound notebook with lined paper and a divider (1 per participant)
- Overhead slide projector
- DVD player and television or a computer and video projector with a DVD player

Science Equipment for Activity 1 (per group)
- 2 paper containers (8 oz. and 32 oz.) with lids
- 3 plastic containers (1 oz., 8 oz., and 32 oz.) with lids
- 2 wide-mouth glass containers (16 oz. and 32 oz.) with lids
- Metal containers (1 coffee can with plastic lid and 1 tuna can with foil for cover)
- Paper plate
- Newspaper
- 15 mini ice cubes and a cooler to keep them in
- Stopwatch

Science Equipment for Activity 2
- Chart paper with findings from Activity 1
- Chart paper with description of activity (see below)
- Data-table chart (created by participants during the activity)
- 1 composition notebooks with divider per participant (from Activity 1)
- Data table: prepared chart for groups to record their data
- Journal Prompts overhead

Science Materials
- Each table group (3 participants per group) needs a set of plates of different sizes and materials, (1 large and 1 small): paper, plastic, aluminum foil, glass (Pyrex plate, custard cup)
- Aluminum foil (1 square foot per group)
- Paper plate for the ice cubes (1 per group)

- Newspaper
- 20 mini ice cubes per table or enough mini ice cubes so that each group has 4–6 ice cubes
- Stopwatch (1 per group)
- Chart paper and markers (1 per group)

Media List

Overheads

1 Not a Profession Versus a Profession
2 Venn Diagram—Making Sense of Science
3 Science Notebook Prompts
4 Inquiry Learning Cycle
5 Inquiry Protocol: Exploratory Phase and Infrastructure
6 Journal Prompts

Handouts

1 Article: "Teaching for Conceptual Change: Confronting Children's Experience" by Bruce Watson and Richard Konicek
2 Article-Reading Discussion Prompts
3 Inquiry Learning Cycle
4 Inquiry Protocol, Exploratory Phase and Infrastructure
5 Viewing Tool—DVD Note-Taking Form
6 Journal Prompts

DVD

Ice Cream Making: Brenda—Classroom Observation

Welcome and Orientation (1¼ hours)

Building a Community of Mentors (30 minutes)

Overview

Because this is the first in a series of sessions, spending time initially on building a community and learning about the mentors in the group is worthwhile. If time is limited, you can carry out this activity in table groups. The purpose of this activity is to help participants introduce themselves by selecting self-definition criteria. Inform participants that you will be operating in an open, collegial way that fosters discussion and challenges assumptions.

Before Beginning

Materials: chart paper, marker, sticky notes

Training Tip

People define themselves in different ways. These can include birthplace, religion, personal or professional interests, family, ethnicity, occupation, and life experiences. Offer a few ways that people define themselves and brainstorm these and others with the group.

Steps

1   Have participants offer their suggestions for ways people define themselves and record these on chart paper.
2   Ask participants to look at the list and choose four for themselves, as a way of introducing themselves and to offer, along with that, what they'd most like to get out of the sessions.
3   Record what they'd like to learn on chart paper.

Discussion Points

Communicate your understanding that participants might be taking this course of instruction for a variety of reasons, such as

•   The principal asked me, or

•   I have been mentoring informally and wanted some training.

Some may already be involved in mentoring, while others are just thinking about mentoring as something interesting to do later. Some may find themselves far advanced in some topics and some ahead in others. Diversity of backgrounds and goals can help make for an interesting group experience.

Introducing the Parking Lot (5 minutes)

Overview

The Parking Lot—a piece of chart paper on which participants record their questions, concerns, and feedback—is one of your most valuable facilitation tools. You can use the Parking Lot to take the pulse of participants and to gauge the effectiveness of each training session. One caveat: It is very important to monitor and respond to participants' Parking Lot comments frequently. When you do so, you create an environment in which participants feel heard and respected as valued members of a learning community.

Before Beginning
Materials: Parking Lot chart; sticky notes on tables.

Steps
1   Introduce the Parking Lot chart that you posted on the wall.
2   Ask participants to use the sticky notes on the tables to write any questions that come to mind or to jot feedback on the Parking Lot paper throughout the day.
3   Tell them that you value their questions and feedback and will check the Parking Lot throughout the day to be as responsive as possible.

Putting Mentoring Into a Broader Context (20 minutes)

Overview
In this section, your objective is to put mentoring into the broader context of teacher professionalization.

Before Beginning
Materials: Overheads 1, 2.

Discussion Points
Use the following discussion points as you explore the topic of mentoring:
1. Classroom teachers are isolated, and mentoring can help create a supportive culture built on collaboration.
2. Mentoring programs can help develop a norm of collaboration in a professional community.
3. Mentoring is an opportunity for well-prepared mentors to pass along years of accumulated wisdom, and to find ways to organize that wisdom and to articulate it in practical ways.
4. Working with a mentee is a responsibility to teach another person and a chance to exercise leadership as teachers carve out new roles and make important decisions that will affect future generations of science teachers.
5. Mentoring provides an opportunity to learn from, and with, a less-experienced teacher.

Steps

1 Show Overhead 1.
2 Discuss how mentoring helps overcome one of the most pernicious cultural aspects of current teaching practice—isolation.
3 Show Overhead 2.

Establishing Norms (20 minutes)

Overview

It is more likely that groups will support work group norms if they are part of developing the norms. So, the time you spend on this activity is an important investment in establishing a supportive, trustful, and collaborative culture in which sometimes-difficult conversations can take place. Some norms will probably include the following: prompt starting and ending times, respectful listening, confidentiality, giving space and time to quieter voices, pausing before responding, not interrupting, and supporting open and honest discussions.

Before Beginning
Materials: chart paper and marker

Steps

1 Brainstorm norms for successful group work.
2 Ask participants to suggest how the group might ensure that it meets these norms.
3 After the session, organize the norms, write them on chart paper, and post them at every session.

Science (2½ hours)
An Extended Investigation on Heat and Heat Transfer
Source: *Ice Cream Making and Cake Baking* (Zubrowski 1994)

Overview

In the next four sessions, participants engage in investigations from a physical science unit entitled *Ice Cream Making and Cake Baking.* They investigate how ice cubes melt in different kinds of containers and on different kinds of surfaces. They collect data on the cooling rate of hot water in different kinds of containers surrounded by three different water environments. Finally, they use this data to decide in which container to make ice cream and the best cooling environment in which to freeze it. Through the context of this unit, participants experience the phases of the inquiry learning cycle—exploration, investigation and data collection, and sense making. Participants can consider how they do or can incorporate each of these phases into their own teaching.

Activity 1: The Inquiry Learning Cycle (20 minutes)

Before Beginning
Materials: Overhead 4

Steps
1   Introduce participants to the inquiry learning cycle (see Figure 1).
2   Discuss each of the phases and ensure that participants understand each of them.
3   Ask participants to give an example of each of the phases from a lesson they have taught.

Figure 1: Inquiry Learning Cycle

Exploration
- Teacher introduces the inquiry
- Students get acquainted with a problem or phenomenon and decide what kind of experiment they will set up

Investigation and Data Collection
- Students carry out experiments and make measurements and/or observations
- Students collect data on their experiments
- Students report their measurements or observations

Sense Making
- Teacher and students analyze the usefulness and meaning of the data
- Teacher and students develop explanations and conceptualizations

Infrastructure and assessment elements are present throughout the whole cycle.

Infrastructure
- Teacher decides how to manage materials
- Teacher decides when and how students will work with other students
- Teacher develops routines and procedures

Assessment
- Teacher determines what students will need to know and be able to do
- Teacher decides how and when he or she will assess students

---

Points to Address

The first few lessons in this unit are explorations.

1. Because the parts of the cycle are inherent in all of the phases, participants also collect data and make some interpretations.
2. As the unit progresses, lessons focus more on one phase, but once again aspects of the other phases are present.
3. In this first session, participants will work with a variety of containers and plates made of different materials.
4. Their task is to gather some initial data about the effect of these containers on the melting rate of ice cubes.

Activity 2: Introduction to the Exploratory Phase (40 minutes)

Overview

Participants investigate ice cubes melting in containers of different materials and sizes to see how these factors influence melting rate.

Science Background

The warm air of the room contacts the ice cubes and causes them to melt. The heat in the air is conducted through the material of the container as well. The density of a material contributes to its thermal conductivity. Low-density materials, such as air, have the poorest thermal conductivity. Dense metals conduct heat better than light metals. The heat capacity of the container is also a factor. The *heat capacity* is the ability of an object to hold heat. Some materials hold heat better than others at any given temperature.

Before Beginning

- Write the activity on chart paper and post the chart paper.
- Before beginning this section of the day, place all materials on the tables, except the ice cubes; leave these in the cooler until you have finished giving directions.
- Divide participants into groups of three for this activity.

Steps

1 Focus participants on the steps of this exploration.

2 Point out that on participants' tables are containers of different sizes and materials. They will examine the containers' effect on the melting rate of ice cubes.

3 Begin by asking participants to discuss and then predict which containers allow ice cubes to melt most quickly and most slowly. Have participants record their predictions and the reasons for their predictions in their science notebooks. Once they are finished, begin the exploration.

4 Distribute at least 15 mini ice cubes on a paper plate to each group.

5 Allow about a half an hour for this exploration. During the exploration, spend time interacting with each group. Make sure that participants record all of their data by asking them questions such as

- What are you noticing?
- Why do think this is happening?
- Are there differences among containers?
- Does anything that is happening surprise you?

6 Listen to participants' comments and jot them down. The purpose here is twofold: This knowledge helps focus the kinds of questions you ask in the follow-up discussion and elicits the kinds of student science discourse that occurs during exploratory activities. As the exploration nears the end, remind participants to observe closely, because the pieces of ice are transparent and participants might not be able to see them easily, even when the cubes have not yet completely melted.

Training Tip

While the groups are working, prepare a data table for the groups to use to record their data. The table should list each container used in the exploration and have a column for each group to record its melting times. This is an example:

Group	1	2	3	4
Container				
Metal (coffee)				
Metal (tuna can)				
Plastic (1 oz.)				
Glass (16 oz.)				
Paper (8 oz.)				

Discussion

During the exploration, participants collected data about melting ice cubes. This discussion will help you and the participants determine what and how they are thinking about melting and the factors that contribute to melting.

Steps

1 As each group finishes the exploration, remind participants to put their group's data on the data table.

2 Once every group has recorded its data, ask each group to report their findings relevant to their observations.

3 Facilitate a group discussion about conclusions participants might make based on the data. Do not correct participants' thinking or give them the right answers. It is not important that participants' thinking is totally accurate at this point. Remember that this is the exploratory phase of inquiry, in which participants access their prior knowledge and become familiar with the materials and how they interact.

4 Ask participants the following questions:
   - What are some preliminary explanations for the results?
   - What effect does the material of the container have on the melt time?
   - How does the data compare to their predictions?
   - What surprised you about this experiment?
   - What data does not fit and how do you explain this?

5 Record participants' thinking on chart paper and post the paper. Participants may suggest that a metal container will allow the ice cube to melt more quickly because it is a better conductor of heat. Questions about size of the container as a variable may arise.

6 Ask participants the following questions:
   - What science concepts did you investigate in this exploration?
   - In which direction do you think the heat is moving? Is heat going into the ice cube or is cold going into the container? (Participants will most likely say that the cold is going into the container.)
   - What is the evidence?

7 Record participants' thinking on chart paper and post the paper.

Training Tip

At this point give participants a 15-minute break.

Activity 3: Investigation and Data Collection (60 minutes)

Overview

This activity moves participants more formally into the investigation and data collection phase. In this phase, participants carry out measurements or observations and report them. In this second investigation, participants experiment with plates made of different kinds of materials and different sizes plus the small ice cubes. They discuss and make predictions about relative melting rates of ice cubes on the different plates. During the second part, they design experiments that identify the variables that affect melting rate.

Before Beginning
–   Make sure that the data table from the previous activity is still posted.
–   Post chart paper with the next exploration: Do ice cubes melt faster on paper, plastic, glass, or metal?
–   Place all materials on the tables, except the ice cubes; leave these in the cooler until you have finished giving directions.
–   Plan to divide participants into groups of three for this activity.

Science Background

This exploration continues to develop ideas about the relationship between properties of different materials and conduction, but it introduces new variables. Participants now consider the effect, if any, the shapes and amounts of the materials have on melt time.

Steps
1   As with any beginning investigation, participants begin by discussing and making predictions about the relative melting rates of ice cubes on plates of different materials and sizes.
2   Refer participants to the chart paper with the investigation: "Do ice cubes melt faster on paper, plastic, glass, or metal?"
3   Have participants review the findings from the first activity, referring to the data table from the previous activity.
4   Ask them what information from the data table is relevant for this challenge.
5   Be sure to have them make a prediction.
6   Have participants record their predictions and the reasons for their predictions in their science notebooks.

7   Point out that a variety of plates of different sizes and materials are on participants' tables. They will use these plates to continue to explore the effect of different materials on the melting rate of ice cubes.

8   Remind participants that, during this investigation and data collection phase, they should take careful notes of their observations in the first section of their science notebooks so they can share their data after they've completed the exploration. Groups will transfer their data onto the chart paper so all participants can compare the findings among the groups.

9   Tell groups to experiment with the different plates to try to determine the effect of their material and size on the melting rate of the ice cube. Allow about 20 minutes for this activity.

Training Tip

During the exploration, spend time interacting with each group by asking the following questions:

- **What are you noticing?**
- **How might you organize the data?**

Discussion

This discussion will help participants make sense of their findings.

Steps

1   When participants have completed the experiment, tell each group to rank the melting times.
2   Collect each group's results, post them on chart paper, and save them for the next session.
3   Ask the following questions:
   - How do these results correlate with the previous activity?
   - What are some tentative explanations?

Activity 4: Classroom Connections and Science Pedagogy (30 minutes)

Overview

This section helps participants connect their work to their classrooms. Here they think about how they begin or open a learning experience for their students. They consider similarities to and differences from what they experienced in the science investigation.

Before Beginning

Materials: Overhead 3. Make sure that participants have their science notebooks.

Steps

1 Tell participants they will now have an opportunity to write in the second part of their science notebooks and call it "Classroom Connections and Science Pedagogy" (see science notebook description in the "The Program in Detail," under Program Components," p. XXX).
2 Put Overhead 3 on the overhead projector.
3 Ask participants to answer the following questions in their journal. They will have 10 minutes to complete the journal.
   - How do you introduce a unit, investigation, or activity in your own classroom?
   - How is this similar to and different from the way this investigation was introduced?
4 Use the remaining 20 minutes of this segment to hold a whole-group discussion to elicit participants' ideas and strategies.

Mentoring (2¼ hours)

In the last part of this session, you will focus on mentoring. Participants will reflect upon their notion of standards-based, inquiry teaching so they can begin to establish a consistent vision among the group members.

Activity 1: Qualities and Characteristics of Good Science Teaching (45 minutes)

Overview

We designed this activity to help participants envision what good inquiry science teaching looks and sounds like in a classroom. It is important for mentors to examine the principles behind inquiry science before they begin their mentoring work.

Before Beginning

Materials: Sticky notes, 4 pieces of chart paper with each of the phases of inquiry—*exploration*, *investigation and data collection*, and *sense making*—and *infrastructure* written on each sheet.

Steps

1 Initiate a general discussion explaining that it is important for teachers to have a vision of those qualities and characteristics that make for good science teaching.
2 Ask participants to think of an excellent science teacher who provides the kind of instruction that promotes increased student science achievement for all students.
3 Ask the following two questions:
   - What specific qualities does this teacher bring to her or his teaching?
   - What are the characteristics and instructional approaches of the science teachers whom we are proud to have as colleagues?

4 After a brief explanation, ask participants to write one quality each on a separate sticky note.

5 Suggest participants think about the science activity they just experienced.

6 Ask participants to think of some of a good teacher's characteristics they have noticed.

7 Encourage participants to write down at least five characteristics.

8 Point to the chart paper and introduce the three phases of inquiry and infrastructure.

9 Explain that you are going to put their ideas of good teaching in the context of a larger conversation that has been going on around the country about the standards-based inquiry approach to teaching science. Participants will decide where to place their sticky notes—under which inquiry phase or infrastructure element each of their qualities fits.

10 Have participants, group by group, come up to the charts and affix their notes. Some qualities may belong on more than one chart, but encourage participants not to be too worried about placing their sticky notes correctly. The point of the exercise is to create visions of what inquiry science teaching and learning looks like. If they can't decide where to put a note, tell them to place it on the side of a chart and the group can decide where it belongs.

Training Tip

After all the sticky notes are on the charts, have participants look at the chart paper and write down their thoughts about any sticky notes whose position they question. Facilitate a conversation about any questions that participants raise. Highlight some sticky notes that reinforce the phases of inquiry. Explain that these phases are based on the inquiry standards they will study in a subsequent session. This is a starting point for having participants think about inquiry phases and standards. Be sure to take time to explain the concept of infrastructure and what kinds of rules, routines, and procedures need to be in place for teachers to be able to engage in inquiry science in classrooms.

After the session is over, type up the sticky note comments on each chart to use in Session 5. You will use this activity as a reference point for the discussion during that session. Help participants understand that these phases are based on national standards, that they are part of a national conversation about what constitutes best practice, and that there is curriculum existing, with these standards serving as a framework, that will also address state standards.

Activity 2: Introduction to Inquiry Protocol (30 minutes)

Overview

During the science section, participants learned about the phases of the inquiry learning cycle. This activity will introduce them to the inquiry protocol. The inquiry protocol delineates classroom activities and behaviors that occur during each phase of inquiry. The focus here is on the exploratory phase.

Before Beginning

Materials: Chart paper, Handout 3

Steps

1   Explain that today the focus is on the exploratory phase of the inquiry protocol.
2   Participants will work with a partner to unpack the specifics of that phase and to gain a clearer understanding of it.
3   Ask participants to select a partner and, with that partner, look carefully at the components of the exploratory phase and the infrastructure component to prepare for the next activity.
4   Encourage mentors to talk about specific examples of what this might look like in the classroom.
5   Ask partners to highlight elements that are either new or challenging to them.
6   Distribute Handout 3.
7   Close by asking partners to share their insights and what they learned.

Activity 3: Introduction to the Exploratory Phase of Inquiry in the Classroom (1 hour)

Overview

During this section, participants look at a science classroom during the exploratory phase of an inquiry project and learn more about how this phase of inquiry looks in practice. Provide the following background information:

- This 28-minute clip was filmed in Brenda Busta's classroom in Lowell, Massachusetts. The introduction is 6:30 minutes; the group work is just under 12 minutes; the wrap-up and sense making is 9 minutes.)
- This is the introduction to the ice cream–making unit, which focuses on the science concepts of heat transfer and properties of different materials.

Before Beginning

Materials: DVD, DVD player and TV, Handouts 4 and 5, Overhead 5.

Steps

1   Prepare the environment for participants by explaining that it is important to bring a spirit of curiosity about teaching and learning to the task of watching this DVD.
2   Instruct participants to view the video assuming that the teacher whose class they are observing is watching the video with them. The purpose of watching the clips is to examine the exploratory phase of the inquiry protocol in practice.
3   Ask participants to consider the following question: What instructional strategies does the teacher use and what infrastructure is already in place prior to this lesson? Even if they might have taught the lesson differently, suggest they ask themselves what the teacher was trying to do and how she was addressing the exploratory phase of inquiry.
4   Divide the group into two. Ask Group A to watch the DVD and focus on finding evidence of the exploratory phase. Instruct Group B to look for infrastructure.
5   Distribute Handouts 4 and 5. Use the note-taking Handout 5 as a guide for observation.
6   Use Overhead 6 to clarify the elements of the exploratory phase and infrastructure.
7   Use the ice cube science lesson to give specific examples.

Reflection and Next Steps (30 minutes)

Reflective Journal (15 minutes)

Overview

In this session, and in others to come, you give participants time for reflective writing and conversation—areas of professional practice too rarely offered to teachers. Following activities, participants share some of their reflective writing and discuss areas and topics that stimulated new thoughts and ideas. This session began with a discussion of the professionalism of teaching. This journal segment now provides you with an opportunity to bring the session back to that topic. Because reflective journals are powerful tools for teachers to focus on their concerns and track their professional growth, they can provide a vehicle for thinking critically about classroom practice. In this exercise, you position the reflective journal as a device for assessing progress, summarizing knowledge, and providing direction for the next steps in the process of becoming a science mentor.

Steps

1 Distribute Handout 6 and put up Overhead 6 (Journal Prompts).

2 Ask participants to direct their thoughts toward the following questions:

  • Why am I interested in science mentoring and what's in it for me?

  • What qualities and skills do I bring?

  • What skills do I need to develop so I can work more effectively with my colleagues?

  • How might I introduce the investigation if I used this ice cream–making unit in my classroom?

  • What infrastructure would I need to have in place before I could begin an exploration?

3 At the end of the day, before participants leave, we strongly recommend that you collect the journals, make copies, and return the journals to participants. In this way you will be able to keep a pulse on the needs of the group.

For Next Time (5 minutes)

Steps

1 Give participants Handout 1, the article "Teaching for Conceptual Change: Confronting Children's Experience" by Bruce Watson and Richard Konicek, and Handout 2. Ask them to read the article and to write in the Classroom Connections section of their science notebook their ideas about the following questions:

  • How did the teacher begin her unit on heat?

  • How did the teacher use what she learned about her students' prior knowledge about heat?

  • What concepts about heat was the teacher trying to develop?

  • What might the teacher have done differently?

  • What are the implications of everyday language for the development of students' science conceptual understanding?

2 Ask participants to prepare to discuss the article at the next session.

Evaluation (10 minutes)

Overview

This activity is an important source of information for you as you prepare to facilitate future sessions.

Steps

1 Ask participants to write "Highlights" on one side of a page of their journals and "Wishes" on the other side.

2   Ask participants to write on the highlights side about what they enjoyed and found beneficial about the work of the day.

3   Ask participants to write on the wishes side about things they wish had happened today or they hope will happen in the future.

4   Ask participants to give you their journals. Make copies of their entries, and return their journals to them. Also, encourage participants to stick their sticky notes with questions or concerns on the Parking Lot as they leave.

SESSION 2

Planning is what you do before you do something,
so that when you do it, it is not all mixed up.

Winnie the Pooh, by A. A. Milne

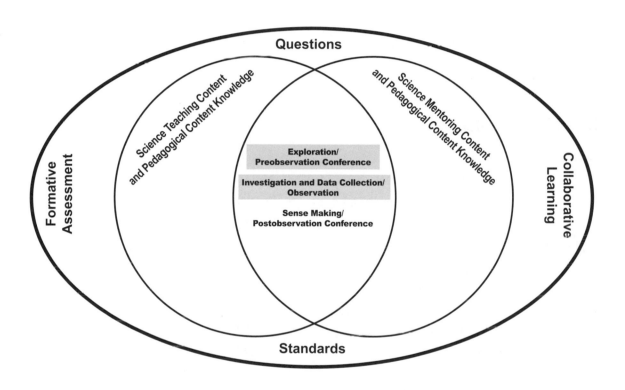

Overview

Mentoring, like teaching, demands skills. Mentors need to learn how to best develop a mentee's professional growth. This goes far beyond the idea of emotional support that many generic mentoring programs advocate. The content-specific mentoring that this mentoring program emphasizes is educative mentoring and requires mentors to think seriously about the method of teaching they want novices to learn and what that teaching entails. During this session, mentors learn mentoring strategies and practices to help them be effective in their new role.

Outcomes

- Gain an understanding of the skills and behaviors of effective science mentors.
- Develop a stance for mentoring.
- Enrich and refine teachers' pedagogical content knowledge.
- Communicate with colleagues about issues of teaching and learning science.
- Develop a common language to give and receive ideas and receive assistance from colleagues.
- Experience the sense of belonging to a culture of peers in which it is safe to discuss instructional problems.
- Experience the investigation and data collection phase of inquiry.
- Engage in designing investigations.
- Consider variables that affect heat transfer.

Session Snapshot

Agenda

20 minutes	**Welcome and Check-In**
	Reconnecting with Each Other and the Program
	Sharing Journal Entries
2¼ hours	**Mentoring**
	Activity 1: Mentor Skill Development
	Activity 2: Visions of Mentoring
	Activity 3: Preobservation Conference DVD
	Activity 4: Reflective Journal
3½ hours	**Science**
	Activity 1: Sharing Homework
	Activity 2: Heat Transfer: Experimental Design
	Activity 3: Classroom Connections and Science Pedagogy
	Activity 4: Heat Capacity—Investigation and Data Collection
30 minutes	**Reflection and Next Steps**
	For Next Time
	Evaluation

How to Prepare for Session 2

What You Need to Do

– Read all introductory and background information in this session, with a particular focus on Preobservation prompts and Viewing Tool: DVD note-taking form.

– Scan through the session and review all of the directions and sidebar notes. These include activity descriptions and directions, the science background sections, the training tips, and the discussion points.
– Do the activities if you haven't done them before as a participant.

What You Need to Make

– Write the Agenda on chart paper and hang the paper on the wall where participants can see it and you can refer to it throughout the day.
– Write the session's Outcomes on chart paper, and hang the paper on the wall.
– Make all overheads.
– Duplicate all handouts.
– Post the Norms and Parking Lot charts.
– Make science Activity Cards 1–4 using the text that follows.
– Freeze mini ice cubes

Activity Card 1: Amount of Metal

Take five 12 × 12 in. sheets of aluminum foil. Stack four sheets of foil, shiny side facing up, on top of one another. Press down firmly to make sure there are no air bubbles. Put one ice cube on top of the stacked sheets and one on top of the single sheet at the same time. Carefully observe and time how long it takes the ice to melt. After you have set up the experiment, predict in your science notebook which ice cube will melt first and why. Did all the ice cubes melt at the same rate? Record the results in your notebook.

Activity Card 2: Amount of Surface Area

Take four 12 × 12 in. sheets of foil, shiny side facing up. Leave the first sheet as is. Fold the second sheet in half, the third sheet twice, and the fourth sheet four times. Make sure to flatten the layers of each sheet so that no air bubbles or lumps remain in the final fold. Place one ice cube on each sheet at the same time. Carefully observe and time how long it takes the ice to melt. After you have set up the experiment, predict in your science notebook which ice cube will melt first and why. Did all the ice cubes melt at the same rate? Record the results in your notebook.

Activity Card 3: Size of Metal Sheet

Line up four sheets of different sizes, shiny side facing up: 24 × 12 in., 12 × 12 in., 6 × 12 in., and 3 × 3 in. Place an ice cube in the center of each of these sheets at the same time. Carefully observe and time how long it takes the ice to melt. Predict in what order the ice cubes will melt and record in your notebook. Record the results in your notebook.

Activity Card 4: Shape of Metal

(Activity card 4 will be used by the entire group after the first three activities have been discussed.) With a partner, design an experiment to melt an ice cube as quickly as possible or as slowly as possible. You have a 12 × 12 in. piece of foil. Decide with your partner what shape would best facilitate or delay the melt rate of the ice cube. In your science notebook, draw the shape and explain why you chose that shape to reach your desired outcome of quickly or slowly melting the ice. As a control, place an unfolded 12 × 12 in. sheet of foil next to the foil you have shaped, and place an ice cube on each piece of foil. Carefully observe and time how long it takes the ice to melt.

What You Need to Acquire
- Chart paper and markers
- Sticky notes
- Science data chart from Session 2
- 4 blank data charts labeled Activity 1, 2, 3, and 4
- Overhead slide projector
- DVD player and television

Science Materials
Each table group needs:
- 1 100 ft. roll of aluminum foil to make the following:
  - 13 pieces of aluminum foil, 12 × 12 in.
  - 1 piece of aluminum foil, 12 × 24 in.
  - 1 piece of aluminum foil, 12 × 12 in.
  - 1 piece of aluminum foil, 3 × 3 in.
- Newspaper to cover work surface
- 4 trays of mini ice cubes
- Stopwatches

Media List

Overheads

1 Journal Prompts
2 Why Does Peer Support Work?
3 Three Mentoring Goals
4 Components of Good Mentoring
5 Components of Observation: Preobservation Prompts
6 Viewing Tool—DVD Note-Taking Form
7 Journal Prompts
8 Activity Card 4: Shape of Metal
9 Classroom Connections Prompts
10 Abilities Necessary to Do Scientific Inquiry, Grades 5–8
11 Evaluation Form

Handouts

1 Journal Prompts
2 Why Does Peer Support Work?
3 Three Mentoring Goals
4 Components of Good Mentoring
5 Components of Observation: Preobservation Prompts
6 Viewing Tool—DVD Note-Taking Form
7 Activity Cards 1–3
8 Journal Prompts
9 Evaluation Form

DVD

"Ice Cream Making: Cindy—Preobservation Conference"

Welcome and Check-In (20 minutes)

Reconnecting With Each Other and the Program (5 minutes)

Overview

The purpose of this time is to help mentors reconnect to the group and the work of science mentoring and to orient them to Session 2.

Before Beginning

Materials: agenda: list of outcomes; norms from Session 1

Steps

1   Review the Agenda.
2   Review the opening quote and talk about the theme of this session: the importance of planning.
3   Go through the Outcomes chart that contains the foci for the day.
4   Review the Norms from Session 1.

Sharing Journal Entries (15 minutes)

Overview

This is an opportunity for mentors to share their reasons for wanting to mentor, the qualities and skills they bring to the task, and the skills they need to develop.

Before Beginning

Materials: Overhead 1, Handout 1

Steps

1   Give participants an opportunity to reread their journal entries from the previous session.
2   Put the journal writing prompts overhead on the overhead projector.
3   Invite participants to turn to a tablemate and share something they wrote about.
4   If time permits, you might want to invite participants to share with the group any insights they had as a result of writing in their journal, focusing on science mentoring skills participants were interested in developing.
5   Record on chart paper and ask participants to think about the list and categorize it by:
    •   I have the skill already—I know how to do this.
    •   That skill is not on my list—I have too much to do to set aside time to learn that skill.
    •   I want to learn that skill.
6   As you wrap up this section, try to address any relevant questions that were posted on the Parking Lot from Session 1.

Mentoring (2¼ hours)

Activity 1: Mentor Skill Development (1 hour)

Overview

During this segment, you present information about the importance of mentoring and collaboration. You also engage participants in discussions of the key elements of effective mentoring.

Before Beginning
Materials: Overhead 2, 3, 4, Handouts 2, 3, 4

Discussion Points

Use the following discussion points to help you reinforce the importance of mentoring and emphasize this program's approach to mentoring:

1. The nonroutine nature of teachers' work requires complex, contextual decision making and an inquiry-oriented approach to practice.

2. Just as we talk about inquiry-based science, so, too, do we want to focus on an inquiry approach to mentoring.

3. This inquiry approach helps develop problem-solving skills as teachers examine their experience, generate alternatives, and evaluate actions.

Steps

1 Acknowledge that everyone in the room is there because they believe in the importance of working with beginning teachers or teachers who are new to inquiry-based science teaching.

2 Reinforce the importance of mentoring and say that participants are taking on the role of teacher educator. Their new role is to work with beginning teachers and to help them become more effective.

3 Explain that learning to talk about teaching and learning may be a new experience for the participants, even if they are experienced teachers.

4 Explain to participants that school reforms require collaborative cultures in which practitioners reflect on their practice together (this is a continuation of the theme and discussion found in Session 1).

5 Say that mentoring or peer coaching can increase teachers' comfort with such professional inquiry and support continued experimentation and professional growth.

6 Show Overhead 2, Why Does Peer Support Work?

7 Show Overhead 3, Three Mentoring Goals, and elaborate on each goal. Explain that this framework will help participants support the work of mentees.

8 Draw a parallel between the three goals and creating a classroom culture that reflects the goals. (Ask participants to think about ways in which they build trust with their students.)

Training Tip

If some of your participants will work with more experienced teachers, you might explain the value of peer coaching. Teachers who have engaged in both mentoring and peer coaching report that no other form of professional development has had such a great impact on improving their teaching performance and that it has validated positive aspects of their teaching. Both mentoring and peer coaching are ways for teachers to reflect on practice, share successful practices, learn from and with colleagues and, most important, break down the isolation of teachers.

Discussion Points

Use the following points to help engage participants in a consideration of the three mentoring goals.

Trust

Establishing trust is crucial. If establishing trust is not made a high priority, reaching the next, and further, goals will be difficult. Attention to trust must be ongoing.

We know the following facts about communication:

- Fifty-five percent of communication consists of nonverbal clues.
- Thirty-eight percent of communication consists of tone of voice and rate of speed.
- Only seven percent of communication consists of actual words spoken.

That's important to keep in mind when building communication skills and establishing relationships with colleagues and mentees.

Ask mentors how they might build trust with a colleague. Record their responses on chart paper.

Learning

To be able to learn from another person, we have to be willing to expose our vulnerabilities as well as our strengths. A helpful strategy is for you to share with the mentors the issues with which you personally struggle as well as the things you believe you do well (and why).

[continued on page 30]

Reflective Teaching

The ultimate goal is for teachers to be reflective practitioners, with the ability to self-monitor, self-analyze, and self-evaluate. A high priority is to support a colleague toward becoming a self mentor—that is, to be able to ask questions of themselves, even in the mentor's absence. The relationship ultimately should not be dependent. Thinking independently is an important prerequisite for being a successful mentor.

Steps (continued)

9   Show Overhead 4, Components of Good Mentoring.

10 Explain the components of becoming a good mentor.

Discussion Points

Use the following points to help deepen participants' understanding of the key components of good mentoring:

Consciousness

Emphasize the importance of self-awareness. Teachers can't teach on automatic pilot. If you want to support a colleague's professional growth, you must be able to articulate your practice and support your decision making.

Precision in thinking

Many teachers believe they teach from intuition; however, that is not the best strategy for improving student achievement. Decisions should be based on data, knowing students well, and understanding the learning needs of each student.

Flexibility

An important teaching strategy is always to have backup options. Developing a teaching repertoire, and having lots of possibilities at one's fingertips is a mentoring goal.

Interdependence

Fostering interdependence by looking to others for help in learning and growing is a way to break down the isolation of teaching while supporting teacher accountability.

(continued on page 30)

Efficacy

Efficacy is a mentoring goal—a way to bring mentees from where they are to where they want to be. It is at the center as a locus of control. It is important for teachers to understand that everything they do makes a difference. This is true for mentees, as well as for mentors. Mentors must feel a sense of efficacy: "I believe I have the capacity to develop someone else."

Steps (continued)

11 Tell participants that it is important for mentors to work toward the three goals: trust, learning, and reflection. When working with a partner, it is important to ask, "How have we moved toward the three goals of mentoring?"

12 Ask participants: "If it's critical to have trust to support learning, what are some things you can do to establish and maintain a trusting environment?" (Examples are maintaining confidentiality and being responsive to the mentees' needs.)

13 Brainstorm reactions with the group and record them on chart paper.

14 Tell participants that, at this point, you will move to the learning segment of the three mentoring goals. There are different kinds of conferences, but you will start with a preobservation conference.

Activity 2: Visions of Mentoring (15 minutes)

Overview

In this session, participants examine and reinforce the importance of observation in the development of the mentoring relationship. You share with participants how the observation process helps to transform teaching from a private to a public act.

Before Beginning
Materials: Overhead 5, Handout 5

Steps

1. Tell mentors that the purpose of the preobservation conference guide is to invite teachers to share their thinking—not only on the lesson itself but also on key issues such as how the teacher thinks about teaching and learning (including prior knowledge and potential problems).

2. Connect the preobservation conference to the exploratory phase of inquiry. Both are open-ended—that is, designed to gather information about a phenomenon.

3. Show Overhead 5. Components of Observation: Preobservation Prompts, and ask participants to look at the questions quietly.

4. Highlight some important components. Reinforce that these questions are for a lesson in which students conduct experiments in order to collect data.

5. Ask participants if they need clarification or have any concerns or questions about the types of questions asked.

Activity 3: Preobservation Conference DVD (45 minutes)

Overview

Participants gain insight into the preobservation conference meeting by watching a video in which a mentor and teacher go through the process.

Before Beginning

Materials: Overhead 6, Handout 6. Two pieces of chart paper with the headings: "Building Trust/Mentor Language" and "Questions/Probes: 'DVD: Ice Cream Making: Cindy—Preobservation Conference'"

Steps

1   Explain that participants are going to watch a video of an interaction between a mentor and mentee to model how mentors might do a preobservation conference prior to observing a lesson.

2   Tell participants that the videotaped conversation will help identify some important features of a productive preobservation conference that can ultimately contribute to the mentor's effectiveness and move a less experienced teacher's practice forward. This preobservation conference is authentic and is in preparation for the observation of a lesson during the investigation and data collection phase of the physical science curriculum unit, Ice Cream Making and Cake Baking. The mentee, Cindy, teaches eighth grade in Fall River, Massachusetts. (For additional examples of preobservation conferences, use "Ice Cream Making: Brenda" or "Investigating Pond Organisms: Mike.")

3   Point out that this is only one example of a preobservation conference. This one is shown because it identifies some key elements of a good conversation. You may want to stress the following points:

    • The importance of uncovering potential misconceptions during a preobservation conference
    • The suggestion that data be posted for all to see
    • Science goals of the lesson

4   Tell participants they should look for the following examples:

    • Language the mentor uses and any evidence of moves to build trust
    • Questions and probes the mentor uses to move the teacher's practice forward

5   Ask mentors at each table to divide themselves into two groups: those who will observe for mentor language and mentor moves that build trust and those who will watch for examples of mentor's questions and probes.

6   Show Overhead 6, Viewing Tool—DVD Note-Taking Form and distribute Handout 6 for note taking.

7   Play the video—"Ice Cream Making: Cindy—Preobservation Conference."

8   After showing the DVD, ask participants to discuss their general observations at their tables

and then offer specific observations based on the prompts.

9 Post two pieces of chart paper on the walls with the following headings: "Building Trust/ Mentor Language" and "Questions/Probes."

10 Ask participants to share their observations. You can use the following prompts:
   • Examples of moves the mentor made that supported the relationship.
   • Examples of questions and probes the mentor used.
   • How did the mentor clarify concepts and ideas along the way? What were some of her listening behaviors?
   • How did the mentor help the teacher to focus on potential misconceptions?
   • What were some questions and probes the mentor asked that might lead to an improved lesson? (Examples are revealing student misconceptions, how data will be collected, what the mentee expects to hear from students about movement of heat, and how the mentee will know if he or she achieves goals.)
   • How does the mentor probe for specificity in supporting the mentee's goals for her own learning?

11 Record examples on the appropriate chart paper.

12 Wrap up this section by explaining that the questions asked during a preobservation conference come from trying to understand what is inside another teacher's head. This is hard work: Mentors must listen carefully, clarify along the way, and visualize the lesson as they unpack mentees' thinking.

Activity 4: Reflective Journal (15 minutes)

Overview

One of the purposes of journal writing is to give a sanctioned time for reflection. At the end of this mentoring segment, you'll want to provide a short amount of quiet space to have participants consider some of the issues that were raised.

Before Beginning

Materials: Overhead 7, Handout 8

Steps

1 Ask participants to respond to the prompts provided in Overhead 7.

2 Again, collect participants' journals and copy them—during the science section if possible—so you can have a copy and participants can also have a copy.

Science (3½ hours)

An Extended Investigation on Heat and Heat Transfer (continued)
Source: *Ice Cream Making and Cake Baking* (Zubrowski 1994)

Overview

This next science segment begins with participants discussing the homework article they read. They design their own experiments to determine the effects of a particular variable on heat transfer. Next, they continue their investigation on the melting rate of ice cubes with a focus on data collection and representation.

Activity 1: Sharing Homework (20 minutes)

Overview

Participants have the opportunity to share their insights about the article they read and its implications for their practice with their colleagues. This activity, and others in which mentors discuss their ideas and experience, are an important part of creating a culture of peers in which it is safe to discuss instructional problems.

Before Beginning

Make sure that participants have their homework assignments from Session 1.

Steps

1   Review the homework assignment from Session 1. Participants will have read the article, "Teaching for Conceptual Change, Confronting Children's Experience."
2   In table groups, have participants share their thinking about the following questions they considered:
    • How did the teacher begin her unit on heat?
    • How did the teacher use what she learned about her students' prior knowledge about heat?
    • What concepts about heat was the teacher trying to develop?
    • What might the teacher have done differently?
    • What are the implications of everyday language for the development of students' science conceptual understanding?
3   After 10 minutes, conduct a whole-group discussion about the questions.
4   Have participants write in their science notebooks any new ideas they gained from the discussion.

Activity 2: Heat Transfer: Experimental Design (1 hour)

Before Beginning
Materials: Chart paper, markers

Overview

In the previous session, mentors explored the melting rate of ice cubes using containers (can, jars, and cups) of various sizes and made of different materials (aluminum, glass, paper, and plastic). They then carried out a similar exploration with plates made of the same materials as the containers. Although participants made predictions about what container or plate they believed would melt the ice cubes fastest and timed the melting rate, the activity was primarily exploratory, a way to gather information about how the ice cubes behaved with these different materials and containers. You did not give participants directions to follow, nor did participants plan the activities carefully from a scientific point of view. Both activities were a quick way to gather some preliminary ideas about ice and the variables that affect its melting rate. In this session, participants begin by designing an experiment to obtain more reliable data. This is an important activity, because it gives teachers practice with the process of experimental design. The National Science Education Standards (NRC 1996, p. 145) recommend that designing and conducting experiments be among several important inquiry skills that middle grades students should develop. Having the experience of doing this activity should help mentors incorporate this practice more readily into their science lessons.

Steps

1   Ask participants how they can design more controlled experiments. (Participants might suggest using containers of different sizes but the same material or containers of different materials but the same size.)
2   Have participants, as a group, design one experiment to determine the effect of a single variable on the relative melting time of ice cubes. Emphasize that these are to be rigorous and controlled designs.
3   Have participants put their experimental designs on chart paper and post their designs.
4   Once all designs are posted, have participants do a gallery walk, reading each design in turn and noting their questions in their science notebooks.
5   Gather participants and, in a large-group discussion, ask them to share the questions that

were prompted by the gallery walk. Taking into account the questions about their designs, give groups an opportunity to revise their experiments.

Activity 3: Classroom Connections and Science Pedagogy (30 minutes)

Before Beginning
Materials: Overhead 9, Overhead 10

Steps

1   Because mentors have just completed their own experimental designs, this is a good time to discuss how they incorporate this practice into their lessons and units. Have mentors discuss the questions that appear below (Overhead 9) in table groups. If they are currently classroom teachers, mentors should answer the first question. If they do not have their own classrooms, they should answer question two.

   • What opportunities do you currently give your students to design their own investigations? What challenges do students encounter?

   • What are some potential challenges for students when they are asked to design their own investigations?

2   Have participants, as a group, discuss any experiences they have had with their students designing their own experiments. Have them share specific lessons they use and their students' successes and challenges with these lessons.

3   Ask participants to explain their strategies for helping students become more proficient at designing experiments.

4   Show participants the overhead of the Abilities Necessary to Do Scientific Inquiry, Grades 5–8 from the National Science Education Standards (Overhead 10). Ask how the unit Ice Cream Making and Cake Baking provides opportunities for students to develop these abilities.

5   If no participants have had students design their own experiments, encourage them to try it before the next session and to be ready to report back on their experiences. Participants for whom this is a common practice will be an invaluable resource to others about potential challenges and problems. (One strategy is to have students design an investigation as a group and then share their design with the class. The class can then ask questions about the design aimed at improving it. This becomes a model for students to critique their own investigation designs.)

Activity 4: Heat Capacity—Investigation and Data Collection (1½ hours)

Overview

In this investigation, participants explore the concept of heat capacity. They work with different numbers of sheets of aluminum foil. Aluminum foil allows them to experiment with variables while keeping the material constant.

Before Beginning

Materials: Handout 7, Activity Cards 1–3, Overhead 8, Activity Card 4 (see What You Need to Make, p. 23, for directions), chart paper, and a marker. Post the data chart from Session 2 and the four blank data charts.

Science Background

Each single sheet of foil holds a certain amount of heat. Three sheets of foil have more heat capacity than one sheet of foil and will melt the ice cube more quickly. Heat is conducted from the material into the ice cube. The warmth of the air in the room also contributes to the melt time.

In the previous activity, ice cubes should have melted more quickly on aluminum than they did on paper or plastic. Metal should have proved to be the best conductor of heat. But the ice cubes in the two cans melted at different rates. Teachers saw that materials alone do not determine how quickly heat is transferred. Other factors that influence heat transfer are size, shape, and total mass of the container.

Steps

1 Begin by reviewing the data from Session 1. Refer to the posted chart and ask the following questions:
   - What did we learn about the effect of different materials on the melting rate of ice cubes?
   - What effect did the size of the melting container have on the melting rate of the ice cubes?
   - What other variables do you think would affect melting rate?

2 Record participants' answers on chart paper.

3 Tell participants that they will investigate three variables that affect melting rate: the amount of metal, the amount of surface area, and the size of the metal sheet. (If participants have identified other variables, encourage them to set up those investigations as well.)

4 Explain that each pair of participants will conduct a different investigation and share data with the rest of the table. Each pair should select one investigation card and take the materials they need from the center of the table.

5 Tell participants that when they finish the investigation, they should share the data from the three investigations. Then have each group post its data on the appropriate data charts.

6 Have each group record its data on the data chart.

7 Participants' data should suggest the following: Four sheets of foil melt the ice more quickly than one sheet; thick (multiple) sheets of metal hold more heat than thin (single) sheets, thus melting the ice faster; and a smaller surface area reflects less heat than a large sheet, which causes the ice to melt faster.

Training Tip

This activity features three simultaneous investigations, and the whole group conducts a fourth investigation together. One way to do this would be in table groups of six people each with each pair at the table conducting a different investigation. In this way, participants will be able to observe what is happening in each case. During lunch or another break, place the following materials and the activities cards 1–3 on each table. (For activity card directions, see the following and the included CD-ROM.)

Sense-Making Discussion (10 minutes)
This discussion will help participants analyze the data they collected in their investigation.

Steps

1 Draw mentors' attention to the charts.

2 Have them analyze the data from the various investigations and draw conclusions about the effects of the amount of metal, surface area, and size of metal sheet on the melting rate.

3   Ask the following questions:
- Does the amount of metal affect the melting rate of the ice cubes? If so, how?
- Does the amount of surface area affect the melting rate? If so, how?
- Does the size of the metal affect the melting rate? If so, how?

4   Say to participants: "Taking into consideration the results of the previous three activities, what effect would the shape of the metal have on the melting rate of the ice cube?"

5   Capture participants' ideas on chart paper and introduce the next investigation.

6   Show Overhead 8.

Training Tip

During the melting process, circulate among groups and probe participants' decision-making processes. Note any interesting ideas, and ask these teachers to share these ideas during the general discussion.

Steps (continued)

7   Ask mentors to draw the shape they made and record the melting rate on the posted Activity 4 chart paper.

8   Facilitate a conversation that includes the following questions:
- Which shapes and sizes melted the ice cube fastest and which the slowest?
- How do you think the shapes caused the given effect?
- What conclusions can we make about heat transfer?

Notes for Facilitator

At this point, mentors should be able to articulate their understanding of heat transfer. Have them describe their ideas about heat transfer, using the various investigations to support their thinking. Collect their ideas on chart paper. Depending upon their familiarity with heat transfer, they may or may not use terms, such as *conduction* and *radiation*. If they do, have them give examples of conduction and examples of radiation from other contexts. (Examples could be that of a metal pot on a stove burner, snow melting on the street, and frozen food thawing in the refrigerator.)

Reflection and Next Steps (30 minutes)

For Next Time (20 minutes)

Steps

1   Ask participants to think about the following questions:
    - What kinds of opportunities do the mentors provide students to generate and collect data?
    - In what ways do students organize and represent their data?
2   Ask them to jot down their ideas in the Classroom Connections part of their science notebook to share at the next session.

Evaluation (10 minutes)

Overview

This activity is an important source of information for you. Participants' feedback will help you prepare for future sessions.

Steps

1   Hand out, and show as an overhead, the Evaluation Form (Overhead 11, Handout 9).
2   Encourage participants to write any questions or concerns they have on sticky notes and stick them on the Parking Lot paper as they leave.

SESSION 3

You can observe a lot by just looking around.

Yogi Berra

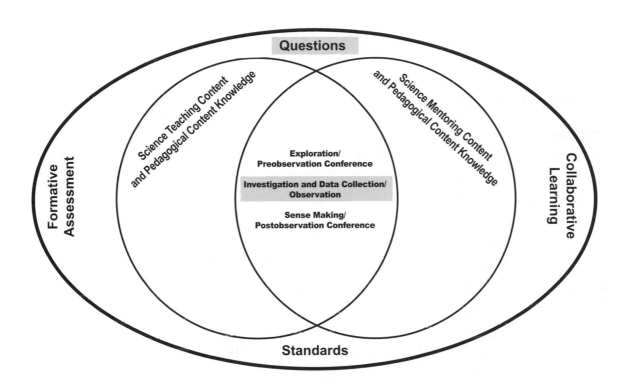

Overview

In this session, you introduce participants to the second phase of the inquiry protocol—investigation and data collection. They have an opportunity to delve deeply into the specifics of that phase through a virtual classroom observation. In this video segment, a teacher works with her students on the same investigations as those in which participants engage in the science section of this session. In the science section, participants explore cooling hot water with three different solutions: cold water, ice water, and ice-salt water.

Outcomes

- Develop a repertoire of mentoring skills and strategies, such as coplanning, preobservation, observation and postobservation frameworks.
- Begin to appreciate collaboration and experimentation as tools for ongoing improvement of teaching.
- Gain an understanding of the second phase of the investigation and data collection phase in the inquiry protocol.
- Explore cooling hot water with three different solutions: cold water, ice water, and ice-salt water.
- Create and analyze cooling curves.

Session Snapshot

Agenda

10 minutes	**Welcome and Check-In**
	Reconnecting With Each Other and the Program
2 hours	**Mentoring**
	Activity 1: Introduction to the Second Phase of the Inquiry Protocol: Investigation and Data Collection
	Activity 2: Investigation and Data Collection in the Classroom
	Activity 3: Video Discussion
3 hours	**Science**
	Activity 1: Classroom Connections and Science Pedagogy
	Activity 2: Cooling Capacity: Investigation and Data Collection
	Sense-Making Discussion
40 minutes	**Reflection and Next Steps**
	Reflective Journal
	Optional: For Next Time
	Evaluation

How to Prepare for Session 3

What You Need to Do

- Read all introductory and background information for this session, with a particular focus on the Second Phase of the Inquiry Protocol: Investigation and Data Collection (Handout 1).
- Scan through the session and review all of the directions and sidebar notes. These include activity descriptions and directions, the science background sections, the training tips, and the discussion points.
- Do the activities if you haven't done them before as a participant.

What You Need to Make

– Write the session's Agenda on chart paper, and hang the paper on the wall where participants can see it and you can refer to it throughout the day.
– Write the session's Outcomes on chart paper, and hang the paper on the wall.
– Make all overheads.
– Duplicate all handouts.
– Post the Norms and Parking Lot charts.
– Make science investigation cards 1–3.

Investigation 1

Using the 8 oz. paper container to measure, pour 16 oz. of hot water into the container you selected. Then pour 32 oz. of cold tap water into the plastic bucket. Place the hot water container in the bucket so that the cold water surrounds it. Quickly place one thermometer in the bucket of cold tap water and one in the container of hot water. Try to position the thermometers so you can read them without removing them. Keeping the thermometers in place, take temperature readings every 30 seconds and record the readings. Keep taking the readings until the temperatures of the two liquids remain the same for three or four readings. Record your results on a data table, and plot the data for the hot water and the data for the cold water on a line graph.

Investigation 2

Using the 8 oz. paper container to measure, pour 16 oz. of hot water into the container you selected. Then pour 32 oz. of cold tap water into the plastic bucket. Fill the bucket half full with ice. Place the hot water container in the bucket so that the ice water surrounds it. Quickly place one thermometer in the bucket of cold tap water and the other in the container of hot water. Try to position the thermometers so you can read them without removing them. Keeping the thermometers in place, take temperature readings every 30 seconds and record the readings. Stir the hot water occasionally between readings. Continue to stir and take the readings until the temperatures of the two liquids remain the same for three to four readings. Let the small container

(continued on page 44)

sit undisturbed in the ice and water. Do not take any more temperature readings. Record the hot water temperature data for your container on a graph. (Before you leave for the day, look inside your small container while you slowly pour out the water. Record your observations.)

Investigation 3

Measure 4 oz. of cold tap water and 4 oz. of salt into a plastic bucket. Fill the bucket halfway with ice and then mix thoroughly. Place a thermometer into the solution so you can read the thermometer without removing it; take a reading immediately. Measure 16 oz. of hot water, and pour it into the container you chose. Place the hot water container into the bucket so that the ice-salt water solution surrounds the hot water container. Be careful not to get any salt in the hot water.

Place the second thermometer into the container with the hot water. Try to position it so you can read the thermometer without removing it. Take temperature readings every 30 seconds and record the temperatures in the data table. Stir the hot water occasionally between readings. Continue to stir and take the readings until the temperatures of the two liquids remain the same for three to four readings. Let the container sit undisturbed in the ice-salt water solution without taking any further temperature readings. Observe any changes in the container for at least 5 minutes. Before the end of the session, look inside the container while you pour out the water. Record your observations and make a graph of your results.

What You Need to Acquire
- Chart paper and markers
- Sticky notes
- Overhead slide project
- DVD player and television
- Optional reading: "The Right Question at the Right Time," by J. Elstgeest, for discussion in Session 4, Science Activity 1. Source: Chapter 4 of *Primary Science: Taking the Plunge* (1985) (see "Resources" at the end of the book for full information). If you choose to carry out optional Activity 1, you will need to make enough copies of this article for all of the participants.

Science Materials
- 1 container from Activity 1
- 2 thermometers
- 1 8 oz. paper container
- newspaper to cover the work surface
- 16 oz. hot water
- 32 oz. cold water
- 1 1 gal. plastic bucket
- 1 watch
- Ice to fill the bucket halfway
- 4 oz. rock salt
- Stirrers
- Stopwatches

Media List

Overheads
1 Second Phase of Inquiry Protocol: Investigation and Data Collection
2 Investigation and Data Collection: Possible Areas of Focus for Observation
3 Components of Observation: Doing the Observation . . . Data Collection
4 Reflecting on the Observation
5 Journal Prompts
6 Evaluation Form

Handouts
1 Second Phase of Inquiry Protocol: Investigation and Data Collection
2 Investigation and Data Collection: Possible Areas of Focus for Observation
3 Components of Observation: Doing the Observation . . . Data Collection
4 Journal Prompts
5 Science Activity cards
6 Evaluation Form

DVD
"Ice Cream Making: Cindy—Classroom Observation"

Welcome and Check-In (10 minutes)

Reconnecting With Each Other and the Program (10 minutes)

Overview

The purpose of this time is to help mentors reconnect to the group and the work of science mentoring.

Before Beginning

Materials: posted agenda; posted list of outcomes; posted Norms.

Steps

1 Review the agenda.
2 Review the opening quote and talk about the theme of this session: observation.
3 Go through the Outcomes chart that contains the foci of the day.
4 Review the Norms from Session 1. Ask participants if they have other Norms that they want to add. Look at the Parking Lot and respond to any pressing issues.

Mentoring (2 hours)

Activity 1: Introduction to the Second Phase of the Inquiry Protocol: Investigation and Data Collection (15 minutes)

Overview

Participants gain a better understanding of the second phase of the inquiry protocol: investigation and data collection.

Before Beginning

Materials: Handout 1, Overhead 1; charts from Session 2

Steps

1 Explain that today the focus is on the second phase of the inquiry protocol: investigation and data collection. Mentors have an opportunity to work with a partner to unpack the specifics of that phase and gain a clearer understanding of it.
2 Have seatmates look carefully at the components of the data collection phase to prepare them for the next activity.
3 Show Overhead 1; ask mentors to turn to Handout 1. They will use the inquiry protocol to determine areas for focus before they watch the video of the postobservation conference.
4 Remind mentors that they saw the preobservation conference for this lesson in Session 2. Review the charts from Session 2, on which you recorded specific observations from the preobservation conference.

Activity 2: Investigation and Data Collection in the Classroom (1¼ hours)

Overview

Before viewing a classroom video clip, participants identify what to observe. They use the inquiry protocol to determine areas for focus. Next, participants script a classroom observation. Participants viewed the preobservation conference for this lesson in Session 2.

Before Beginning

Materials: Handout 2, Overhead 2; Handout 3, Overhead 3; DVD: "Ice Cream Making: Cindy—Classroom Observation"

Steps

1   Explain that teachers will use this video as an opportunity to learn how to script an observation.
2   Tell participants that this video is of an eighth-grade class in Fall River, Massachusetts, taught by Cindy. She is teaching Activity Four, "Cooling Hot Water With Cold Water," of the ice cream making and cake baking unit. Her focus is the investigation and data collection phase in the inquiry protocol. The clip runs 31 minutes.

> ### Video Cue
> You may choose to begin the clip at 8 minutes, 30 seconds, after the review from the session before. The first 8½ minutes of the clip review the data collected during the previous lesson and provide a strong example of sense making during the data collection phase.

Steps (continued)

3   Show Overhead 3.
4   Point out that the line down the middle of the page ensures that participants keep their interpretations separate from the observational data they collect.
5   Ask participants to try to script as much of the lesson as possible. Tell participants that scripting is a classroom observation data collection technique whereby the observer writes down exactly what is said by both teacher and students. Most observers use their own form of shorthand and then rewrite their notes into full sentences to share with the teacher who was observed. Most people find that with practice scripting becomes easier. Remind participants that there is a certain focus for any observation, so the observer would only script the agreed-upon area for focus. (A possible focus might be the types of questions the teacher asks.)

6 Explain that scripting is extremely worthwhile because this kind of data-driven feedback can improve teaching and learning.

7 View the video segment.

Training Tip

Emphasize that observational data should be specific, not general, and objective, not interpretive. This emphasis maximizes learning outcomes. This phase of the mentoring cycle is akin to the data collection phase of the inquiry cycle. It is important for mentors not to interpret data prematurely.

Activity 3: Video Discussion (30 minutes)

Overview

Participants share their observation scripts and reflect on how they might hold a postconference discussion with this teacher.

Before Beginning

Materials: Overhead 4

Steps

1 Ask the mentors what they observed. If participants make evaluative or interpretive statements, be sure to ask what data supports that interpretation and encourage them to rephrase an opinion into an objective statement. This is not to say that we never give opinions or suggestions, but it is essential to start by considering the data. As participants contribute to the discussion, record their observations.

2 After recording the observations, pose the questions on Overhead 4.

3 Record participants' responses to the questions on chart paper. Save this paper for the next session. In Session 3, you refer to their responses to Overhead 4 when you show the postobservation conference video that occurred between Cindy Wrobel and the mentor.

Science (3 hours)

Activity 1: Classroom Connections and Science Pedagogy (30 minutes)

Overview
In the last session, you asked mentors to think about the opportunities they provide their students to generate, collect, and represent data. In this segment they share their reflections.

Before Beginning
Ensure that participants brought their science notebooks with them.

Steps
1   Begin by asking mentors share their reflections about how they have their students generate, collect, and represent data.
    - What kinds of opportunities do you provide that enable students to generate and collect data?
    - In what ways do students organize and represent their data?
2   Process the prompts by asking mentors to share their ideas with each other.
3   Question whether they have students create their own tables, charts, and graphs, or if they provide a ready-made template for students to use.
4   Ask why they might use a particular graph versus another and what kinds of charts and tables students create and the purposes of the charts and tables.
5   Be sure to collect on chart paper the different strategies mentors use to help students organize and represent data.

Activity 2: Cooling Capacity: Investigation and Data Collection (1¾ hours)

Overview
In the previous activities, participants explored the concept of heat capacity—the amount of heat an object already possesses—through experiments using aluminum foil. They examined the effect of the amount, surface area, and size of the metal sheet on melting ice cubes. In the next three activities, mentors explore cooling hot water with three different solutions: cold water, ice water, and ice-salt water.

Before Beginning
Materials: data charts from Session 2; Handout 5, Science Activity Cards (Investigations 1, 2, and 3) you prepared during your advance preparation work (see What You Need to Make, p. 43).

Steps

1   Begin by reviewing the data from the previous session. Refer to the posted chart and ask the following questions:
   - What did we learn about the effect of the amount of metal on the melting rate of ice cubes?
   - What effect did the size of the metal have on the melting rate of the ice cubes?
   - How did surface area affect the melting rate of the ice?
2   Tell participants that they will investigate which of three solutions will cool hot water most quickly. The three solutions are cold water, ice water, and ice-salt water.
3   Suggest that table groups divide into three subgroups. Each subgroup will conduct one of the investigations.
4   Tell each subgroup to select one investigation card from the table and to collect the materials they need.
5   When they finish the investigation, ask participants to share the data and graphs from the three investigations in table groups and compare their results.
6   Next, have each subgroup post its data on the appropriate data charts.

Sense-Making Discussion (45 minutes)

This discussion will help participants interpret the data they collected in their investigations.

Steps

1   Have one or two table groups transfer each of the three graphs onto a transparency or piece of chart paper.
2   Display the graphs (cooling curves) so that the entire group can see it.
3   For Investigation 1: Ask mentors to compare the curves and determine which container is the best choice for cooling hot water.
4   For Investigation 2: Have mentors compare the graphs of hot water cooled with tap water and hot water cooled with ice water.
5   For Investigation 3: Have mentors compare the results of this investigation with the previous two and plot the cooling curves for hot water in the metal containers in the three different environments.
6   Engage the mentors in a discussion of the differences, and indicate what implications this has for making ice cream in a metal container.

Science Background

In the first investigation (Activity Card 1), heat leaves the hot water in the container rather than being conducted into it. Metal is still the best conductor. In the second investigation, there is a greater temperature difference between the hot water and the ice water, so the heat transfer happens more quickly than in the first investigation. The ice-water solution does not change temperature because the heat melts the ice rather than raising the temperature of the solution. In the third investigation, the heat is leaving the hot water quickly and eventually reaches 0°C. The hot water and the water begins to freeze.

Reflection and Next Steps (40 minutes)

Reflective Journal (15 minutes)

Before Beginning
Materials: Handout 4, Overhead 5

Steps
1   Remind mentors that establishing a culture of reflection is important.
2   Explain that during these training sessions, you want to model the importance of allotting sanctioned time for reflection. At the end of the day, you want to provide a short amount of quiet time to have mentors consider some of the issues that they raised during this session.
3   Distribute Handout 4.
4   Ask mentors to respond to the journal prompts (Overhead 5).
5   Collect mentors' responses so that you will know what you need to address in the next session.

Optional: For Next Time (15 minutes)

Before Beginning
Materials: Optional reading, "The Right Question at the Right Time" by J. Elsgeest, for discussion in Session 4, Science Activity 1. (See "Resources" for full information.)
If you would like to explore questioning strategies with participants, completing optional Activity 1, including the reading of this chapter, will provide a deeper understanding of the kinds of questions that teachers should use to help students develop their understanding of science concepts.

Discussion Points

The following ideas will help participants lay the groundwork for their exploration of the sense-making phase of inquiry in the next session:

1. During this session, you had the opportunity to dig deeper into the sense-making phase of inquiry. Determining what ideas and understanding students have developed following an investigation is a critical component of inquiry teaching. This sense-making process should incorporate questions that not only give teachers data about student understanding and thinking but also help students develop concepts and higher-order thinking skills.

2. In many classrooms, students do not have the opportunity to participate in sense-making sessions. Many teachers follow up investigations and hands-on activities by having students read about the targeted concept(s) in a textbook. The idea seems to be that if students did not develop the conceptual understanding through the activity, the text will fill in the gaps in their understanding.

3. Knowing what the best or right question is in a particular instance is not easy. Many educators learned that the best question to ask students is, "Why?" Explaining the "why" of a particular concept is, however, very difficult and requires deep understanding. If you have chosen to use the optional article "The Right Question at the Right Time" by J. Elsgeest, mentors may read that teachers must scaffold questions—building a bridge of "what" and "how" questions that help students reach the "why."

The article will help participants with these kinds of questions and ideas.

Steps

1   Share the discussion points with mentors.

2   Ask them to read the optional article "The Right Question at the Right Time" by J. Elsgeest for next time (see "Resources" for a complete reference). Request that they consider the following questions as they read:

- What are the three most important new ideas to come to you as a result of reading this article?
- How would you categorize the questions that you typically ask your students?

- What new categories or kinds of questions will you try to incorporate into your sense-making discussions with students?

3   Ask mentors to record their responses in their science notebooks and come to Session 4 prepared to share their thoughts about these questions.

Evaluation (10 minutes)

Overview

This activity is an important source of information for you. Participants' feedback will help you prepare for future sessions.

Before Beginning

Materials: Handout 7, Overhead 6

Steps

1   Distribute and show as an overhead, the Evaluation Form (Overhead 6, Handout 6).

2   Encourage participants to write any questions or concerns they have on sticky notes and stick them on the Parking Lot paper as they leave.

SESSION 4

Communication leads to community, that is, to understanding, intimacy and mutual valuing.

Rollo May

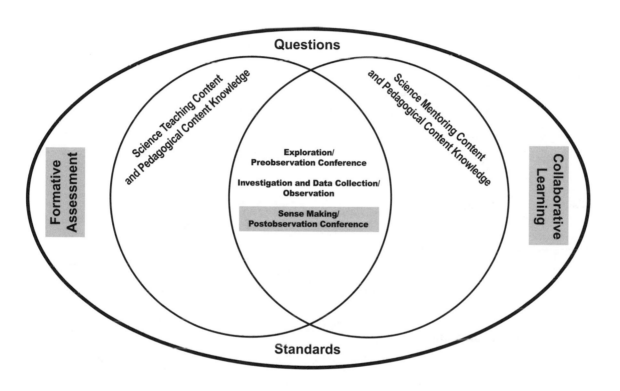

Overview

In this session, participants view and have an in-depth discussion about a postobservation conference for a lesson from the ice cream–making unit in Cindy Wrobel's class. They fill out a mentoring journal, and they evaluate the mentoring journal from the video conference. Participants identify the best container in which to make ice cream, make ice cream, and enjoy the fruits of their labors. They also examine components of communication and assess their own communication skills. The session ends with your introducing participants to the Mentor-Mentee Handbook and the Planning Guide which will guide their interactions.

Outcomes

- Develop a repertoire of mentoring skills and strategies, such as coplanning and preobservation, observation, and postobservation frameworks.
- Learn communication skills, including active listening.
- Create an individual mentor-mentee plan.
- Gain familiarity with the mentoring handbook.
- Apply concepts relating to heat transfer to making ice cream.

Session Snapshot

Agenda

10 minutes	**Welcome and Check-In** Reconnecting With Each Other and the Program
1 hour, 20 minutes	**Mentoring** Activity 1: Postobservation Conference—Ice Cream Making: Cindy Activity 2: Mentoring Journal
2¾ hours	**Science** (Optional) Activity 1: Classroom Connections and Science Pedagogy I—Sense Making Activity 2: Making Ice Cream Activity 3: Classroom Connections and Science Pedagogy II—Formative Assessment
2 hours	**Mentoring** Activity 1: Communication: The Components of RARE (*Reflect* the facts, pay *Attention*, *Reflect* feelings, *Encourage* the other person to talk) Activity 2: Communication Skills Self Assessment Activity 3: Mentor-Mentee Handbook Activity 4: Planning Guide: Creating an Individual Mentoring Action Plan
25 minutes	**Reflection and Next Steps** Reflective Journal Evaluation

How to Prepare for Session 4

What You Need to Do

- Read all introductory and background information with a particular focus on discussing the postobservation conference.

- Scan through the session and review all of the directions and sidebar notes. These include activity descriptions and directions, the science background sections, the training tips, and the discussion points.
- Do the activities if you haven't done them before as a participant.

What You Need to Make
- Write the Agenda on chart paper, and hang it on the wall where participants can see it and you can refer to it throughout the day.
- Write the Outcomes on chart paper and hang the paper on the wall.
- Make all overheads.
- Duplicate all handouts.
- Post the Norms and Parking Lot charts.

What You Need to Acquire
- Chart paper and markers
- Sticky notes
- Overhead slide projector
- DVD player and television

Science Materials
Each table group needs:
- 1 1 gal. plastic bucket
- 4 oz. cold water
- 4 oz. rock salt
- 4 oz. cream (or milk or half-and-half)
- 2 tsp. sugar
- ½ tsp. vanilla flavoring
- Ice to fill the bucket halfway
- 1 large metal spoon
- Spoons (1 for each group member)
- 1 coffee can with cover
- Cups (1 for each group member)
- 1 stirrer
- Newspaper (to cover the work surface)

Media List

Overheads
1 Reflecting on the Observation
2 Postobservation Conference Protocol
3 Postobservation Video Questions
4 Blank Mentoring Journal
5 Components of RARE
6 Communications Potholes
7 12 Roadblocks to Communication
8 Journal Prompts
9 Marian Wright Edelman Quote
10 Evaluation Form

Handouts
1 Blank Mentoring Journal
2 Procedure for Making Ice Cream
3 Components of RARE
4 Listener Card 1
5 Listener Card 2
6 Listener Card 3
7 Communications Skills Self-Assessment
8 Mentor-Mentee Handbook
9 Planning Guide
10 Evaluation Form

DVD
"Ice Cream Making: Cindy—Postobservation Conference"

Welcome and Check-In (10 minutes)

Reconnecting with Each Other and the Program (10 minutes)

Overview

This check-in sets the context for the day's work on communication. Participants discuss issues and questions raised in their reflective journals.

Before Beginning

Materials: agenda, list of outcomes, Norms from Session 1.

Steps

1 Explain that today's work is a continuation of the previous session.
2 Highlight a few of the more compelling or often-repeated issues and questions that participants raised in the journal reflections from the previous session and assure mentors that you will spend some time answering questions and addressing concerns.
3 Review the opening quote and talk about the theme of today's session: communication.
4 Review the Outcomes (the foci of the day).
5 Refer to the posted Norms and ask people how they think you're all doing regarding the Norms. Probe so that participants will realize you are asking the question to get real answers and want to ensure that voices are being heard. Look at the Parking Lot and respond to any pressing issues.

Mentoring (1 hour, 20 minutes)

Activity 1: Postobservation Conference—
Ice Cream Making: Cindy (1 hour)

Overview

Participants begin by reviewing suggestions they made for issues to be raised during the postobservation conference. They observe the videotaped mentor's actions in the postobservation conference of the classroom video from Session 3.

Before Beginning

Materials: Overheads 1, 2, 3; chart paper from Session 3, Activity 4 video discussion; DVD: "Ice Cream Making: Cindy—Postobservation Conference."

Discussion Points

1. Point out the importance of processing observations. It isn't enough just to observe; mentor and mentee need an opportunity to make sense of the observation.
2. Just as sense making is an essential phase of the inquiry process, the postobservation conference is essential to the mentee's growth.
3. Postobservation conferences give the mentor and mentee an opportunity to reflect on the lesson from the perspective of student learning.
4. The more specific the mentor's feedback is in relating teaching to student learning, the more likely it will be useful to the mentee.
5. It is important to have postobservation conferences within a day or two after observations.

Steps

1. Show Overhead 1 (also used in Session 3). Direct participants' attention to the chart paper from the Session 3, Activity 3, video discussion. Review suggestions made for issues to be raised during the postobservation conference. Note that, although it is important to address the focus requested by the mentee, the data will probably raise additional issues. If participants believe that many of the issues are important, suggest that the group prioritize them.
2. Use the discussion points provided to introduce the postobservation conference.
3. Introduce the protocol for the postobservation conference (Overhead 2). The overhead shows a generic postobservation form. The data should relate to the specific area of interest (focus) that the teacher and mentor agreed upon in the preobservation conference. Teacher and observer analyze the lesson using data gathered by the observer, probing for specificity.
4. Show the DVD. Ask the group to watch as closely as possible for the videotaped mentor's actions and to script as much of the conversation as possible. Use Overhead 3, Postobservation Video Questions as a way to frame the observation. (For additional examples of postobservation conferences, use "Ice Cream Making: Brenda" or "Investigating Pond Organisms: Mike.")

Video Cue

Stop the DVD at #17:49 before the mentoring journal is completed.

Steps (continued)

5   Use the following questions to engage participants in a discussion of the postobservation conference they viewed:
- What are the core issues that the mentor and mentee discussed?
- What was—and what was not—addressed in the postobservation conference?
- What do you think the teacher might have learned as a result of the postobservation conference?
- How does the mentor help the mentee foster student learning in the lesson?

6   Suggest to mentors that a good way to end a postobservation conference is for the mentor to ask for specific feedback about the use of conferencing strategies and how the three goals of mentoring (trust, learning, reflection) are progressing. At the end of every conference, the mentor should hand the data collected (the scripting of the observation) to the mentee. The mentee can then review and reflect upon the data at his or her leisure.

7   Tell participants that the final step in a postobservation conference is to complete the mentoring journal. They will learn more about the mentoring journal in Activity 2, but right now, they will see an example of the journal.

> **Video Cue**
> Restart the DVD at #17:49.

Activity 2: Mentoring Journal (20 minutes)

Overview

The mentoring journal is a formative assessment tool and is used to support the work of both the mentor and the mentee. It is a way to keep a record of the mentoring conversations, recording both the content and the outcomes of the conversation.

Before Beginning
Materials: Overhead 4; Handout 1

Steps

1   Show the blank mentoring journal on the overhead (Overhead 4) and point out the different components. Use the discussion points provided to describe the purpose of the journal.

2   Have partners fill out the mentoring journal based on the postobservation conference they just observed.

3   After they complete this task, take suggestions from participants.

4   Using Overhead 4, complete a sample mentoring journal on the overhead.

5   Tell mentors that the homework for the next session will be to fill out a mentoring journal after each meeting they have with their mentees. Remind them that they should meet with their mentees at least once a month.

Discussion Points

1. Highlight that the goal of using the mentoring journal is to support both the mentor and the mentee, not to have it be an intrusive or evaluative document.

2. Explain that this is an opportunity to summarize insights gained during the meeting and record possible solutions, next steps, and who is responsible for what.

3. Point out that the mentoring journal is not limited to recording observations but is useful to keep a record of all mentor-mentee meetings.

4. Keeping a mentoring journal provides focus and clarity for the collaborative work of the mentor and mentee and guidance for the kind of support the mentor should make available.

Science (2¾ hours)

Activity 1: Classroom Connections and Science Pedagogy I— Sense Making (1 hour)

NOTE: If you choose not to carry out this optional activity with participants, add this hour, as necessary to the remaining two activities.

Overview

An optional activity at the end of the last session was to ask mentors to read as homework the chapter "The Right Questions at the Right Time" by Jos Elstgeest and to think about three questions: What are the three most important new ideas to come to you as a result of reading this article? How would you categorize the questions that you typically ask your students? and What new categories or kinds of questions will you try to incorporate into your sense-making discussions with students?

Steps

1   First, have mentors do a think-pair-share and then share their thinking in table groups.

2   After 15 minutes or so, conduct a whole-group discussion focusing on the third question above.

Activity 2: Making Ice Cream (1¼ hours)

Overview

In this final physical science session of the institute, mentors apply to making ice cream what they have learned in previous sessions.

Before Beginning

Materials: Handout 2

Steps

1   Begin by reviewing the data from the previous session. Post the cooling curves created in the previous session and ask:
    - What are the implications for making ice cream?
    - What container is the best for making ice cream and why?

2   Divide each table into groups of three or four and have participants gather materials to make ice cream.

3   Distribute the Procedure for Making Ice Cream (Handout 2) to each group. (The recipe is a guideline and does not need to be rigidly followed.)

4   Every three to four minutes, have participants scrape the sides of the container with a spoon to remove the ice. Once the ice cream is made, participants can enjoy the fruits of their labor and learning.

5   A good way to end this section is to have a conversation about how the five activities mentors have experienced address the following National Science Education Standards (NSES) and their own state standards (while states and districts have their own science frameworks, most are based upon the NSES). You should, of course, connect these activities to the local standards more specifically. Discuss that
    - Energy is a property of many substances and is associated with heat, light, electricity, mechanical motions, sound, nuclei, and the nature of a chemical.
    - Heat moves in predictable ways, flowing from warmer objects to cooler ones, until both reach the same temperature.

Science Background

Making ice cream illustrates several concepts. These include the following: Heat from a hot material always travels to a cooler one; the greater the difference in the temperatures between the two materials, the faster the heat transfer occurs; and using containers of different materials also can slow down or speed up the transfer of heat. For ice cream to freeze properly the transfer must happen quickly.

Activity 3: Classroom Connections and Science Pedagogy II— Formative Assessment (30 minutes)

Overview

There are many opportunities throughout these investigations to assess students' understanding of heat transfer and related concepts and process skills. The teacher can ascertain what progress the students are making and use this information to adjust lessons accordingly. The most common way to assess informally is through observation and discussion, but there are other ways to informally assess students' conceptual understanding and process skills development. For example, teachers can determine how well students conduct their investigations by looking at their data tables. In this activity, mentors identify opportunities for formative assessment for each of the investigations they experienced.

Before Beginning

Materials: chart paper and markers for each table

Steps

1 Begin by having a discussion about formative assessment and the various techniques participants use to informally assess their students. You may want to have mentors describe a particular type of assessment they use and for what purpose.

2 Once mentors have discussed the different ideas, have them work in pairs to identify: what concepts and skills in each of the activities they think would be important to assess and how they would go about assessing them.

3 Assign each pair of participants one investigation and have each pair design an assessment. You may have several pairs working on the same investigation. This will allow several different types of assessment to be generated for each investigation.

4 Have groups report on the concepts and skills they identified as being important to assess, as well as the different assessment ideas they produced. Mentors should write up their assessments on chart paper and display them around the room.

Mentoring (2 hours)

Activity 1: Communication—The Components of RARE (45 minutes)

Overview

Professional relationships are complex; building a positive relationship is key to the success of mentoring. Introduce this section by stressing that communication is fundamental to establishing a positive relationship with a colleague. Lines of communication need to be kept open, so that shared, coherent views about teaching and learning can be created over time.

Before Beginning

Materials: Overheads 5, 6, 7; Handouts 3, 4, 5, 6, 7

Discussion Points

1. As busy people, we often want to close conversations as quickly as possible and, for teachers in particular, finding adequate time to have meaningful conversations with one another is difficult.

2. Closing conversations quickly does not enhance communication. Instead, the goal should be to keep the conversation going. Think of detective work. The detective's goal is to keep the suspect talking.

3. Sometimes people want to have a conversation with you, but it's at an inopportune time. It's appropriate to say, "I want to have this conversation with you, but not right now."

4. We tend to want to solve problems, instead of stepping back and letting people know we've heard what they're saying. Stepping in to solve a problem shows a desire or attempt to change the other person—to influence, rather than to accept. Our experience indicates that it can slow down or inhibit problem solving and that it can prevent good communication.

(continued on page 66)

5. The next activity is designed to highlight the importance of listening to being a good communicator and emphasizes common pitfalls to communication. Professional relationships are complex. Building a positive relationship is key to the success of both coaching and mentoring. Introduce this section by stressing that communication is fundamental to establishing a positive relationship with a colleague. Lines of communication need to be kept open so that shared coherent views about teaching and learning can be created over time. There are two essential ingredients in any relationship of one person fostering growth in another—empathy and acceptance. Active listening performs both functions and creates a climate that facilitates problem solving.

Steps

1   Use the discussion points to introduce this activity to participants.

2   Explain to participants that RARE is an acronym for good communication skills: *Reflect* the facts, pay *Attention, Reflect* feelings, *Encourage* the other person to talk.

3   Show participants Overhead 5 and distribute Handout 3 describing RARE.

4   Invite mentors to group into trios for this activity, ideally with colleagues they haven't worked with yet.

5   Explain that there are three roles. One of each trio, whom you will call A, will think of a problem or issue he or she wants to share with someone; another partner, B, will be the listener and will meet with the facilitator for a few minutes while the As are planning their story. C will be the observer in the group.

6   Clarify to the As that this should not be a story about a serious problem, but that it should be a real issue they would like to discuss with someone. The problem or issue may or may not be connected to school and work and could be about something such as mothers-in-law, children, or travel plans.

7   Ask trios to identify themselves, and make sure that every trio has an A, a B, and a C.

8   Ask the B group to meet with you, outside the room if possible. Bring the listener cards, Handouts 4–6, with you when you meet with the Bs. Divide the number of Bs by three, and copy that number of each listener card, Handouts 4–6. For example, if you have nine B participants, make 3 copies of Handout 4, 3 copies of Handout 5, and 3 copies of Handout 6.

9   Give each third of the B group copies of one of the listener cards for each member. You will now have one-third of the B group with Handout 4, one-third with Handout 5, and one-third with Handout 6. Give everyone a moment to look over the directions. Bring the Bs back in the room and have them rejoin their groups.

Steps (continued)

10 Ask the As to tell their stories, and, after about two minutes, interrupt the group. Some people will have figured out that this is a game, but others will not.

11 Begin the discussion with the As. They were the "victims" in the game, so we want to give them the opportunity to speak first.
   - What did they notice?
   - What was it like to tell their problems to these partners?

12 Then ask the Bs how it was for them to play a nonlistener. (The responses will vary, depending on how seriously the Bs took their nonlistening role.) At this point, give the Bs an opportunity to show their handout to their partners.

13 Now ask the C group for their observations. Explain that this was an exaggerated, artificial scenario, but, in truth, these are roadblocks to communication that happen in real-life conversations. Sometimes someone just wants a good listener—no advice, no jokes, no interruptions. For many people, the role of listener is a difficult one to play.

14 Summarize for mentors that communication skills cannot be minimized in successful mentoring. We have to stop talking and start listening if we're to find out what's on the other person's agenda.

15 Ask participants, "What gets in the way of listening?" Possible responses include thinking our own thoughts and wanting to solve the other person's problem.

16 Show overheads—Overhead 6, Communications Potholes, and Overhead 7, 12 Roadblocks to Communication.

17 Highlight a few points from these lists. You might want to supply personal anecdotes to give mentors a flavor of how the potholes and roadblocks prevent communication and undermine trusting relationships.

Activity 2: Communication Skills Self-Assessment (15 minutes)

Overview

This activity helps participants analyze their communication skills. They identify their strengths and those areas that could be improved.

Before Beginning
Materials: Handout 7

Steps
1   Explain to mentors that they are now going to assess their communication skills. As they assess their strengths and weaknesses, they should think about themselves as communicators not only in a school setting but also in more general terms.
2   Distribute Handout 7. Tell participants not to agonize about the exact numbers. The exercise is just intended to get a sense of their strengths and weaknesses.
3   Tell participants they have about five minutes to fill out the page.
4   Process the experience with the whole group by discussing which aspects of communication are strengths and which present challenges. In our experience the following three areas are often challenging for teachers: stating preferences, confrontation, and expressing feelings.

Activity 3: Mentor-Mentee Handbook (30 minutes)

Overview

This activity provides an opportunity for mentors to understand the components of the handbook and to gain insight into how using these documents will support their mentoring and their mentee's learning. Emphasize that the Mentor-Mentee Handbook is a collection of tools that supports their work as mentors.

Before Beginning
Materials: Handout 8

Discussion Points

1. Both the mentor and the mentee receive a copy of the Mentor-Mentee Handbook (Handout 8).

2. Remind mentors that they have already seen most of these documents at different sessions, but you want them to look at the whole handbook.

3. The whole is more than the sum of its parts—that is, as a whole, the handbook creates a platform or climate for mentoring.

4. Highlight the importance of the inquiry protocol and the importance of keeping it front and center. Suggest that, at the first meeting between mentor and mentee, they spend time understanding what is in the handbook and the purpose of each document.

Steps

1   Use the discussion points provided to introduce the Mentor-Mentee Handbook. Invite mentors to work in pairs to question the documents and suggest revisions, so the handbook can be more context-specific and reflect the realities of their settings.

2   As partners finish their examination of the handbook, ask them to discuss their insights.

3   If participants suggest revisions, record them, and let participants know that you will talk with your colleagues and committee about revising the document.

Activity 4: Planning Guide: Creating an Individual Mentoring Action Plan (30 minutes)

Overview

In this activity, participants receive a planning guide to help them structure their mentoring work. They review the components of the guide and make revisions according to their own particular context and needs.

Before Beginning

Materials: Handout 9

Discussion Points

1. Explain that you are going to hand out a suggested framework or planning guide for the mentor-mentee relationship.

2. Two major pitfalls for any mentor program are a lack of time for teachers to work together and a lack of clarity of the role of mentor.

3. Reiterate that this model of mentoring is educative mentoring—with a mentor who goes beyond being supportive, to providing active assistance for teacher learning.

4. Go over the idea that teaching science effectively is a complex skill. It involves juggling a lot of competing interests and unpredictable events, all while making decisions on the fly. These factors contribute to making teaching "messy," which is one reason why it's difficult for the novice to understand how an effective teacher manages to be effective.

5. Teachers use implicit knowledge to solve problems, but mentees need that to become explicit. That's one reason it's so important for mentees to observe mentors and vice versa.

Steps

1   Use the discussion points provided to introduce this activity. Distribute Handout 9. Explain that this is a draft.
2   Ask participants to examine this document with a partner (a colleague from their school, if possible) and determine what makes sense in the context of their schools and what would be challenging or not applicable.
3   Highlight the importance of context in this work. Tell mentors that it is important to determine what in their schools supports this mentoring work and to identify the obstacles they still need to address.
4   Suggest they write on the handout itself and make additions to the boxes marked "Other."
5   Give pairs 25 minutes to examine the document carefully.
6   After mentors have had an opportunity to examine and edit the planning guide, facilitate a group conversation about positive aspects of the guide and potential pitfalls.
7   Record responses on chart paper and look for patterns.

Reflection and Next Steps (25 minutes)

Reflective Journal (15 minutes)

Overview

The goal of this final section is to bring closure to the first four sessions of the institute and to ensure that mentors fully understand that working with novice teachers will improve their own teaching practice. Reinforce the notion that the potential for growth among veteran teachers who mentor others is profound, and that mentors report that their own teaching practice improves in significant ways as a result of their mentoring other practitioners.

Before Beginning

Materials: Overheads 8, 9

Steps

1   Ask mentors to think about the following prompts and write in their journals (Overhead 8).
    • How will I benefit from my work as a science mentor?
    • How might my students benefit from my work as a science mentor?
2   After five minutes, ask a few participants to share some of their predictions about how they will benefit from their new roles as mentors.
3   Remind mentors that they are to complete the mentoring journal each time they meet with their mentees.

4   Tell them that these will be used in Session 5 and that it is important that they bring copies to that training session.
5   Close by showing the Marian Wright Edelman quote about mentors (Overhead 9).
6   Emphasize the importance of the work of mentoring and that we all need to work together to improve the instruction of beginning teachers.
7   Relate the conversation to Session 1, when you first talked about mentoring as critical to the professionalism of teaching, and how mentors are adding new value and knowledge to the teaching profession.

Evaluation (10 minutes)

Overview

This activity is an important source of information for you. Participants' feedback will help you prepare for future sessions.

Before Beginning
Materials: Overhead 10, Handout 10

Steps
1   Hand out, and show as an overhead, the Evaluation Form (Overhead 10, Handout 10).
2   Encourage participants to write any questions or concerns they have on sticky notes and stick them on the Parking Lot paper as they leave.
3   End with a quick taking of turns, asking mentors to share actions they'll take.

Session 5

*The important thing in science is not so much to obtain new facts
as to discover new ways of thinking about them.*

Sir William Bragg, Nobel Prize in Physics 1915

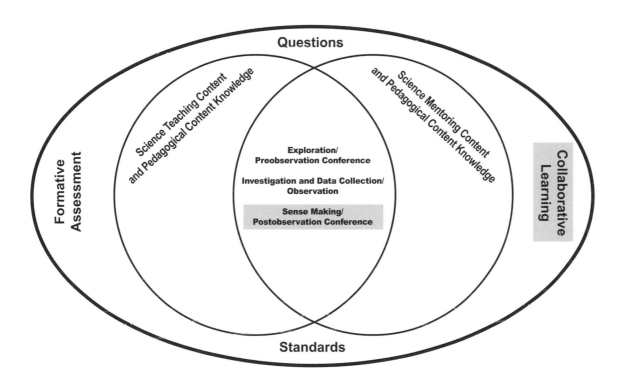

Overview

The session begins with having mentors reflect on their mentoring experience thus
far. You re-introduce the mentoring journal, and they consider difficult mentoring
issues. Next, participants view a virtual classroom observation with a focus on the
sense-making phase of inquiry, and they review the inquiry protocol. The session
ends with you introducing, and engaging participants in, a discussion of the phases
of new teacher development.

Outcomes

- Study pedagogical content knowledge with a colleague or colleagues.
- Develop a deeper understanding of the role of the inquiry protocol in science teaching and teacher development.
- Become familiar with the third phase of the inquiry protocol: sense making.
- Gain a heightened awareness of what the phases of inquiry look like in classroom practice.
- Continue to develop a repertoire of mentoring skills and strategies, such as coplanning, preobservation, observation and postobservation frameworks, and formative assessment.

Session Snapshot

Agenda

25 minutes	**Welcome and Check-In** Reconnecting with Each Other and the Program
1 hour, 35 minutes	**Mentoring** Activity 1: Mentor Update Activity 2: Mentoring Journals Activity 3: Burning Issues
3 hours	**Science** Activity 1: Introduction to the Third Phase of the Inquiry Protocol: Sense Making in the Classroom Activity 2: DVD: Video Analysis—Sense Making Activity 3: Studying the Inquiry Protocol
25 minutes	**Mentoring** Activity 4: Phases of New Teacher Development
25 minutes	**Reflection and Next Steps** Reflective Journal Evaluation

How to Prepare for Session 5

What You Need to Do

- Read all of the introductory and background information with a particular focus on the sense-making phase of the inquiry protocol.
- Scan through the session and review all of the directions and sidebar notes. These include activity descriptions and directions, the science background sections, the training tips, and the discussion points.

What You Need to Make

- Write the Agenda on chart paper and hang it on the wall where participants can see it and you can refer to it throughout the day.
- Write the Outcomes on chart paper and hang the paper on the wall.
- Make all overheads.
- Duplicate all handouts.
- Post the Norms and Parking Lot charts.

What You Need to Acquire

- Chart paper and markers
- Sticky notes
- Index cards
- Overhead slide projector
- DVD player and television

Media List

Overheads

1 Mentoring Journal
2 Inquiry Protocol, Sense-Making Phase
3 Studying the Inquiry Protocol
4 Stages of New Teacher Development
5 Viewing Tool—DVD Note-Taking Form
6 Possible Areas of Focus for Observation: Sense Making
7 Journal Prompts
8 Mentoring Journal: Mike
9 Mentoring Journal: Brenda
10 Mentoring Journal: Cindy

Handouts

1 Mentor Update Prompts
2 Inquiry Protocol
3 Video Note-Taking Organizer
4 Viewing Tool—DVD Note-Taking Form
5 Stage of New Teacher Development
6 Evaluation Form

DVD

"Ice Cream Making: Cindy—Classroom Observation"

Welcome and Check-In (25 minutes)

Reconnecting With Each Other and the Program

Overview

This may be the first session after training sessions held in the summer, or it may be a continuation of school-year sessions. If it is the former, it is worthwhile to spend some time reconnecting with the group and reestablishing the community. Spend about 15 minutes on the warm-up activity provided below (or one of your choice), then spend the remainder of your time reviewing the agenda and preparing participants for the day's activities.

Before Beginning

Materials: index cards on each table, one per participant; Agenda written on chart paper; Outcomes written on chart paper; Norms from Session 1.

Steps

1 Ask mentors to take an index card from the center of the table and jot down two truths and one lie about themselves. Explain that people will take turns in table groups.

- Step 1: One person tells the table group three statements about himself or herself. Two are true and one is a lie. Others at the table try to guess which one is the lie. For example, the person could say, "I won a prize in spelling in second grade. My favorite food is sushi. I got lost at the zoo when I was little." To be extra tricky, ask participants to word the lie so it contains a truthful element.

- Step 2: Everybody else at the table then holds up one, two, or three fingers to show which statement they think is the lie. The player sets the record straight; then the next person takes a turn. If time permits, each table can share the best lie with everyone.

2 Review the agenda with participants.

3 Revisit the Norms that participants developed in Session 1. Spend a little more time on the Norms if it has been a while since the group last met.

4 Review the quote and talk about the theme of today's session: The inquiry protocol and the sense-making phase.

5 Highlight the Outcomes (the foci of the day).

6 Look at the Parking Lot and respond to any pressing issues.

Mentoring (1 hour, 35 minutes)

Activity 1: Mentor Update (30 minutes)

Overview

Participants share with one another their initial mentoring experiences. As a group, they troubleshoot scheduling challenges.

Before Beginning

Materials: Handout 1

> **Training Tip**
>
> This may be the first time the group has met since taking on mentees. If the mentors have mentored mentees (or are practicing with peers), proceed with the following update. If not, perhaps use only Question 3, below, as a prompt.

Steps

1. Distribute Handout 1, which contains the following prompts:
   - What is something you have learned about being a mentor that has surprised, pleased, or annoyed you?
   - Have you managed to set up a regular meeting time? If so, when? If not, what is getting in the way?
   - Do you have some burning issues that you'd like to discuss today?

2. When participants have completed the handout, ask them to share their answers to Question 1 (or 3) with their tablemates.

3. After participants have completed this phase of the check-in, ask for any insights they gained from this sharing. Were there any patterns that stood out?

4. Ask participants to raise their hands if they are having trouble setting up a regular meeting time with their mentees. Depending on how many are having a hard time finding a meeting time, spend some time brainstorming solutions. (Mentors and mentees have met during preparation periods, lunch, and before or after school.)

5. Record on chart paper possible strategies for scheduling consistent meeting times with mentees.

6. In their table groups, ask mentors to first categorize and then prioritize the burning issues raised. Invite groups to share their top two or three issues.

7. Record issues on chart paper.

Activity 2: Mentoring Journals (20 minutes)

Overview

This activity reintroduces mentoring journals and their value. Participants review their journals and look for any patterns that might have emerged.

Before Beginning

Materials: Overhead 1

Steps

1 Remind mentors of the importance of using mentoring journals to keep track of the focus of their evolving mentor work.

2 Ask the mentors to indicate by a show of hands whether they have begun using the mentoring journals this year.

3 Ask for specifics. How have they used them? Have they found the journals a worthwhile tool in their mentoring?

4 Tell mentors that they should consistently use these mentoring journals in their mentoring.

5 Explain that research shows that ongoing and systematic measure of a teacher's professional growth—this is known as formative assessment—can have a significant impact on the teacher's professional development and the mentor's ability to offer appropriate support. Formative assessment guides beginning teachers as they develop teaching practices, habits, and skills that improve student learning. Using the inquiry protocol, mentors give feedback in context that enables teachers to improve their practice and become more reflective.

6 Show the mentoring journal (Overhead 1) on the overhead, and remind mentors of its different components.

7 Explain that this is an opportunity to summarize insights gained during the meeting and record possible solutions, next steps, and who is responsible for what.

8 In groups of four, have participants look at the data they have in their mentoring journals.

9 Ask groups to look for patterns they notice.

10 Ask groups to report patterns and any insights they gained from looking at other examples of mentoring journals. (Mentoring journal examples are in Overheads 8, 9, and 10.)

11 Let mentors know that during the next training session you will spend some time discussing how mentors use these journals, and they will have an opportunity to discuss the challenges and benefits of using them. Ask every mentor to bring in at least two completed journals to the next session.

Activity 3: Burning Issues (45 minutes)

Overview

In this brainstorming activity, participants generate numerous potential solutions to their identified mentoring issues and challenges. It reinforces the group as a community of learners and the value of shared problem solving.

Before Beginning

Materials: posted chart paper with one issue recorded on each chart, markers (one different colored marker per group).

Steps

1 Tell mentors that the next activity will be a Carousel Brainstorm.
2 Explain that the Carousel Brainstorm process is good for generating large numbers of responses to questions or issues.
3 There should be one group for every issue that is posted on chart paper. Count off by the number of groups you need. If you have six issues, ask participants to count off by sixes and form six groups. The ones become a group, the twos another group, and so on.
4 Ask participants to brainstorm solutions to each issue listed on the chart paper. Tell them to spend a few

minutes at each station to brainstorm as many solutions to address the issue as possible.

5 At the signal, ask each group to rotate to the next station. Each group should then read what the previous group or groups wrote. For each comment on the paper, instruct them to put a check mark if they agree, an "X" if they disagree, and a question mark if they need clarification.

6 Assign each group to a different chart paper to begin the brainstorming process. After a few minutes of brainstorming in small groups, signal the groups that they need to move on to the next station and repeat the brainstorming process, discussing what others have written and adding new thoughts to the charts. The carousel continues to turn until each group has had time to work at each station.

Training Tip

Begin the processing of this activity by clarifying any questions that were raised. Ask what stood out for people. Encourage mentors to use some of the ideas generated to address some of the challenges and issues they face in this new role as mentor.

Science (3 hours)

Activity 1: Introduction to the Third Phase of the Inquiry Protocol: Sense Making in the Classroom (1 hour)

Overview

During this section, participants will view a science classroom during the sense-making phase of an inquiry project and learn more about how this phase of inquiry looks in practice.

Before Beginning
Materials: Overhead 2, 6; Handout 2

Training Tip

Tell participants that they will view another clip from Cindy's classroom. Explain that her students have just completed the same investigation done by participants in which they used different containers (paper, plastic, glass, and metal) to cool hot water with cold water and created cooling curves for each of the containers. A short review of what they did and what they learned would be helpful.

Steps

1   Tell participants that today the focus is on the third phase of the inquiry protocol, the sense-making phase. Participants will work with a partner to unpack the specifics of that phase and to gain a clearer understanding of it.

2   Show Overhead 2 and ask mentors to turn to Handout 2. Clarify the elements of the sense-making phase.

3   Have seatmates look carefully at the components of the sense-making phase to prepare them for the next activity.

4   Ask participants to come up with possible areas of focus for this sense-making session. Record their ideas on chart paper.

5   Show Overhead 6. Discuss the possible areas of focus from the overhead.

Activity 2: Video Analysis—Sense Making—"Ice Cream Making: Cindy—Classroom Observation." (1 hour)

Overview

By watching the DVD, participants will have an opportunity to examine the sense-making phase of inquiry in practice.

Before Beginning

Materials: Handouts 3 and 4; Overhead 5; DVD: "Ice Cream Making: Cindy—Classroom Observation."

Training Tip

Remind participants once again that it is important to bring a spirit of curiosity about teaching and learning to the task of watching a DVD. Caution them to resist temptations to make judgments about the teacher but rather to look at the DVD as a source of interesting ideas about science teaching. Even if they might have taught the lesson differently, suggest they ask themselves what the teacher was trying to do and how she was addressing the sense-making phase of inquiry.

Steps

1   Divide the group into two. Ask Group A to observe the DVD with a focus on finding evidence of the sense-making phase, and request that Group B observe for infrastructure.

2   Distribute Handouts 3 and 4. Instruct participants to use the note-taking Handout 3 as a guide for observation and to record their observations on Handout 4.

3   Review the Viewing Tool—DVD Note-Taking Form, Overhead 5.

4   Show the DVD.

5   After showing the DVD, ask participants to discuss their general observations at their tables and then offer specific observations based on the prompts.

6   Ask participants to share observations. (Participants should comment on the teacher's questioning strategies and skills and how well the student groups collaborated.)

Activity 3: Studying the Inquiry Protocol (1 hour)

Overview

Participants review the inquiry protocol. You clarify in more detail the purpose of the protocol—the three phases of inquiry, infrastructure, and assessment (see the first section of this guide for further details). Mentors also use the science they experienced during the heat transfer (ice cream–making) unit as a way to illustrate how the inquiry protocol is exemplified in practice.

Before Beginning

Materials: Overheads 2, 3; Handouts 2

Training Tip

Throughout this segment, be sure to highlight the place of assessment in instruction and give specific examples from the science content participants have experienced in earlier sessions.

Steps

1   Explain that today participants will have an opportunity to work with a partner to unpack the specifics of each phase and to gain a clearer understanding of the use of the inquiry protocol in science teaching. This activity will help them consider the importance of having an agreed-upon protocol to inform the planning and observations of science lessons.

2   Emphasize that these phases are not discreet but rather interrelated parts of a cycle. They represent a holistic view of science teaching and should not be viewed as a checklist.

3 Introduce this activity as an opportunity to gain familiarity with the language and concepts of the phases of inquiry and the infrastructure that frame good science teaching and learning. Ask participants to take out the inquiry protocol (Handout 2).

4 Review the instructions on the overhead transparency (Overhead 3).

5 Both partners silently read Phase 1—Exploration.

6 Partner A summarizes the description.

7 Partner B gives examples of what that phase might look like in a classroom or instances of how the phase was exemplified during the science components of the training sessions.

8 Repeat the process for Phase 2, reversing roles.

9 Repeat switching roles back and forth for Phase 3—sense making.

10 Repeat switching roles back and forth for infrastructure and assessment.

11 As partners finish their review of the inquiry protocol, ask them to discuss what they have learned.

12 At this point, participants have experienced each of the phases of inquiry through the science investigations in the ice cream–making unit. They also have experienced how each of the phases looks in a classroom. They have had the opportunity to review the inquiry protocol and reflect more deeply on each of the phases. Suggest that, if possible, participants use this unit with their students to have firsthand experience with an extended inquiry investigation.

Mentoring (25 minutes)

Activity 1: Phases of New Teacher Development (25 minutes)

Overview

In this activity, you explain the different phases that teachers go through during their careers, and, in particular, new teachers experience in their first year of teaching. Mentors will be better able to support novices and teacher new to a situation—such as teaching at a new grade level or teaching a new subject—if they understand the different needs of the teacher. It is important for mentors to understand that they need to adapt their support for mentees to respond to the phases of new teacher development.

Cycles of Teacher Development

Researchers have documented the stages and cycles that teachers move through as they develop in their careers (Hord et al. 1987, Fuller and Brown 1975, Katz 1972, Moir 1990). Teachers move through a predictable cycle, represented by the spiral below, in response to each new challenge and change they experience (see Figure 5.1). This cycle begins with feelings of anticipation and even excitement with the prospect of experiencing success. As teachers becomes involved in the change, they begin to struggle with the reality of the challenge. Once teachers are able to move beyond mere survival with the new situation, they begin to ascend the spiral again, experiencing more success.

Figure 5.1. Cycle of Change

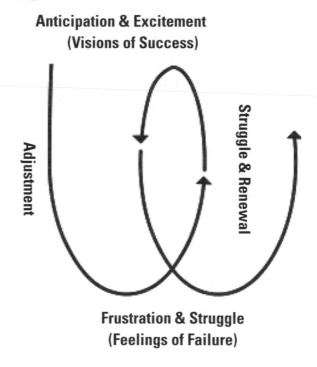

Teachers also move through stages over time during their careers as teachers. Even these stages are characterized by periods of less comfort preceding and directly following change. However, teachers still try new situations, strategies, and curricula with increasing focus on understanding student learning. While beginning teachers focus on coping, more-experienced teachers focus on instruction, and mature teachers focus on student learning and ways to further refine their teaching in response to individual student needs. This progression can be represented by the spiral narrowing over time to a focus on student learning (see Figure 5.2).

Figure 5.2. Spiral of Teacher Growth

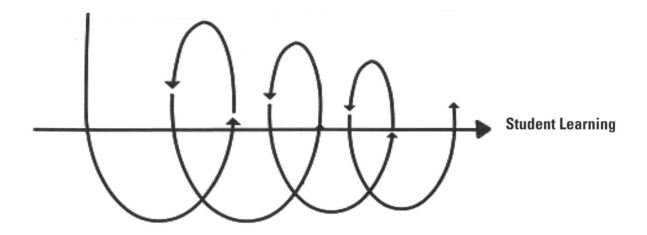

Before Beginning

Materials: Overhead 4, Handout 5, chart paper for each group.

Steps

1   Show Overhead 4 and explain that the description of stages is based on research of teachers in all phases of career development.
2   Describe the different stages of new teacher development.
3   To help participants understand that different stages require different types of support, assign each table a different phase (except for "Anticipation and Excitement, Revisited"). If you have fewer than five tables, divide tables in half; if you have more than five tables, give the same phase to more than one group.
4   Ask mentors to brainstorm specific needs a teacher, especially a new teacher, might have during this phase. For each need, suggest some strategies a mentor could use to support teachers with this need.
5   Encourage participants to be very specific and to try to address every need they can anticipate.
6   Have participants record these ideas on chart paper in two columns as shown.
7   After groups have finished, ask them to post their chart papers.
8   Tell participants to do a gallery walk and read other charts.
9   After mentors have had an opportunity to read the charts, ask what stood out for them? What surprised them? What might they think about next year?

Example of Chart Paper Columns

Stage of New Teacher Development_____

Need of teacher/mentee	Support strategy for mentor
1.	1.
2.	2.

Reflection and Next Steps (25 minutes)

Reflective Journal (15 minutes)

Before Beginning
Materials: Overhead 7

Steps

1   Ask mentors to respond to the following prompts in their journals:
    - As you think about implementing inquiry science in your own classroom, what areas will be good entry points for you and your students?
    - Which areas of the inquiry protocol will be most challenging to implement in your particular context? Why?
    - What is one thing you would like your mentee to work on?
    - How can you help him or her learn that?
    - What will progress look like?
2   Collect the journals, make copies, and return them to participants. That way, you will be able to keep tabs on the needs of the group.

Training Tip

If, in your group, there are peers practicing mentoring in pairs, reframe the last several prompts in the journals. For example, "What is one thing you would like to work on together?"

For Next Time

Beginning with Session 6, participants will engage in a pond study. If possible, have participants go to the pond to collect their pond water and organisms. That way, they will have a good idea of the kind of pond from which the organisms came and they will develop experience in collection techniques that will enable them to try a pond unit with their students. Try to schedule the visit to the pond at a time other than that of a scheduled mentoring session. If not, this could serve as the science portion of this fifth session.

Evaluation (10 minutes)

Overview

This activity is an important source of information for you. Participants' feedback will help you prepare for future sessions.

Before Beginning

Materials: Handout 6

Steps

1   Hand out the evaluation sheet (Handout 6), and ask participants to choose to write about one of the following prompts as a way of reflecting on their work today:
    - One thing I'm thinking about differently as a result of today's session is ....
    - One thing I am struggling with in thinking about today's session is ....
2   Encourage participants to write any questions or concerns they have on sticky notes and stick them on the Parking Lot paper as they leave.

References

Fuller, F. and O. Brown. 1975. Becoming a teacher. In *Teacher education* (74th Yearbook of the National Society for the Study of Education. Part 2, ed., K. Ryan, pp. 25–52. Chicago; University of Chicago Press.

Hord, S. M., W. L. Rutherford, L. Huling-Austin, and E. Gene. 1975. Taking charge of change. Alexandria, VA: Association for Supervision and Curriculum Development.

Huberman, M. 1989. The professional life cycle of teachers. *Teachers College Record 91* (1): 31–57.

Katz, L. G. 1972. Developmental stages of preschool teachers. *Elementary School Journal 73* (1): 50–54.

Moir, E. 1990. Phases of first-year teaching. California New Teacher Project Newsletter. Sacramento, CA: California Department of Education.

SESSION 6

*The most important measure of how good a game I played
was how much better I'd made my teammates play.*

Bill Russell, Boston Celtics

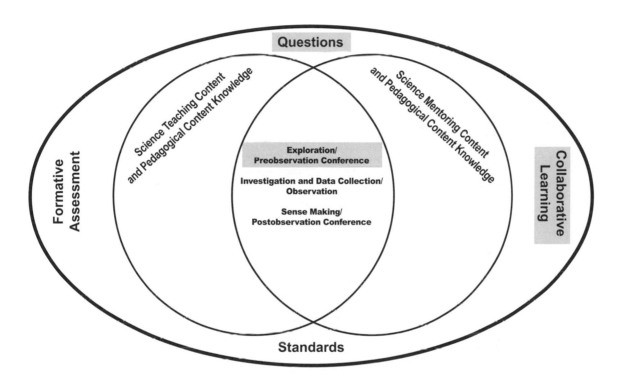

Overview

In this session, participants share their mentoring experiences thus far. They watch
a video clip of a sixth-grade classroom where students are engaged in a pond
study. Participants take on the role of the mentor and mentee and role-play the
postobservation conference. Next, they investigate life science concepts through
the context of a pond from the same unit used in the videoclip. Finally, they develop
questions about a pond organism to further investigate and discuss how they might
help students develop investigable questions.

Outcomes

- Experience how collaboration among teachers can contribute to a teacher's efficacy and professional growth.
- Develop an increased understanding of pedagogical content knowledge through virtual classroom observation and discussion with a colleague or colleagues.
- Establish a culture for addressing instructional problems.
- Become familiar with a schema for selecting appropriate mentoring strategies.
- Continue to build a learning community that builds trust in the sharing of ideas.
- Become familiar with the diversity of pond organisms.
- Increase ability to develop investigable questions.
- Create criteria for developing investigable questions.

Session Snapshot

Agenda

15 minutes	**Welcome and Check-In**	
	Reconnecting With Each Other and the Program	
3 hours, 40 minutes	**Mentoring**	
	Activity 1: Mentor-Mentee Reflections	
	Activity 2: Mentoring and Observation Strategies	
	Activity 3: Video Viewing and Discussion	
	Activity 4: Mentor-Mentee Role-Playing and Debriefing	
1 hour	**Science**	
	Activity 1: Exploring the Pond	
	Activity 2: Classroom Connections and Science Pedagogy	
10 minutes	**Wrap-Up and Next Steps**	
	Homework	
	Evaluation	

How to Prepare for Session 6

What You Need to Do

— Read all introductory and background information with a particular focus on the content-student-teacher triangle. You may also want to review the work of Joseph Schwab. (The curriculum model most universally applicable to a broad range of educational settings was developed by Joseph Schwab, a science educator fascinated by the practical aspects of curriculum-making. He codified the dimensions of curriculum change into a "language" for curriculum discourse. He identified four *commonplaces* of every encounter—subject matter, teacher, students, and milieu—and suggested that they are equally salient aspects that can be addressed independently in curricular discussions.)

— Become familiar with the organisms that are in the sample of pond water that you collected and make sure that there is a diversity of organisms present.

— Review the Grades 5–8 Inquiry Standards of the National Science Education Standards as well as your state's middle grades life science standards to identify the concepts that the pond study unit would support.

— Scan through the session and review all of the directions and sidebar notes. These include activity descriptions and directions, the science background sections, the training tips, and the discussion points.

What You Need to Make

— Write the Agenda on chart paper and hang it on the wall where participants can see it and you can refer to it throughout the day.

— Write the Outcomes on chart paper and hang the paper on the wall.

— Make all overheads.

— Duplicate all handouts.

— Post the Norms and Parking Lot charts.

What You Need to Acquire

— Chart paper and markers

— Sticky notes

Science Materials

— Pond organisms: several 5 gal. buckets with pond water containing both plants and animals, large and small. You may wish to involve mentors in the collection of the pond organisms.

— Tips on collecting organisms: Make sure to collect organisms (plants and animals) from the top, middle, and bottom layers of the pond, as organisms differ among the layers. Also, be sure to collect mud and sand for the bottom dwellers.

— The organisms in the pond water are easy to maintain. Make sure to find a suitable place to keep the water samples over the course of the next five sessions. Make sure that you have a simple aquarium pump with aerator to provide oxygen and place the water in an area where it will receive at least partial sunlight.

— If you do not have access to a pond, you can order pond organisms from a biological supply house. You will need to order snails, dragonflies, nymphs, damselfly nymphs and mayfly nymphs; caddisfly larvae, isopods, amphipods; copepods, daphnia, planaria, beetles, and backswimmers. Use spring water to store these organisms. Regular tap water has chemicals that will kill them.

Materials per Group
- Wallpaper soaking trays (not black)
- Aquarium aerators
- Small pail
- Hand magnifiers, one for each person
- Microscope
- Microscope slides, several per group
- Aluminum pie plates, several per group
- Large spoon or ladle
- White plastic plate
- Kitchen strainer
- Coffee stirrers, several per group
- Newspaper to cover tables

Media List

Overheads
1 Reflections
2 Observation Form
3 CST (content, student, teacher) Triangle
4 A Framework for Interpreting Observation
5 Feedback Focus
6 Evaluation Form

Handouts
1 Reflections
2 Observation Form
3 CST (content, student, teacher) Triangle
4 A Framework for Interpreting Observation
5 Feedback Focus
6 Evaluation Form

DVD
"Investigating Pond Organisms: Mike—Classroom Observation"

Welcome and Check-In (15 minutes)

Reconnecting With Each Other and the Program

Overview

The purpose of this time is to help mentors reconnect to the group and the work of science mentoring.

Before Beginning

Materials: session agenda, session outcomes, Norms from Session 1

Steps

1   Review the Agenda.
2   Review the opening quote and talk about the theme of this session: collaboration and observing and analyzing practice.
3   Go through the Outcomes chart that contains the multiple foci of the day.
4   Review the Norms from Session 1. Ask participants if they have any Norms they would like to add to this list.

Mentoring (3 hours, 40 minutes)

Activity 1: Mentor-Mentee Reflections (30 minutes)

Overview

This activity guides participants to review their mentoring journals with a focus on the science concept(s) that were taught.

Before Beginning

Materials: Overhead 1, Handout 1

Steps

1   Give participants an opportunity to reread the mentoring journals from their homework assignments.
2   Show Overhead 1.
3   Ask participants to select a partner and reflect on their classroom observations for approximately 20 minutes.
4   Bring the group together as a whole, and ask participants to share any insights they gained as a result of the observations and conversations. Some of this debriefing should focus on the science concept they taught and the difficulties of teaching that concept.

SESSION 6

Activity 2: Mentoring and Observation Strategies (2 hours)

Overview

The activity prepares participants for viewing a classroom videoclip by reinforcing the importance of collecting descriptive data.

Before Beginning

Materials: Overheads 2, 3, 4, 5; Handouts 2, 3, 4, 5

Discussion Points: Data

1. There is real power to having data points. They provide the supporting framework for rich conversations about practice.

2. Conversations between mentors and mentees can deteriorate into an opinionated back-and-forth, such as: "Here's my way. Well, here's my way. No, this is the way." But data represent a third, impartial source of information.

3. Consider the sentence, "The patient has a fever." It is an impartial observation. There's no quibbling with it, no room for argument. However, "The patient has an infection" is an inference or an opinion that can be challenged. In these mentor-mentee exchanges, it's crucial to separate observation from inference and keep the discussion based on factual observations recorded (scripted) by the mentor.

Steps

1. Begin this activity by sharing with participants the discussion points about data. Then, introduce the activity by explaining that participants will have an opportunity to watch a video, practice selective scripting, and prepare for a postconference.
2. Show Overhead 2 and point out the line in the middle of the page.
3. Review the importance of keeping descriptive data separate from interpretations and opinions; hence, the vertical line separating the two sections.
4. Tell participants to write in the left column as much of what is happening as possible, restricting their notes to data and not including interpretations.
5. Instruct participants to write questions, thoughts, and interpretations in the right column. Remind participants to use shorthand such as T = teacher, and G = girl. The column on the far left is to note the time so participants can see how long a particular activity took.

6   Tell participants that the purpose of watching this video is to collect data to give feedback to the teacher that would be most helpful in improving his practice.

7   Use the discussion points about the video to describe the video clip.

8   Before showing the videoclip, remind participants to use the video observation form. You may want to share the sample observation form with them first.

9   Show the videoclip.

Discussion Points: Video

1. This video is of a sixth-grade class in Danvers, Massachusetts, taught by Mike. He is teaching the pond study unit during the investigation and data-collection phase.

2. The video shows a portion of Mike's class including whole-class directions and students working in groups to observe "critters" and develop questions for further experimentation. Mike is working on facilitating students' ability to come up with investigable questions.

Activity 3: Video Viewing and Discussion (1½ hours)

Overview

Participants observe and script a videoclip of students making observations of pond organisms, using a "descriptive data" observation form. They watch the video a second time and focus on one of three perspectives—the teacher, the student, or the content.

Before Beginning

Materials: chart paper and marker; Overhead 3, Handout 3; Overhead 4, Handout 4; DVD: "Investigating Pond Organisms: Mike—Classroom Observation"

Training Tip

Before this discussion begins, encourage participants to think of the teacher whose work they are examining as a silent member of their group. In other words, they don't want to be overly critical of a colleague's work. Promote respectful conversation and be careful not to allow the conversation to become overly critical.

Part 1: Steps (30 minutes)

1   After the video, ask participants "What have you noticed about the lesson?"
2   Record participants' answers on chart paper.
3   After you've collected observations, try to categorize them. For example, which observations were about the teacher, which were about the students, which were about the content, and which were about the context (e.g. physical space, logistics, culture of class). Put letters next to what you've recorded on the chart paper, such as T = teacher, S = students, and C = content.

Training Tip

This categorizing is a way to highlight what stands out for teachers when they script an observation. Usually teachers focus on "teacher talk." It is important to raise teachers' consciousnesses to the importance of highlighting the science and also the students' conversations in their scripting. It is impossible to focus on all three simultaneously.

Steps (continued)

4   Explain to participants that it is worthwhile to rotate the focus as you continue to observe a colleague's practice.
5   Ask the following questions:
   •   Why do you think you noticed the particular things you did notice?
   •   What does this help you learn about yourself as a teacher?
6   Show Overhead 3 and explain that this is the instructional triangle. Use the discussion points provided to describe the triangle.
7   Explain that you can observe from any one of these perspectives.
8   Ask the following question: "What is the worthwhile science that is being taught here?"
9   Inform participants they will have an opportunity to view the video again, this time with a particular focus—teacher, students, or content.
10   Reshow the video.

Training Tip

Before showing the video for the second time, have participants count off by threes to form groups. Assign one focus to each group. Encourage participants to practice scripting again (on a clean copy of the observation handout) as they watch the video, this time from the particular perspective that was assigned.

Discussion Points

1. The triangle (Overhead 3, Handout 3) comes from Joseph Schwab, a science educator who was fascinated by the practical aspects of curriculum making. He codified the dimensions of curriculum change into a "language" for curriculum discourse. He identified four commonplaces of every encounter—subject matter, teacher, students, and milieu—and suggested that they are equally salient aspects that can be addressed independently in curricular discussions.

2. Teaching and learning are the interaction of all three—teacher, student, and content—all in a milieu (context). Effective observations take into account the interaction of the three components in this triangle, which is based on Schwab's commonplaces of education.

3. Content usually gets the shortest amount of attention, and most of the observation focuses on the teacher's actions. Since this is content-specific mentoring with a focus on science, it is important to pay attention to content.

Part 2: Steps (60 minutes)

After reshowing the video:

1. Have everyone who rewatched it with the focus on the teacher get together in one group.
2. Have everyone who rewatched the video with the focus on students get together in one group.
3. Have everyone who rewatched the video with the focus on content get together in one group.
4. Have the people in these groups discuss briefly (10 minutes) what they observed the second time they watched the video, with their particular focus. What did they notice that they didn't see the first time?
5. Form groups of three people each, mixed so that each perspective will be represented in each trio. In each group, there should be one person who focused on the teacher, one person who focused on the students, and one person who focused on the content.
6. Tell participants that, working in these trios, they will prepare feedback to the teacher in the video. Handout 4 will help them frame their scripted observations (from either observation sheet) so they can decide what feedback they'll give and how they will do it. Emphasize the importance of having evidence to support their statements.
7. Distribute Handout 4. Allow 20 minutes for the discussion and to complete the sheet.
8. When mentors and mentees have completed the sheet, focus their attention on giving feedback by asking, "What would you talk about with the teacher in the video and why?"

MAKING SCIENCE MENTORS

9 Tell them to use the protocol and identify an area of practice that could be contributing to the problem. For example, if the teacher on the video is asking unclear questions, it could be due to poor science content knowledge, inexperience with the unit, or with asking questions that are too open-ended.

10 Emphasize the importance of grounding the practice in the protocol.

11 Distribute Handout 5 and suggest participants choose one topic to address and record that under the "what" column. The next step is for participants to decide how they would begin the conversation.

12 Suggest participants draft some questions or prompts that could help focus the mentee on the issues or its causes.

13 Record these in the "how" column. The "why" column is a rationale for choosing a topic as a focus for the conversation. Allow 10 to 15 minutes.

14 When participants complete this activity, explain that you're asking them to create a curriculum and pedagogy for improving practice. This is an important part of mentoring—what we're talking about here goes beyond supportive mentoring. It is educative mentoring, and the mentor assumes a role as teacher educator.

15 As groups finish this activity, ask participants to share out—"popcorn" style (quick go-around)—topics, questions, or prompts they chose as a focus. Record these on chart paper with the same headings as the handout and discuss common ideas. Look for patterns and highlight them.

Activity 4: Mentor-Mentee Role-Playing and Debriefing (25 minutes)

Overview

This activity gives participants an opportunity to practice a postobservation conference based on the classroom video they just watched.

Before Beginning

Ask for two volunteers to role-play a postobservation conference.

Steps

1   Explain that one person will play the teacher on the video (the mentee) and the other will be the mentor. The person acting in the mentor's role will receive support from the other participants.

2   Allow the mentor to open the postconference, and, after a couple of statements, freeze the action and ask the group to give some suggestions of what the mentor could say next.

3   Collect three responses and then tell the mentor to either choose one of the suggested responses or respond as she or he chooses.

4   Continue in this mode for about 10 minutes.

5   After role-play is completed, ask participants to offer any insights they gained from observing or participating in this process. Highlight the importance of learning as a goal for these kinds of mentor-mentee conversations.

6   Ask if the mentee learned a new strategy, gained insight into his or her teaching practice, or has a plan to improve a teaching skill.

7   In table groups, have participants discuss the questions from the Framework for Interpreting Observation.

8   Tell them to use their observation notes to answer the questions about the lesson. Remind them to provide evidence.

Science (1 hours)

Overview

In the first five sessions, participants engaged in a physical science guided inquiry about concepts relating to heat transfer through the context of making ice cream. Over the next several sessions, they will investigate life science concepts through the context of a pond. This inquiry is less guided. Participants design and implement investigations, based on questions they have about the pond organisms they observe. A pond contains a wide variety of organisms that interact in complex ways. Additionally, the makeup of a pond changes drastically from season to season. A pond therefore provides a rich context for investigation.

Science Background

The pond environment lends itself to the development of many different life science concepts relating to populations and ecosystems, structure and function in living systems, and diversity and adaptation of organisms. The focus over the next five sessions will be on macroinvertebrates and concepts relating to structure and function.

Activity 1: Exploring the Pond (30 minutes)

Overview

The unit begins with an open exploration of the pond. Participants share their observations and any questions they have about the pond organisms.

Before Beginning

Materials: a wallpaper soaking tray, newspaper to cover the workspace, several white plastic plates, a small pail, and a kitchen strainer for each group.

Steps

1 Introduce the unit and explain that over the next five sessions participants will engage in a pond study.

2 Tell participants that these investigations are an example of a less-guided, extended inquiry investigation and that they will have an opportunity to discuss the differences between the two kinds of inquiries later during the Classroom Connections section.

3 Begin by asking if anyone has used a pond study with their students. If so, ask them to describe their unit by talking about such things as the concepts they were targeting, their approach, and the amount of time they spent on the unit. This is a good way to find out what participants know about ponds and to highlight the different topics and concepts that teachers can address using ponds as the context.

4 Post their comments, particularly those relating to the concepts they were trying to develop, on chart paper. If no one has done a pond study with their students, postpone the discussion of

potential topics for study until after the exploratory phase when participants will have a better idea of topics that might be explored.

5   Make sure that each group has a wallpaper-soaking tray, newspaper to cover their workspace, several white plastic plates, a small pail, and a kitchen strainer. Explain that each group will have its own pond environment to study.

6   Invite each group, one at a time, to come get a supply of pond water and organisms of varying size to study during the session. Make sure that they collect a bit of mud as well for the bottom dwellers.

7   Tell participants that this first activity is to get them familiar with the organisms in the pond. The purpose is for them to find out how many different kinds of living things are in their pond water samples. Give groups about 30 minutes to explore and examine their "ponds."

8   Suggest to participants that they place a few organisms at a time on the white plastic plates to observe them more easily. Be sure they include enough pond water to keep the organisms viable.

9   Have participants record their observations and findings in their science notebooks.

10 Bring the groups together, ask what people noticed, and have each group share its observations. Ask participants to talk about the following:
   • Which creatures were the most interesting to you? Why?
   • What did you notice about each of these organisms?

11 If you were unable to have participants come to the pond and collect samples, have them try to describe the pond based on the variety and range of organisms they have observed in their and other groups' samples.

12 Working in table groups, have participants discuss and try to describe the pond. After 15 minutes, ask groups to share their thinking. Make sure groups give evidence to support their ideas.

13 Have participants place their wallpaper trays with pond water samples in an appropriate place until the next session. Make sure that there is enough light, not necessarily direct sunlight, and that the aerator is working properly.

Training Tip

Listen for comments about the organism's size, structure, ways of moving, and behavior.

If possible, place some pond water and organisms in a flat transparent container on the overhead projector. Participants can point to the organism projected on the wall as they are reporting.

At the end of the reporting, make sure to point out the variety of living things that are present in the pond water.

Activity 2: Classroom Connections and Science Pedagogy (30 minutes)

Overview
Participants have an opportunity to talk about the kinds of questions they had about the organisms during their initial exploration of pond life. They consider how their questions will help them support students in developing questions to investigate.

Before Beginning
Materials: chart paper and a marker to write down participants' questions

Steps
1   Instruct participants to pair up with a partner and think about one or two organisms that they observed and found particularly interesting.
2   Ask pairs to develop three to five questions about the organism that they think they might be able to investigate.
3   Conduct a whole-group discussion and have participants share their questions. Make sure they tell you which organism(s) they are talking about. Collect their questions on chart paper.
4   Have pairs, working in table groups, look at the list of questions generated and ask them to decide if each question can be investigated and answered. Ask them to give their reasons about why or why not a question can be investigated and answered.
5   Conduct a whole-group discussion, and develop a set of criteria about what makes a question investigable. This will be a good resource for both mentors and mentees when they engage in this practice.
6   As a whole group, discuss any experiences participants have had with asking their students to develop questions to investigate. Have them share specific lessons they use, and ask them to share their students' successes and challenges with this practice. Ask them to explain their strategies for helping students become more proficient with this skill.

Wrap-Up and Next Steps (10 minutes)

Training Tip
This last activity, unlike in Sessions 1 through 5, does not have a Reflective Journal activity. Participants engaged in reflection in an earlier activity.

Homework

Remind participants to bring in the completed mentoring journals for next time. They will be used during the workshop.

Evaluation (10 minutes)

Overview

This activity is an important source of information for you. Participants' feedback will help you prepare for future sessions.

Before Beginning

Materials: Handout 6

Steps

1   Distribute Handout 6 and ask participants to comment on today's session. Collect participants' completed handouts before they leave.
2   Encourage participants to write any questions or concerns they have on sticky notes and stick them on the Parking Lot paper as they leave.

SESSION 7

Learning is not attained by chance. It must be sought for with ardor and attended to with diligence.

Abigail Adams, 1780

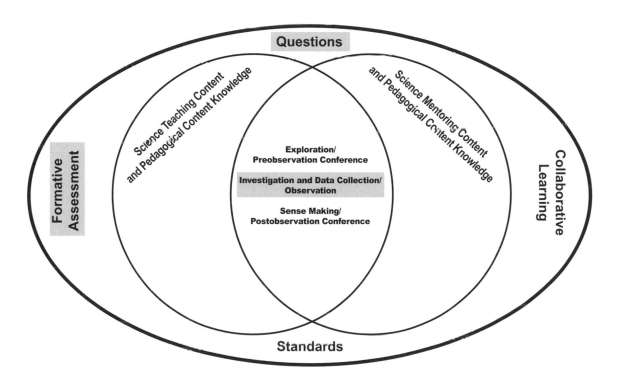

Overview

In this session, participants review the purposes of the mentoring journals and develop a minicurriculum to use in their work with mentees. They explore issues around giving and receiving help. They do a more in-depth investigation of a pond organism, choosing one question developed in Session 6 to investigate. Finally, they examine the literacy and formative assessment opportunities embedded in these kinds of pedagogical practices.

Outcomes

- Understand the role of formative assessment in new teacher development.
- Practice goal setting and implementation of formative assessments.
- Identify with the role of mentor as instructional coach.
- Be aware of the variety of complicated issues involved in helping a colleague.
- Gain an increased ability to design and implement an investigation.
- Recognize the value of group critique and analysis to improve and refine student work.
- Understand the differences between a life science and physical science investigation, guided and open-ended inquiry, and the kinds of data collection and representation done in life science and physical science.
- Realize the many different concepts that can be developed through a pond study.

Session Snapshot

Agenda

10 minutes	**Welcome and Check-In** Reconnecting With Each Other and the Program
1½ hours	**Mentoring** Activity 1: Using Formative Assessment to Improve Practice and Developing Minicurriculum
2½ hours	**Science** Activity 1: Pond Study—Investigable Questions and Experimental Design Activity 2: Investigating and Collecting Data Activity 3: Classroom Connections and Science Pedagogy—Formative Assessment and Literacy Connections
1 hour	**Mentoring** Activity 1: Issues Around Helping
35 minutes	**Reflection and Next Steps** Reflective Journal For Next Time: Homework Volunteers Evaluation

How to Prepare for Session 7

What You Need to Do

– Read Activity 1: "Using Formative Assessment to Improve Practice and Developing a Minicurriculum" section, and especially familiarize yourself with step 3.
– Review the "Issues Around Helping" section.
– Check the investigable questions developed by participants in the last session.
– Scan through the session and review all of the directions and sidebar notes. These include activity descriptions and directions, the science background sections, the training tips, and the discussion points.

What You Need to Make

– Write the Agenda on chart paper. Hang it on the wall where all can see it and you can refer to it throughout the day.
– Write the Outcomes on chart paper and hang the paper on the wall.
– Make all overheads.
– Duplicate all handouts.
– Post the Norms and Parking Lot charts.

What You Need to Acquire

– The pond organisms from the previous session containing both plants and animals, large and small.
– Materials per Group
  • Wallpaper soaking trays (not black)
  • Aquarium aerators
  • Small pail
  • Hand magnifiers, one for each person
  • Microscope
  • Microscope slides, several per group
  • Aluminum pie plates, several per group
  • Large spoon or ladle
  • White plastic plate
  • Kitchen strainer
  • Coffee stirrers, several per group
  • Newspaper to cover tables

Media List

Overheads

1   Developing Minicurricula for Learning to Teach
2   Issues Around Helping—1
3   Issues Around Helping—2
4   Reflective Journal Summary
5   Evaluation Form

Handouts

1   Developing Minicurricula for Learning to Teach
2   Issues Around Helping—1
3   Issues Around Helping—2
4   Protocol for Presenting Student Work
5   Reflective Journal Summary
6   Evaluation Form

Welcome and Check-In (10 minutes)

Reconnecting With Each Other and the Program (10 minutes)

Overview

The purpose of this time is to help mentors reconnect to the group and the work of science mentoring.

Before Beginning

Materials: agenda, list of outcomes, Norms from Session 1

Steps

1   Review the agenda and the list of session outcomes.
2   Talk about the themes of today's session: formative assessment and deepening the necessary skills to give effective feedback.
3   Refer to the posted Norms and ask participants how they think they are doing regarding the Norms.
4   Look at the Parking Lot and respond to any pressing issues.

Mentoring (1½ hours)

Activity 1: Using Formative Assessment to Improve Practice and Developing a Minicurriculum (1½ hours)

Overview

During this segment, you review the purposes of the mentoring journal, and you give participants an opportunity to examine the challenges and benefits of using these journals with their mentees.

Before Beginning

Materials: Overhead 1, Handout 1

Discussion Points

1. Reiterate that the purpose of the mentoring journals is to identify goals and to monitor the progress of the mentee. Point out that the idea of formative assessment parallels a guiding principle of teaching: the cycle of plan-teach-reflect.

2. The consistent use of the mentoring journals, together with the process of examining evidence through the lenses of the inquiry protocol, allows novice teachers to reflect upon their teaching in systematic ways and become more consciously aware of effective science instructional practices.

3. Learning to teach is a career-long developmental process that involves a continuous cycle of planning, teaching, and reflecting. The heart of the work is to respond to each new teacher's developmental and contextual needs and to promote the ongoing examination of classroom practice. The idea is to create a vision of quality teaching.

4. The mentoring journals are going to be used to create a curriculum for mentees.

Steps

1   Ask participants to review the mentoring journals they completed during the month. Ask them to share what they wrote for "current focus" with their tablemates.

2   Have each table prioritize the top three foci. When they have completed this, ask each group to report which foci they have decided are the most worthy of attention. List the foci on chart paper and, by a show of hands, ask mentors to choose which one(s) they'd like to work on during the next half hour. In groups of three or four, have mentors work on one or two foci that were mentioned on the mentoring journals.

3   Explain that what they are doing now is creating a minicurriculum to use in their work with their mentees. Just as assessments are used in teaching to inform next steps with students, mentors should use assessment to create lessons for their mentees. Emphasize that this is a way for mentors to determine their curriculum and pedagogy. Just as teachers need both curriculum and pedagogy, mentors need curriculum and pedagogy to use with their mentees.

4   Show Overhead 1. Model how a group might complete this worksheet, using the discussion points provided for reference. Choose a focus from the list of suggestions that were included on the mentoring journals and write it in the "What" column.

Discussion Points

1. Remind participants of the importance of grounding the practice in the protocol. For example, if holding students' attention is a focus, you would write that in the "What" column.

2. Point out that this is too generic a focus and that it needs to be refined if it is to be used to teach the mentee.

3. Suggest that there are different causes for disruptions, and, therefore, the first step might be to diagnose the cause. The next step might be to develop ways to respond to specific situations.

4. Another possible focus might be framing effective inquiry questions. Again be specific—which phase of inquiry, what are the goals of the questioning?

5. The "How" column includes specific ways you might work on this focus, such as modeling, giving specific suggestions in order to build a repertoire of responses, and then following up with observations and feedback, and videotaping.

6. Highlight the importance of being concrete when completing the "Success" column. What will success look like? How will mentors know when the mentee has accomplished this goal? If the focus, for example, is "less telling, more

(continued on page 111)

inquiry," then the how might be that the teacher and mentor coplan inquiry questions to ask during group work to uncover student thinking (e.g., in a pond study, "Why do you think that organism has long back legs and short front legs?"). An example of success would be that the teacher independently develops a series of questions to be used during the exploratory and sense-making phases.

7. Encourage mentors to ground the focus of their minicurriculum in the appropriate phase of the inquiry protocol, so that the choice of focus is based not on an idiosyncratic opinion but rather on a recognized pedagogical practice.

Steps (continued)

5   Give participants about 30 minutes to work in their groups. As groups work, encourage them to be specific about what mentors will do to teach this goal and what success will look like. The more explicit mentors can be, the more likely the mentee will succeed.

6   When groups finish, facilitate a conversation highlighting what next steps might be to begin to implement these minicurricula. End by clarifying that this kind of work helps to integrate formative assessment with individualized support based on the assessment results. Ask mentors to keep a record of what they tried and how it went for next time.

Science (2½ hours)

Activity 1: Pond Study—Investigable Questions and Experimental Design (60 minutes)

Overview

In this open inquiry, participants choose one of the questions to investigate that they developed in Session 6. They design an investigation and share it with the group for feedback.

Before Beginning

Ensure that participants have the questions they developed in Session 6.

Training Tip

As noted in the previous session, a pond provides a rich context for investigation and you want to make the most of it. Be careful to ensure that several different questions are being investigated. This way, participants learn about multiple and perhaps diverse concepts. You may want to discuss with each pair or trio what concept(s) it thinks their question targets.

Steps

1   Have participants review the questions they developed in Session 6 and decide which one they would like to investigate.

2   Create groups by putting participants who want to explore the same question into groups of two or three. Try to have as many questions represented as possible. You may, however, have several pairs or trios investigating the same question.

3   Ask pairs and trios to propose and design an investigation to answer their question. Have them write their investigation on chart paper and hang it on the wall. When all groups are finished, have them do a walk-around to read each proposed investigation and note any questions they may have.

4   End with a whole-group discussion about each design. Have participants discuss the strengths and weaknesses of each.

5   Give groups time to refine their design, if necessary; otherwise, they should begin their investigations.

Activity 2: Investigating and Collecting Data (1 hour)

Overview

Participants implement their investigation, collect data, and report their findings to the group. They identify the science concept(s) that their investigations developed. The session ends with a discussion about the differences between a physical science inquiry and a life science inquiry.

Before Beginning

Materials: chart paper and markers for each group of participants. Make sure that participants have their science notebooks and pond-water samples.

Training Tip

As you work with this unit, you should continually highlight the following ideas: the differences between a life science and a physical science investigation, guided and open inquiry, and the kinds of data collection and representation done in life science and physical science.

Life science versus physical science investigations

Typically, life science investigations take more time than physical science investigations. Students need to make observations over time and this can take from a few days to several weeks. For example, it takes time to observe change in plant growth or mealworm behavior.

Most physical science investigations can be completed more quickly, and students can easily repeat the investigation to gather more data.

Guided versus open inquiry

With guided inquiry the teacher has control of the learning environment and establishes parameters and procedures for inquiry. Students are provided with a hands-on problem to investigate as well as the procedures and materials necessary to complete the investigation. If students have not experienced much hands-on science in the elementary grades, we suggest starting with guided inquiry. If they have good hands-on experience, we advocate a less-guided approach in which the teacher provides the problem for investigation and the necessary materials and students devise their own procedure to solve the problem, as recommended by the National Science Education Standards.

In open inquiry students have total control of their learning. They formulate their own problems as well as the procedures to use to investigate them. Although this is an extremely worthwhile practice, it becomes difficult to address grade-level standards when students are investigating questions of interest to them. Teachers can and should provide opportunities within a guided-inquiry unit for students to pursue their own questions and ideas.

(continued on page 114)

Data collection and representation

The data from life science investigations tend to be more qualitative in nature, although students may measure the rate of plant growth or time how long it takes a mealworm to find food in a simple maze. Data from most physical science investigations are more quantitative and can be collected more quickly.

Each kind of data is represented differently. Physical science data is easily represented in charts, tables, and graphs. Life science data is represented visually in diagrams or drawings. For example, students might draw a series of pictures of a tadpole as it develops into a frog.

Engage participants in a discussion of the differences between a guided and open-ended inquiry. These beginning pond investigations—this one and the one from the last session—have taken participants through a complete learning cycle. However, in terms of the entire pond-study unit, they represent the exploratory phase, where participants have the opportunity to explore the organism of their choice, ask their own question, and carry out a preliminary investigation to find an answer.

Steps

1   Have groups collect their pond-water samples and any materials they need to implement their investigation. Remind them to take notes as they work in their science notebooks. Give groups 45 minutes or so to carry out their observations and investigations and to put any data or drawings they have onto chart paper.

2   Have groups hang their chart paper on the wall for a whole-group discussion. When all groups have completed their investigations, ask each group to report to the whole group.

3   Remind them to state the question they were investigating, what they did, and what they found out.

4   Ask participants what concept(s) they were investigating.

5   Encourage the other participants to ask questions of the reporting group.

6   At the end of each report, ask each group the following questions:
    • Did the design of your investigation provide the necessary data to answer your question?
    • If so, how? If not, what would you do differently?
    • What new questions did your investigation raise for you?
    • What would you like to investigate next?

7   After you wrap up the reports and discussion, take some time to revisit the inquiry framework

and discuss how each of the phases—exploration, investigation and data collection, and sense making—differed from the previous physical science investigation into ice cream making. Use the following questions to focus the discussion:

- What differences did you notice between this investigation and the physical science investigation?
- What were the similarities and differences between the two exploratory phases?
- What different thinking and process skills did you need to use during the investigation phase in the pond unit?

Activity 3: Classroom Connections and Science Pedagogy—Formative Assessment and Literacy Connections (30 minutes)

Overview

Participants consider the assessment and literacy features inherent in the Abilities to Do Scientific Inquiry (Grades 5–8) Standards.

Before Beginning

Materials: Make sure that participants have their science notebooks

Steps

1 Explain to participants that many of the strategies that you use in the sessions model ones that they should use with their students. Use the discussion points provided to review with participants the connection between the strategies you have used with them during the last several sessions and their work with students.

2 Divide the group in half and have participants work in table groups to discuss either the formative assessment aspects or the literacy and higher-order thinking skills developed by these practices. Remind them that their science notebooks are a valuable resource for this discussion. Use the following questions to help focus the discussion:

- Formative assessment: What kinds of information about student understanding can you get from a discussion about: the questions students choose to investigate and their experimental design?
- Literacy and higher-order thinking skills: How does a whole-class discussion about each group's questions and experimental design strengthen the development of students' communication skills? What higher-order thinking skills are students required to use as they discuss their questions and experimental designs?

Discussion Points

1. Remind participants of the two strategies you used in the past two sessions:
   - having participants come up with a question to investigate and
   - designing an investigation and reporting on the investigation to the whole group.

   Having students come up with a question to investigate and design an investigation to find an answer are part of the inquiry standards recommended by the National Science Education Standards.

2. Posting and analyzing each group's question and its experimental design (and having a whole group discussion about each) helped each group to refine its question and design. It also promoted reflection, higher-order thinking, and cooperative group learning. This is also good formative assessment practice, because it gives the teacher knowledge about each group's understanding about experimental design.

3. The method for reporting after an investigation is also an important classroom technique. Effective reporting requires students to communicate clearly about their work, to answer questions, and perhaps to defend their data analysis. Although these practices take time, be sure to convey to participants that they help students develop many literacy skills that are often neglected in science classrooms. As with everything, the more opportunity students have to engage with these practices, the better they become at reflecting on their work and communicating clearly about it both orally and in writing.

Mentoring (1 hour)

Activity 1: Issues Around Helping (1 hour)

Overview

Participants gain insights into the nature of successful and unsuccessful helping situations to make the idea of helping more acceptable to novice teachers. Adult development theories establish that for change to occur the professional environment must be supportive.

Before Beginning

Materials: chart paper and marker; Overheads 2, 3; Handouts 2, 3

Steps

1 Note that in the current school culture it is not the norm to expect help from a colleague. Some new teachers think receiving help is a sign of weakness and that they should be able to do it all alone. It is important, therefore, for mentors to be aware of some of the complexities of helping. One of the ways to do this is for mentors to put themselves in the shoes of the teachers being helped.

2 Begin by showing Overhead 2.

3 Explain that you would like participants to fill out the form (Handout 2) so they can think of specific occasions when they have received help.

4 When participants have finished filling out the questionnaire, ask them to share how they felt on each of these occasions. Reinforce the importance of discovering characteristics that are common to successful and unsuccessful helping situations.

5 After participants have shared their helping experiences in their table groups, collect a few examples. Distribute Handout 3 and put up Overhead 3. Explain that the goal is to look for characteristics common to successful helping situations.

6 Ask participants to analyze their experiences in their table groups in light of these questions.

7 Have groups share examples.

8 Wrap up by asking participants how they might use the insights gained from this activity in a mentoring relationship. Jot down participants' suggestions on chart paper and collate them for participants. Use the discussion points provided to leave participants with some final thoughts about issues around helping.

Discussion Points

1. The set of issues surrounding the process of one teacher coaching, helping, or mentoring another teacher illustrates one of the unacknowledged complexities of teaching.

2. Often, even among teachers themselves, teaching is thought of as a relatively straightforward task. Yet, experienced teachers know this is simply not so.

(continued on page 118)

3. Provide this example: We all understand that the job of a child psychologist is a difficult one. But, think about it. Child psychologists prepare for their 50-minute meetings with children by having time to reflect, review notes, do some research. They get 50 minutes alone, uninterrupted, to work with a single client. Following the session, psychologists get time to review notes, reflect again, consult with colleagues, and perhaps do more research—all this for one single child.

4. Now think of the work-life of the teacher with a classroom full of children, all with different needs, different skills, different problems, and all demanding attention at the same time.

5. Once we understand the complexity of the teacher's many challenges, we can be more accepting of the notion that every teacher can use help. Accepting help is not a sign of incompetence, but merely an acknowledgement of the many demands and requirements of the job.

Reflection and Next Steps (35 minutes)

Reflective Journal (15 minutes)

Overview

In this segment, you continue to support mentors' reflection and processing of their training experience by encouraging them to respond in writing to a series of prompts.

Before Beginning

Materials: Overhead 4, Handout 5

Steps

1   Show Overhead 4 and distribute Handout 5. Ask participants to complete the 3-2-1 summary shown in Overhead 4.

2   Collect participants' responses so you can have a copy and participants can have a copy.

For Next Time: Homework Volunteers (10 minutes)

Before Beginning
Materials: Handout 4

Steps

1 Ask for two participants to volunteer to submit three samples of student work to you, for your review. Tell them that you will need one sample of a strong student's work, one sample of an average student's work, and one sample of a weak student's work. The samples need to be from the same lesson in the same classroom. Make sure that students' names have been removed.

2 Ask to receive these samples far enough in advance of Session 8 so you can select which ones you will use, and make the appropriate number of copies.

3 After you receive the samples, select which group of three you will use in the next session. That participant will present the samples of student work for the rest of the participants to evaluate. You want to have two volunteers, so that you can have at least two selections from which to choose.

4 Do not give out Handout 4 during class time. Instead, e-mail it to the volunteer you have chosen to present the three samples of student work. Make arrangements with the volunteer you have chosen to meet before the next session and review the Protocol for Presenting Student Work. Review the presentation format, going over each step so that the volunteer understands what he or she needs to focus on. This should take no more than 20 minutes.

5 Preview for participants that during the next session they will focus on analyzing student work as a powerful tool to guide instruction.

6 Describe the kind of work that is helpful to use for this kind of activity—work that shows student thinking and work that calls for student products or performances. Typically, worksheets, quizzes, or tests don't provide much of a basis for analyzing student work.

7 Remind all participants to bring in the completed mentoring journals for next time and also to work with their mentee on the focus they developed during the formative assessment component of the day.

Evaluation (10 minutes)

Overview
This activity is an important source of information for you. Participants' feedback will help you prepare for future sessions.

SESSION 7

Before Beginning

Materials: Overhead 5, Handout 6

Steps

1   Hand out and show as an overhead the evaluation prompts (Overhead 5, Handout 6).
2   Encourage participants to write any questions or concerns they have on sticky notes and stick them on the Parking Lot paper as they leave.

120

Session 8

In the field of observation, chance favors only the prepared mind.

Louis Pasteur

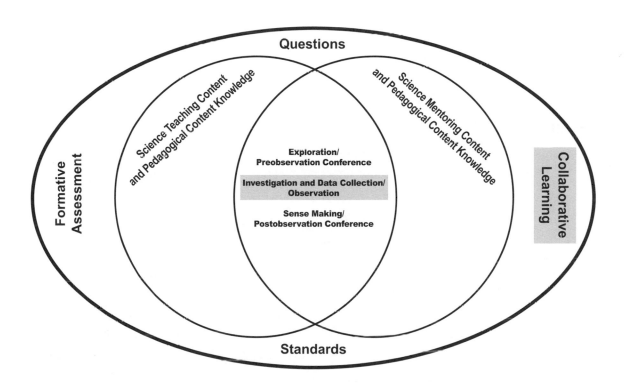

Overview

In this session, participants reflect on their mentor-mentee experiences thus far. They learn a protocol for examining student work, examine several pieces of student work, and discuss implications for the classroom. In the science segment, they study one pond organism in depth and create a schema for sorting pond organisms.

Outcomes

- Become familiar with a process and protocol for examining student work.
- Practice mentoring conversations around the examination of student work.
- Gain an improved understanding of pedagogical content knowledge through discussion of student work.
- Experience an in-depth observation of one pond organism.
- Become familiar with the form of one pond organism and consider the functions of its various structures.
- Construct a schema for sorting pond organisms.

Session Snapshot

Agenda

15 minutes	**Welcome and Check-In**
	Reconnecting With Each Other and the Program
1½ hours	**Mentoring**
	Activity 1: Mentor-Mentee Reflections
	Activity 2: Examining Student Work
3 hours	**Science**
	Activity 1: Investigation and Data Collection—Observing a Single Organism
	Activity 2: Investigation and Data Collection—Identifying Organisms
	Activity 3: Investigation and Data Collection—Sorting Pond Organisms
	Activity 4: Classroom Connections and Science Pedagogy—Science Notebooks
25 minutes	**Reflection and Next Steps**
	Reflective Journal
	Evaluation

How to Prepare for Session 8

What You Need to Do

- Read and become familiar with the Fishbowl Exercise and Tuning Protocol handouts and overheads. Be sure you are clear as to how to set up the fishbowl.
- Make sure that you have a diversity of viable pond organisms.
- Determine if any participants will bring samples of their students' science notebooks.
- Scan through the session and review all of the directions and sidebar notes. These include activity descriptions and directions, the science background sections, the training tips, and the discussion points.

What You Need to Make

- Write the Agenda on chart paper and hang it on the wall where all can see it and you can refer to it throughout the day.
- Write the Outcomes on chart paper and hang the paper on the wall.
- Make all overheads (1–7).
- Duplicate all handouts (1–7).
- Post the Norms and Parking Lot charts.

What You Need to Acquire

- Chart paper and markers
- Sticky notes
- Colored pencils

Materials

- A variety of pond organisms from the previous two sessions
- Materials per group
  - Wallpaper soaking tray (not black)
  - Aquarium aerator
  - Small pail
  - Hand magnifiers, one for each person
  - Microscope
  - Microscope slides, several per group
  - Aluminum pie plates, several per group
  - Large spoon or ladle
  - White plastic plate
  - Kitchen strainer
  - Coffee stirrers, several per group
  - Newspaper to cover tables
  - Field guide
  - Cards with drawings showing common pond organisms drawn to scale, including their common and scientific names

Media List

Overheads

1 Reflections on Your Experience
2 Fishbowl Exercise
3 Tuning Protocol
4 Student Work Analysis Recording Sheet
5 Implications for Classroom Practice

6   Reflective Journal Prompts
7   Evaluation Form

Handouts
1   Reflections on Your Experience
2   Fishbowl Exercise
3   Tuning Protocol
4   Student Work Analysis Recording Sheet
5   Implications for Classroom Practice
6   Reflective Journal Prompts
7   Evaluation Form

Welcome and Check-In (15 minutes)

Reconnecting With Each Other and the Program (15 minutes)

Overview

Participants focus on the purpose and content of the session. They revisit the Norms established in Session 1 to prepare to engage in the day's activities.

Before Beginning

Materials: agenda, list of outcomes, Norms from Session 1

Steps
1   Review the agenda and the Norms from Session 1. Refer to the Norms throughout the day.
2   Go over the list of session outcomes.
3   Review the quote and talk about the theme of today's session: examining student work.

Mentoring (1½ hours)

Activity 1: Mentor-Mentee Reflections (30 minutes)

Overview

This activity is similar to the previous mentor reflections, but it has a different focus. Participants reflect on what they have learned from and the questions they have about their mentoring interactions.

Before Beginning

Materials: Overhead 1, Handout 1

Steps

1 Begin the session by having participants look at the mentoring journals they completed for today's session.
2 Have participants complete Handout 1.
3 Ask participants to share their reflections with their table groups. Encourage them to focus on learnings and next steps.
4 Tell groups that you will ask one person from each table to synthesize the conversation so that all participants can benefit from each other's lessons. Below are possible focus questions for reporting:
   - What new insights have you gained?
   - What will you do next?

Activity 2: Examining Student Work (1 hour)

Overview

You introduce participants to a tool (the Tuning Protocol) and a strategy (the Fishbowl Exercise) to examine student work. These devices emphasize the value of being a community of learners and of group problem solving.

Before Beginning

Materials: enough copies of 3 pieces of student work for every participant (1 strong, 1 medium, 1 weak); Overheads 2, 3, 4; Handouts 2, 3, 4, 5

Training Tip

After you describe the following activity, give participants a break so you can set up the room for a fishbowl interaction. Create the fishbowl by putting one or two tables with chairs in the center of the room to accommodate 12 participants. Create an outer circle around the table(s) and chairs on the outside to accommodate the rest of the participants.

Steps

1 Introduce this activity by recounting the story provided and using the discussion points to amplify upon the article. (See the Sidebar on page 9.)

2 Explain that participants will use a protocol. Note that participants will form a fishbowl and an audience to become familiar with this strategy of examining student work.

3 Ask participants to volunteer to be in the fishbowl. (The mentor who is contributing the student work must be in the fishbowl.) A good number is about 12 mentors, and you should act as the facilitator.

4 Tell fishbowl participants to choose a partner or two (depending on size of group) from the other participants. The purpose is to engage the participants who are on the outside of the fishbowl in the activity.

5 Give participants a break so you can set up the room.

Story

Twenty-three heart surgeons decided to observe each other in action in the operating room over a nine-month period. They wanted to learn about and share each other's approaches and insight through presentation and observation, reflection, and discussion. During the two years following, the death rate among their patients fell by 25 percent. The study showed that, by "emphasizing teamwork and communication instead of functioning like solo practitioners, all the doctors brought about major changes in their individual and institutional practices" (Performance Learning Systems).

Discussion Points

1. Point out that for teachers who, like heart surgeons, traditionally work as isolated professionals, the experience of these doctors holds a powerful lesson.

2. Emphasize that you can compare a teacher's goal and purpose to that of a heart surgeon—a teacher's goal is to lower the death rate of young minds and see them thrive. Many educators now emphatically believe that they can do it better together than by working alone.

3. Like doctors making hospital rounds or lawyers examining clues to build a case, teachers in many school districts have begun purposefully probing the rich evidence that lies immediately at hand in every school, searching for what it can yield about how students best learn.

4. Teachers bring to the table their students' writing, math-problem solving, science projects, artwork, and whatever other evidence they can gather—in written notes or audio or video form—of what students are producing every day.

5. Instead of disappearing into the book bag or the wastebasket, these artifacts become a valuable mirror of how the teacher's practice does or does not reflect its intentions. A benefit of examining student work is that it reflects the work that teachers and students actually do together. The analysis can then translate into informed action: changed perceptions of students, revised curricula and teaching strategies, new goals, and a sense of direction for a faculty.

Steps (continued)

6. Distribute Handout 2 to participants who are sitting outside the fishbowl. Ask them to make sure they are seated in a place where they can see and hear their partners.

7. Distribute copies of student work to all participants both in and out of the fishbowl.

8. Distribute the Student Work Analysis Recording Sheet, Handout and Overhead 4, to all participants.

9. Introduce the Tuning Protocol and Handout and Overhead 3, and explain that you are going to be a strict timekeeper to model a way to use the protocol to support the kind of analysis you would like teachers to do in their schools. Explain that this will feel awkward at first, but

participants should suspend disbelief and participate fully.

10 Distribute Handout 3. Ask the presenting teacher to respond to the prompts in Handout 2.

11 After the presenting teacher gives a context for the work, ask participants whether they have any clarifying questions. A caution—these should be short-answer questions, not the beginning of the analysis.

12 Now it is time for participants to look at the samples of student work. Ask participants both inside and outside the fishbowl to look closely at the three samples of student work you requested from Session 7 for homework and fill out the Student Analysis Recording Sheet (Overhead 4, Handout 4).

13 After participants finish examining the student work, lead them into the warm feedback phase, followed by cool feedback and suggestions. (Warm and cool feedback are described in number 5 of the Tuning Protocol.) Invite a few comments from outside the fishbowl if participants have burning issues they would like to raise.

14 Give the presenting teacher an opportunity to respond and emphasize that the teacher decides which comments he or she will respond to.

15 After completing number 6 on the Tuning Protocol, ask all participants to fill out Handout 5. Debrief the whole group by sharing insights.

16 End this section by discussing the use of the Tuning Protocol itself. You might ask some or all of the following questions:

- What was it like to talk in this way?
- What did you learn?
- What worked well?
- What in the Tuning Protocol led to the discussion that allowed teachers to reflect on their own practice?

17 Explain that, after using a protocol, finding out how it worked is critical. Ask participants what it was like to talk in this way. If no one responds, add that using a protocol supports a certain kind of discourse. How would the conversation have been different if they had not had the protocol? Using collaborative assessment protocols forces us to think in a way we are least likely to do in schools. There is no push to a quick fix or a solution. Often, a protocol raises more questions. Your are asking teachers to wonder. Emphasize that this process parallels the inquiry approach to science.

18 Ask the participants outside the fishbowl to meet with their partners and reflect on their partners' participation in the fishbowl. Encourage them to be frank with one another so each of them can learn how to be a more effective participant in these kinds of conversations.

Training Tip

Work with the presenting mentor so she or he is prepared to present the information in the protocol. Make sure the mentor has a focus question that lends itself to an insightful discussion. In preparation, you can ask the mentor the following questions: "What are you bringing to this work? What do you hope to learn? To what larger question about your practice does this work connect? What might you learn about your practice?"

As you facilitate the group, be prepared to interrupt tactfully when a participant violates the protocol—for example, by speaking out of turn, by jumping to cool feedback, or by mixing warm and cool feedback. Sometimes the presenting teacher wants to respond during the time she or he should be listening. Encourage her or him to be silent and to take notes rather than to engage in a back and forth of why this would not work or similar pitfalls to productive conversations.

Science (3 hours)

Activity 1: Investigation and Data Collection—Observing a Single Organism (45 minutes)

Overview

As noted earlier, the past two science sessions were embedded in the exploratory phase of the inquiry learning cycle and were open inquiries, since participants asked and investigated their own question. This session is a more-guided inquiry. Participants select one organism and make a detailed drawing of it.

Before Beginning

Materials: chart paper, colored pencils, markers. Make sure that participants have their pond water samples and science notebooks.

Training Tip

Depending on the questions participants investigated in the last session, they may or may not have found the answer to their question or anything definitive about their organism. They may want to continue to pursue their question or to research their organism to learn more about them. You should encourage them to continue on their own.

Frequently, students want to continue with an investigation or pursue a related question. Teachers should encourage them to do so and should find ways of supporting student inquiries. For example, it is important for teachers to check in with how a student's work is progressing and help that student make sense about his or her observations or findings. These individual student inquiries make perfect science fair projects because they arise from a student's classroom work and the student's own curiosity.

Steps

1   Divide the group into pairs or trios and explain that they will be doing an in-depth observation of one organism.
2   Ask participants to get their samples of pond water, and give them time to select an organism for an in-depth observation.
3   Be sure that participants include any smaller and microscopic organisms. Usually, these are among the plants and organic matter at the bottom of the containers.
4   Tell participants that first they are to observe and take notes about how their organism moves. They should write their observations in their science notebook.
5   When they finish, ask them to carefully observe the organism's structure and make a drawing of it in their science notebooks. Next, have them make a large drawing of their organism on chart paper. They should use colored pencils or markers, using colors as close to the color of the organism as possible.
6   Have groups post their drawings around the room when they finish.
7   Ask each pair or trio to stand by their drawing and share their observations with the whole group. Request that they describe their organism in as much detail as possible.
8   Encourage the other groups to ask questions and take notes.
9   Finish this activity by asking the following questions:
    • How does your organism move?
    • What structures does it have that facilitates that kind of movement?
    • Why do you think it moves that way?
    • Does its motion indicate anything about how it lives, eats, or any other characteristic?

Activity 2: Investigation and Data Collection—Identifying Organisms (30 minutes)

Overview

Participants identify the organism they observed and examined in Activity 1.

Before Beginning

Materials: field guides and cards with drawings showing common pond organisms drawn to scale, including their common and scientific names. Having internet access also would be valuable.

Training Tip

Typically, at this point in the pond study, the tendency is for learners—both adults and children—to want to know the names of the organisms in their pond water samples. Identifying the organisms is not a goal of this unit, but it is probably a good idea to let participants find out the names of the organisms so that you can continue to develop the targeted concepts. Knowing the names of some of the organisms will make discussions in and among groups easier.

Steps

1   Tell participants they will now have some time to identify the organism they just studied. Explain that identifying the organisms is not a goal of the unit, but that knowing the names of some of the organisms will make discussions in and among groups easier.
2   Show them the resources you have collected, such as field guides.
3   Give participants about 30 minutes to identify their organism. If they have time, they should go on to identify other organisms in their sample.
4   Have groups label their drawings with the name of their organism. Make sure that all participants agree with the identification of each organism.

Activity 3: Investigation and Data Collection —Sorting Pond Organisms (60 minutes)

Overview

Participants develop a schema for sorting the organisms in their pond-water sample.

Before Beginning

Materials: chart paper and markers for each group

Steps

1 Focus participants' attention on the chart papers of different pond organisms that you displayed around the room. Use the following questions to engage participants in discussing the organisms:
   - What similarities and differences do you notice about the organisms?
   - Are the organisms related? If so, in what way do they relate to each other?
   - How might you go about grouping the organisms?
   - What would be the value of sorting the different organisms into groups?

2 Collect participants' ideas on chart paper and post the chart.

3 Ask participants to decide in their groups how they would sort their organisms.

4 Once they make a decision, give groups 45 to 60 minutes to sort the organisms in their pond water samples. Make sure that each group has a good supply of organisms in its sample. Remind participants to put their notes and drawings on a piece of chart paper.

5 When groups complete the task, ask them to think about the following questions:
   - Why did you select that particular characteristic for sorting your organisms?
   - What information does that give you about each organism?

6 Tell them to record their answers in their science notebooks.

7 When everyone has finished, bring the groups together to share their work. Have each group display its chart paper and explain how they sorted the organisms, addressing the questions:
   - Why did you select that particular characteristic for sorting your organisms?
   - What information does that give you about each organism?

8 The remainder of the groups should ask questions of the presenters.

9 After all groups have presented, ask participants the following questions:
   - Do you agree with each group's sorting process?
   - Do you agree with the placement of each organism based on the group's sorting criteria? Explain why you agree or disagree with the placement.

10 Conclude this activity with a discussion about the different concepts and skills that participants developed in these three activities. Take about 15 minutes to discuss as a whole group other standards that they might address using a pond as the context.

Activity 4: Classroom Connections and Science Pedagogy—Science Notebooks (45 minutes)

Overview

Participants consider the value of science notebooks. Those who use science notebooks share examples from their students. They explain how they use the notebooks and for what purposes.

Before Beginning

Make sure that participants brought some of their students' science notebooks to share with their colleagues.

Discussion Points

1. Over the course of the sessions, you asked participants to keep notes about their investigations in their science notebooks.

2. In the ice cream–making unit, they recorded data, made charts and tables, and drew graphs.

3. In the pond-study unit, they recorded their experimental designs and observations of organisms in drawings and words.

4. The science notebook is a record of their work during the sessions. Similarly, requiring students to keep a science notebook is a wonderful strategy for documenting students' work and thinking over the course of any unit.

5. Science notebooks serve as formative assessment.

6. Science notebooks are extremely useful for students; they can go back to previous investigations and review data, graphs, descriptions, and drawings. This allows students to go back, refine their work, and revise their thinking about a particular idea.

Steps

1   Ask if any participants brought samples of their students' science notebooks to share with the group. If so, divide the group into twos or threes depending on the number of samples you receive. If not, skip to Step 3 and discuss how participants might go about having students keep a science notebook, using the bulleted questions to guide the conversation.

2   Have participants examine the notebooks and note the types of entries recorded.

3   Ask participants who have brought the samples to talk about:
   - How do you have students organize their notebooks?
   - What challenges do students have with keeping a notebook?
   - What kind of feedback do you give students about their notebooks?
   - If and how do you use notebooks for assessment purposes?
   - Do you have students share their notebooks with each other and, if so, for what purposes?
   - How do or can the notebooks support literacy in the science classroom?

Reflection and Next Steps (25 minutes)

Reflective Journal (15 minutes)

Overview

You continue to support mentors' reflection and processing of their training experience by encouraging them to respond in writing to a series of prompts.

Before Beginning

Materials: Overhead 6, Handout 6

Steps

1   Distribute Handout 6 and ask participants to respond to the reflective journal prompts on Overhead 6.
2   Again, collect participants' journals and copy them so you can have a copy and participants can have a copy.

Evaluation (10 minutes)

Overview

This activity is an important source of information for you. Participants' feedback will help you prepare for future sessions.

Before Beginning

Materials: Overhead 7, Handout 7

Steps

1   Hand out and show as an overhead the Evaluation Form (Overhead 7, Handout 7).
2   Encourage participants to write any questions or concerns they have on sticky notes and stick them on the Parking Lot paper as they leave.

Reference

Performance Learning Systems. Coaching Skills for Successful Teaching. *www.plsweb.com/resources/newsletters/hot–archives/79/peer–coaching.*

SESSION 9

Only in the vacuum of a nonexistent abstract world can movement or change occur without that abrasive friction of conflict.

Saul Alinksy

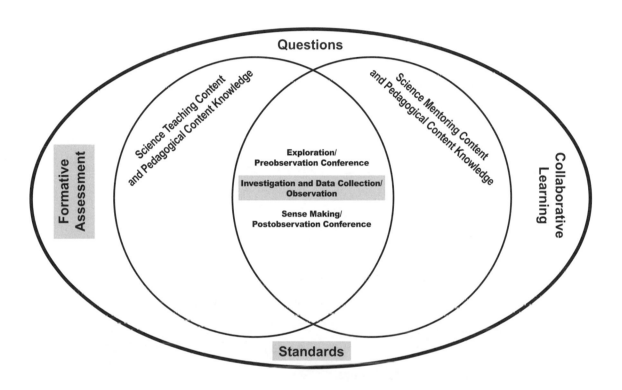

Overview

In this session, participants identify a mentoring situation that has been challenging for them and explore ideas about how to become more effective mentors. They learn about different conflict management styles, identify their own, and consider the potential uses and limitations of each style. They make minipond environments to explore ecological and environmental concepts. They create concept maps and brainstorm various contexts that potentially would support development of the miniponds.

Outcomes

- Expand repertoire of mentoring techniques.
- Identify a preferred style for dealing with conflicts.
- Identify how different conflict styles might be appropriate in different situations.
- Learn how to assess conflict situations and apply new skills in dealing with conflict situations.
- Identify ecological and environmental concepts that can be taught using a pond as the context.
- Create minienvironments.
- Construct a concept map and identify various contexts that could support their development.
- Continue to build a learning community that builds trust in the sharing of ideas.

Session Snapshot

Agenda

25 minutes	**Welcome and Check-In**	
	Reconnecting With Each Other and the Program	
1½ hours	**Mentoring**	
	Activity 1: Strategic Mentoring	
2¾ hours	**Science**	
	Activity 1: Context Setting	
	Activity 2: Creating a Minienvironment	
	Activity 3: Classroom Connections and Science Pedagogy	
1¼ hours	**Mentoring**	
	Activity 1: Your Conflict Management Style	
30 minutes	**Reflection and Next Steps**	
	Reflective Journal	
	For Next Time	
	Evaluation	

How to Prepare for Session 9

What You Need to Do

- Read all introductory and background information with a particular focus on the mentoring section.
- Review your district's and state's middle grades science standards, particularly those relating to the environment and ecology.
- Scan through the session and review all of the directions and sidebar notes. These include activity descriptions and directions, the science background sections, the training tips, and the discussion points.

What You Need to Make

– Write the Agenda on chart paper and hang it on the wall where all participants can see it and you can refer to it throughout the day.
– Write the Outcomes on chart paper and hang the paper on the wall.
– Make all overheads.
– Duplicate all handouts.
– Post the Norms and Parking Lot charts.

What You Need to Acquire

– Your state's and district's middle grades science standards and frameworks
– Chart paper and markers
– Sticky notes
– Overhead transparencies
– 10 to 20 gal. aquarium
– Transparent, 2 L soda bottles, tops removed, rinsed out thoroughly
– Transparent, 1 L soda bottles, tops removed, rinsed out thoroughly
– Pond water
– Mud samples from the pond
– Plants collected from the pond
– Pond organisms
– Hand lenses

Media List

Overheads

1 Inquiry Protocol
2 Trio Activity—Directions
3 Mentoring Worksheet
4 Myths or Misconceptions About Conflict
5 Conflict Management Styles
6 Management Categories
7 Uses and Limitations of Six Different Conflict Management Styles
8 Relationships Versus Issues
9 Reflective Journal Prompts
10 Evaluation Form

Handouts

1 Inquiry Protocol
2 Trio Activity—Directions

Welcome and Check-In (25 minutes)

Reconnecting With Each Other and the Program (25 minutes)

Overview

Participants focus on the purpose and content of the session. They revisit the Norms established in Session 1 to prepare to engage in the day's activities. They also engage in an activity that supports them in reflecting on what they have learned.

Before Beginning

Materials: agenda; list of outcomes; Norms from Session 1

Steps

1   Take about 10 minutes to give participants an overview of the day and re-engage them in the program.

    • Review the agenda.

    • Share the quote and talk about the themes of today's session: formative assessment, deepening the necessary skills to give effective feedback, and conflict management.

    • Go over the Outcomes (the foci of the day).

    • Refer to the posted Norms and ask people how they think they're all doing regarding the Norms. Look at the Parking Lot and respond to any pressing issues.

2   Use the remaining 15 minutes of this segment to engage participants in reflection.

3   Post the following directions on chart paper: "Jot down five words related to last session's learnings or mentoring in general." Choices might include

    • collegial conversation

    • risk taking

    • scaffolding

    • problem solving

    • thought provoking

4   Ask participants to share these words or phrases at their table groups and decide on the three they think are most important. When they have chosen the three, direct them, as a table group, to craft one question or insight.

5   To encourage ideas to flow beyond the table groups, tell participants to hold a "stand-up meeting." Ask that they choose someone from another table and share their words and phrases, questions, or insights.

Training Tip

As you wrap up this section, feel free to take extra time to try to address any relevant questions that were posted on the Parking Lot from Session 1 as well as questions that were raised as a result of this exercise.

Mentoring (1½ hours)

Activity 1: Strategic Mentoring (1½ hours)

Overview

Participants identify a challenging classroom observation and isolate the components of the lesson that affected student learning. Working in small groups, they choose an issue to address with the teacher, using the inquiry protocol as a guide for the conversation.

Before Beginning

Materials: chart paper, markers, highlighters placed on tables; Overheads 1, 2, 3; Handouts 1, 2, 3

Discussion Points

1. Point out to participants that the role of a new teacher mentor is really much bigger than the title implies.

2. As we bring new teachers into the profession, we help to establish new Norms and behaviors for them to break down the traditional isolation that most new teachers face.

3. Reinforce the idea that the norms of isolation are alive and well in school cultures and one of the jobs of the mentor is to begin to break down those walls.

Steps

1 Ask, "What are some professional Norms we want to create as part of our induction program?" Try to get a few responses from the group that focus on the following Norms:
   - collegiality
   - accepted expertise of a colleague
   - trust
   - acceptance of failure, mistakes
   - support for risk taking
   - time for reflection and talking about practice
   - engagement in inquiry and reflection

2 Continue by asking the question, "How many of you have heard from your mentee in response to the question, 'How's everything?' the answer, 'Fine!'?" Given what we know about school culture, why would we be surprised? But, in fact, mentors are frustrated by that response.

3 Explain that the next section will give mentors ideas about how to become more strategic with their coaching.

4 Ask participants to think about a coaching or mentoring situation that has been challenging for them.

5 Ask participants to write down the main points regarding this situation and think about how the teaching they have observed affected the learning of the children. Encourage them to avoid lengthy discussions of personality, personal situation, or school context. Instead, guide them to focus on what they see in the classroom with regard to instructional learning. Give them about 10 minutes to write down their ideas. Some possible focus areas:
   - The science activities are hands-on, but they are not inquiry based. Students are simply following directions using predetermined materials.
   - Much of the class period is spent reading and answering questions in the science text.
   - The teacher spends most of class time telling rather than engaging students in inquiry.
   - The teacher tries to cover too many goals and introduce too many skills; the teacher doesn't target instruction to a particular science concept or skill.
   - The teacher focuses only on a few students and is unaware of the entire class.
   - There is excessive student talk while the teacher is instructing.

6 Ask participants to form trios and choose an issue they would like to address. Push them to move from management issues to science issues. Suggest that often management issues are a result of ineffective teaching strategies, and, therefore, even if management is not perfect, it is helpful to focus on the science teaching.

7 Explain that mentors and mentees can most successfully address issues when they connect to the inquiry protocol. Put the inquiry protocol on the overhead (Overhead 1) and give examples from the list of where a focus area could be addressed in the protocol. For example, if the issue is that the teacher is telling too much, you might highlight a question from the inquiry protocol.

8   With a highlighter, demonstrate highlighting the particular area of the protocol that you want to emphasize.

9   Distribute Handouts 1, 2, and 3.

10 Tell participants to follow the steps listed in the Trio Activity handout to consider strategies to address their challenges. Emphasize again the importance of looking at the different components of the protocol.

11 Ask which aspects of the protocol are applicable to the situation with which the mentors are dealing—with this teacher, their mentee.

12 Emphasize that grounding the issue in the protocol gives it more validity and it takes some of the burden off the mentor. When you use the protocol, you put the teaching issue in a framework of accepted practice, not just mentor opinion. Ask participants to use a highlighter to highlight the aspects of the protocol that apply to the selected issue.

13 Clarify that on page one of the handout are the directions and on page two is the worksheet that mentors complete during the discussion. Remind mentors that it is important to think about what data they want to collect and how they plan to do it. Beginning teachers will value seeing specific data rather than relying on a mentor's opinion.

14 While participants are engaged in this activity, circulate and make a list of the issues. Record them on chart paper. After about 30 minutes, ask participants to put up fingers indicating how much time they still need to complete the task. Give them another five minutes, if necessary, to complete the worksheets and to prepare to share their conversations with the large group. Have a few groups come up and describe the issues they discussed and mentoring strategies they plan to use.

Science (2¾ hours)

Activity 1: Context Setting (1 hour)

Overview

In this session, participants consider the pond environment and communities of organisms. They create and investigate minienvironments. These minienvironments support them in exploring ecological and environmental concepts that they identify and that students can develop through examining the context of a pond. Participants' interest will determine the choice of inquiry. This open inquiry will continue over this and the next session.

Before Beginning

Materials: chart paper and marker

Steps

1   Engage participants in a discussion of the ecological or environmental concepts they teach and the context they use to support students' development of the concepts. Record participants' responses on chart paper.

2   Have participants, working in table groups, brainstorm which concepts they think they could teach using the pond as a context. List the group's ideas on a transparency, and ask them to describe the kinds of pond activities they think would support the development of these concepts.

3   Have each participant choose the concept(s) he or she would like to investigate. If some participants are not responsible for teaching such concepts, pair them with someone who is. Those who are not teaching the concepts will have valuable new ideas to contribute.

4   Create groups of no more than three, based on the participants' choice of concept(s) and have them generate several questions that would address the concept(s) they selected.

5   Given that the group probably represents several grade levels, there should be many interesting questions to investigate. Tell participants that they may need to do some research to determine what resources they will need to answer their question(s). For example, if they want to do chemical testing, they will have to procure the right kind of kit from a pet store that has aquarium supplies.

6   Based on their question(s), instruct participants to plan their observations and design any investigation that they want to carry out over the next two sessions. They may need to modify their questions, depending on the time between this session and the next. Have groups share their ideas. If possible, try to have each group select a different question to explore.

Activity 2: Creating a Minienvironment (45 minutes)

Overview

This activity gives participants an opportunity to explore a different set of concepts—ecological and environmental—that can be investigated using the pond as a context.

Before Beginning

Materials: a 10 to 20 gal. aquarium; sufficient number of clear, 2 L soda bottles, tops removed, rinsed out thoroughly, for participants to work in pairs or trios; pond water; mud samples from the pond; plants collected from the pond; pond organisms; and hand lenses

Steps

1   Based on their questions, have groups set up a minienvironment, using the 2 L soda bottles.

2   Make sure that mud taken from the pond, as well as plants, is included. Add pond water

(be sure not to use tap water because it harms the organisms) and any organism(s) appropriate to the selected inquiry.

3   Because participants have just established the minienvironments, they will not be able to do much investigation. Give them time to make some preliminary observations. Encourage them to take notes and make drawings of what they observe at this point.

4   Tell participants that, since this is an ongoing investigation, it is vital for them to observe and collect data about their minienvironments between this session and the next. Ask them to decide, in their groups, what data to collect, how often they will collect it, and how they will record it (drawings, tables, graphs).

5   Acknowledge to participants that, because they are working in groups, you know it will be difficult for each group member to collect data. If participants work at the same school, they can easily make observations or tests as a group. If not, ask participants to figure out a way to share their minienvironment before the next session, so that every member has an opportunity to make observations and collect data. If this is not possible, request that one group member take on this responsibility for the group.

Activity 3: Classroom Connections and Science Pedagogy— Units That Address Multiple Standards/Develop Multiple Concepts (1 hour)

Overview

In this age of standards, most teachers believe it impossible to do extended, in-depth inquiries that last many weeks. This activity helps participants think differently about teaching contexts, like the pond, which teachers can use to develop multiple concepts with students.

Before Beginning

Materials: state and district middle grades science standards

Steps

1   Participants should now be aware that there are some contexts, like a pond, that lend themselves to the teaching of multiple concepts.

2   Working in grade-level groups of 2 to 3, have participants review the concepts they are responsible for teaching. Distribute copies of your state and district middle grades science standards.

3   Ask participants to think about what concepts from one domain or across domains they might cluster. They may consider creating a concept map to help prompt their thinking. Once they have completed their cluster of concepts or concept map, have the group brainstorm various contexts, like the pond, that they think would support the development of those concepts.

4   Have each group present their ideas to the entire group.

Mentoring (1¼ hours)

Activity 1: Your Conflict-Management Style (1¼ hours)

Overview

This activity raises participants' consciousness of how they react and respond to conflict. This self-knowledge is valuable to mentors who need to establish a trusting relationship with their mentee. Knowledge of the different conflict-management styles also provides insight about the mentee.

Before Beginning

Materials: chart paper and markers for each group; Overheads 4, 5, 6, 7, 8; Handouts 4, 5, 6, 7, 8

Steps

1   Introduce this section by explaining that disagreement by itself is usually not the cause of conflict. More often, failure to listen and to respect alternative views causes conflict.

2   Inform participants that they will have an opportunity to evaluate their own conflict-management style and to analyze the positive and negative aspects of that style. Because positive collaborative relationships are crucial to mentoring and also to breaking down the crippling isolation that exists in today's schools, it is important for teachers to learn to make clear choices about how to deal with specific conflict.

3   Show Overhead 4. Distribute Handout 4 and ask participants to fill it out.

4   After the handout forms are completely filled in, put up Overhead 6. (Do not show categories before participants have completed their forms.)

5   Ask participants to raise their hands to indicate in which column they received the highest score. Divide the group into their preferred conflict styles, making adjustments to try to get relatively even groups. If no one has chosen number VI—defer discussion of that style until later and address it as part of your wrap-up.

6   Tell groups they have 15 minutes to write about potential uses and limitations of their particular conflict styles on chart paper. Ask participants to be as specific as possible about examples of when this conflict style works and when it hinders resolution.

7   Ask groups to hang up their charts, and, after everyone has completed this activity, ask groups to present their work. Facilitate a conversation by asking for differences of opinion, questions, and clarifications.

8   Summarize by saying that it is important to remember that there are many strategies we can use in conflict situations, but each of us tends to habitually use some strategies more often than others. To most effectively resolve a conflict, we should use the strategy that is most appropriate for that particular conflict situation. However, that strategy might not be the strategy that we habitually use.

9   Distribute Handout 5 and ask participants to complete it. Tell them to read each technique listed and decide whether they use that technique frequently, occasionally, or rarely during conflicts. They can think about conflicts with friends, family, and school—whatever they prefer.

10 Give participants five minutes to complete the form.

11 Distribute Handout 7. Give participants a few minutes to read it, and then ask them if they have any comments.

12 Wrap up this section by showing Overhead 8. Use the discussion points provided to describe the graphic image depicted in Overhead 8, Relationships Versus Issues.

Discussion Points: Relationships Versus Issues

1. The vertical axis in Overhead 8 is about the Relationship and the horizontal axis is about the Issue.

2. People make decisions based on which is more important to focus on for that particular conflict.

3. For example, if one is attempting to build a Relationship without regard to the Issue, one focuses on accommodation.

4. In situations where addressing the Issue is of paramount importance, such as in a fire drill, the Relationship is of little importance.

5. Compromise floats in the middle, because often we give up too much when we compromise. No one leaves happy, even though we often ask children in our classes to compromise.

6. The best solution is collaboration, where one can equally address the Relationship and the Issue. But it's the furthest away, because it takes longer to reach.

Reflection and Next Steps (30 minutes)

Reflective Journal (15 minutes)

Overview

In this segment, you continue to support mentors' reflection and processing of their training experience by encouraging them to respond in writing to a series of prompts.

Before Beginning

Materials: Overhead 9, Handout 9

Steps

1   Bring the discussion back to the theme of this session, conflict management, and ask participants to respond to the Reflective Journal Prompts on Overhead 9.
2   Again, collect participants' journals and copy them both, so both you and the participants can have a copy.

For Next Time (5 minutes)

Overview

Participants read and reflect on an article about the use of the questioning cycle during scientific inquiry.

Before Beginning

Materials: Handout 10

Steps

1   In preparation for the next session, ask participants to read the article on questioning, "Questioning Cycle: Making Students' Thinking Explicit During Scientific Inquiry," by Erin Furtak and Maria Ruiz-Primo (Handout 10).
2   Suggest they share this article with their mentees, and encourage them to focus their next observation on practicing the informative questioning cycle described in the article.

Evaluation (10 minutes)

Overview

This activity is an important source of information for you. Participants' feedback will help you prepare for future sessions.

Before Beginning
Materials: Overhead 10, Handout 11

Steps
1   Hand out and show as an overhead the evaluation prompts (Overhead 10, Handout 11).
2   Encourage participants to write any questions or concerns they have on sticky notes and stick them on the Parking Lot paper as they leave.

SESSION 10

Anything worth doing well is worth doing slowly.

Gypsy Rose Lee

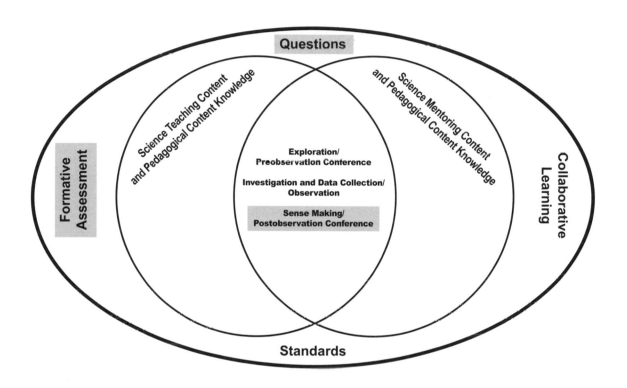

Overview

This is the last session, and you will want to spend time at the beginning on an activity that creates an atmosphere that helps participants bring this series of workshops to a satisfying close. The goal is to have participants leave the last session on an upbeat note, with a feeling of accomplishment and the confidence to help other science teachers improve their practice.

Outcomes

- Improve student achievement by studying pedagogical content knowledge with a colleague or colleagues.
- Understand the many roles of mentoring.
- Determine the most favorable conditions for keeping an organism alive.
- Identify the kinds of understanding an assessment task provides from an analysis of a product designed by students.
- Identify how working with novice teachers can benefit both mentors and novices.

Session Snapshot

Agenda

30 minutes	**Welcome and Check-In**	
	Reconnecting With Each Other and the Program	
1 hour, 40 minutes	**Mentoring**	
	Activity 1: Article Discussion	
	Activity 2: Mentoring Reflections	
	Activity 3: Mentor Roles	
3 hours	**Science**	
	Activity 1: Minienvironments Revisited	
	Activity 2: Assessment: Inventing an Organism	
30 minutes	**Institute Wrap-Up**	
	Closing	
	Evaluation	

How to Prepare for Session 10

What You Need to Do

- Read and become familiar with the article "Questioning Cycle: Making Students' Thinking Explicit During Scientific Inquiry," by Erin Furtak and Maria Ruiz-Primo from Session 9.
- Become familiar with the Read and React worksheet.
- Remind participants to bring their minienvironments to the session.
- Scan through the session and review all of the directions and sidebar notes. These include activity descriptions and directions, the science background sections, the training tips, and the discussion points.

What You Need to Make

- Write the Agenda on chart paper and hang it on the wall where participants can see it and you can refer to it throughout the day.
- Write the Outcomes on chart paper and hang the paper on the wall.
- Make all overheads (1–5).
- Duplicate all handouts (1–4).
- Post the Norms and Parking Lot charts.

What You Need to Acquire

- Overhead projector
- Chart paper and markers
- Sticky notes
- Colored pencils
- Arts-and-crafts materials such as: modeling clay, pipe cleaners, electrical wire of various gauges, and ribbon

Materials

- Hand magnifiers, one for each person
- Newspaper to cover tables
- Field guides
- Cards with drawings showing common pond organisms, drawn to scale and including their common and scientific names

Media List

Overheads

1 Read and React
2 Mentoring Reflections
3 Mentor Roles
4 Benefits of Mentoring
5 Marian Wright Edelman Quote

Handouts

1 Read and React
2 Mentoring Reflections
3 Mentoring Practice Growth Plan
4 Evaluation Form

Welcome and Check-In (30 minutes)

Reconnecting With Each Other and the Program (30 minutes)

Overview

Participants focus on the purpose and content of the session. They revisit the Norms established in Session 1 to prepare to engage in the day's activities. They also engage in an activity that supports them in breaking existing mindsets and internalizing abstract concepts.

Before Beginning

Materials: chart paper and marker; agenda; list of outcomes; Norms from Session 1

Training Tip

The activity in which participants engage in this segment—Synectics Brainstorm— is an approach to creative thinking that depends on looking at what appears on the surface as unrelated phenomena and drawing relevant connections. Its main tool is analogy or metaphor. This activity is an effective opener because there are usually some very funny ideas as well as some more thoughtful and even poignant ones.

Steps

1 Take about 10 minutes to review the posted agenda, session outcomes, and Norms from Session 1. Respond to participants' questions and comments, and then move on to engage participants in this section's opening activity.

2 Ask participants to sit in groups of four.

3 Begin by asking participants to say something they have seen in the last 24 hours. (The success of this activity does not depend on participants choosing the right answer. On the contrary, it does not matter what they shout out.)

4 Choose three responses, and write them on chart paper. On the top of the chart paper, write "Mentoring science teachers is like _____." For example, if *onion* is one of the words recorded, ask participants to write down five ways that mentoring science teachers is like an onion. They might say that sometimes it makes you cry, it makes your teaching more flavorful, or there are many layers to peel. If *telephone pole* is chosen, then participants might say communication is the most important aspect of mentoring, it provides stability and strength or it withstands the rigors of time. (You get the idea.)

5 Give participants 10 minutes to come up with 5 examples for each answer—15 in all.

6 Ask each group to choose its favorite example for each answer.

7 End by having each group report an example for how science mentoring is like ... first word or phrase, then the second, and finally the third.

Mentoring (1 hour, 40 minutes)

Activity 1: Article Discussion (40 minutes)

Overview

This discussion of the article "Questioning Cycle: Making Students' Thinking Explicit During Scientific Inquiry," by Erin Furtak and Maria Ruiz-Primo (*Science Scope*, January 2005) is designed to deepen mentors' understanding of the role of questioning in inquiry-based science. It is a good article for the last session because it focuses on the questioning cycle—the teacher's role in eliciting student thinking and using informative questioning as an assessment for student learning. It also serves to heighten participants' awareness of the breadth of professional literature available on inquiry science.

Before Beginning

Materials: Overhead 1, Handout 1

Steps

1 Ask participants to count off so there will be four mentors in each group. (For example, if you have 48 participants, count by 12.) If you have an odd number, create groups of 3 with those teachers.

2 Once mentors are in their groups, put the directions on the overhead projector (Overhead 1) and ask them to review Handout 1.

3 After mentors complete this activity, ask them to share any insights or learnings that they gained. Then, debrief the participants. Ask them whether they thought this was a useful way to explore ideas in the article and to explore their own thinking. If so, why? If not, why?

Activity 2: Mentoring Reflections (30 minutes)

Overview
The purpose of this activity is to give mentors an opportunity to improve their use of the mentoring journal as a vehicle for increasing the mentee's teaching repertoire as well as a formative assessment tool.

Before Beginning
Materials: Overhead 2, Handout 2

Steps
1 Give participants an opportunity to look over the completed mentoring journals that focused on observing or discussing the questioning cycle with their mentees.
2 Show Overhead 2 and distribute the handouts.
3 Ask participants to meet with a colleague at their tables.
4 Review the tasks shown on the overhead and ask participants to discuss the tasks with their groups.
5 After partners have reflected on their mentoring journals and classroom observations (about 25 minutes), ask participants to share insights they gained as a result of the observations and conversations.

Activity 3: Mentor Roles (30 minutes)

Overview
You engage mentors in considering the varied roles they have played in their first year of mentoring, and you offer ideas of how they can improve their mentoring skills and expand the scope of the work.

Before Beginning
Materials: chart paper; Overhead 3; Handout 3

Steps
1 Begin by saying that, after working as a mentor over the year, mentors are beginning to understand how multifaceted their role is. Brainstorm the roles mentors have taken on during the year.

Steps (continued)

2   Ask participants to write down the top three roles that kept them busy during the year. Explain that different skills are involved in performing these roles.

3   Using Overhead 3, ask mentors to discuss with a partner the roles they assumed.

4   Debrief participants by asking them to give a few examples of what mentors do in different roles. Note that, at any given meeting with a mentee, mentors may have to change hats many times.

5   Close by emphasizing that mentors take on the responsibility of moving a beginning teacher's practice forward. Sometimes mentors are teachers, and sometimes they solve problems. They must be good listeners.

6   Distribute Handout 3 and ask mentors to fill out the growth plan for their mentoring practice.

7   Invite participants to share their growth plans with the group, and engage participants in a discussion of how each mentor is thinking about, and approaching, his or her personal and professional growth in terms of what he or she learned during the past several sessions.

Science (3 hours)

Overview

The previous session shifted the pond study from closely observing a single organism to the pond environment at large and communities of organisms. Participants selected particular ecological and environmental concepts to explore through the minienvironments they created. In this session, participants share findings about their minienvironments and engage in an assessment task in which they invent a viable pond organism.

Activity 1: Minienvironments Revisited (1 hour)

Overview

Participants make final observations of their minienvironments and share their data and findings with the group.

Before Beginning

Make sure that participants have their science notebooks.

Training Tip

You asked participants to observe and record their observations between the last session and this one. Depending on how each group handled this responsibility, participants will need time to share their observations and any other data that they collected.

Steps

1 Give groups time (about 20 minutes) to confer about their minienvironments and observe and record any new observations in their science notebooks.
2 Have each group report on the following:
    • what question or idea they investigated
    • how they set up their minienvironment and why
    • how often they observed their environment
    • the kinds of observations they made and what they think was happening
    • what questions they still have
3 Instruct participants to ask questions of each presenting group.
4 Give groups time to walk around and observe each others' minienvironments and ask specific questions about each investigation.

Activity 2: Assessment: Inventing an Organism (2 hours)

Overview

This session's science segment ends with an assessment task. Working in pairs, participants create an imaginary, but viable pond organism. This task provides a lot of information about what participants have learned about the pond and its organisms.

Before Beginning

Materials: arts-and-crafts materials such as modeling clay, pipe cleaners, and wire; chart paper, markers, and colored pencils for each group

Steps

1   Tell participants that, based on their pond study, they will invent an imaginary, but viable pond organism.

2   Ask them to select partners and to begin by thinking about such issues as where the organism lives in the pond, how it lives, how it eats, how it moves, and what happens to it over the course of the year. They must design an organism that has specific characteristics.

3   Ask pairs to make preliminary sketches in their science notebooks. When they are satisfied with their designs, they may either build 3-D organisms using the art materials or they may do a drawing on chart paper using markers and colored pencils.

4   Give pairs an hour to work on their organisms.

5   When pairs are finished, group two pairs and have them analyze each other's organism. Tell them to begin by taking some time to look carefully at the design and take notes on what they notice in their science notebooks.

6   Instruct each pair to ask questions about the other pair's organism and its design, habits, and other characteristics.

7   Ask each pair to decide what the design of the organism communicates about the other pair's understanding about pond organisms and the pond. Give pairs about 30 minutes to complete this task. They should record their ideas in their science notebooks.

8   End this session by selecting 3 to 4 organisms and discussing with the group at large what understanding about pond organisms each design conveys.

Institute Wrap-Up (30 minutes)

Closing (20 minutes)

Overview

In this section, your objective is to remind mentors about the importance of their role. Much of the literature on mentoring asserts that formal programs produce dramatic changes for new teachers.

Before Beginning
Materials: Overheads 4, 5

Steps

1   Show Overhead 4.

2   Emphasize that mentoring is very difficult work, but the results are clear. Among districts with induction programs involving mentoring and other support, there is a lower drop-out rate and, at this time when 50% of urban teachers leave teaching within the first five years, retention of teachers, and certainly science teachers in particular, is a major goal.

3   Reiterate that the new-teacher mentor is the most important component of any high-quality induction program. No technology, no curriculum, no standardized structures can substitute for the power of a knowledgeable and skillful veteran to move a novice teacher to ambitious levels of teaching.

4   Highlight the idea that researchers also suggest that mentoring can provide valuable experiences for veteran teachers. Formalizing the mentor role for experienced teachers creates another niche in the career ladder for teachers and contributes to the professionalism of education.

5   Remind participants that mentoring is an inquiry into teaching, much the same as inquiry is the foundation of good science teaching.

6   Emphasize the importance of the work of mentoring and that we all need to work together to improve the instruction of beginning teachers. Relate the conversation to Session 1, when you first talked about mentoring as critical to the professionalism of teaching and you discussed how mentors are adding new value and knowledge to the teaching profession.

7   Close by acknowledging the commitment these mentors have made to their mentees, the project, and the teaching profession.

8   As an inspirational review of the importance and impact of mentoring, show the Marian Wright Edelman quote about mentors (Overhead 5) and read it aloud to the group.

Evaluation (10 minutes)

Overview

As this session completes the institutes, it will be helpful to get feedback from the participants to aid in your planning.

Before Beginning
Materials: Handout 4

Steps
1   Distribute Handout 4, and ask participants to comment on their science-mentoring experience.

2   Collect Handout 4 before participants leave. If there is time, you might want to engage in a discussion of any remaining questions or issues that linger in the Parking Lot—particularly if they will have an impact on participants' work with mentees.

Appendix A

The Planning and Observation Protocol

Teachers may choose some of these questions to use as a guide during coplanning or pre- and postobservation discussions, or to help focus observations.

I. Phases of inquiry/learning cycle

Across all phases
- How does each phase promote students' learning of concepts, skills, and ideas?
- How does the teacher give directions to students? (For example, does the teacher use multiple modalities?)
- How and when does the teacher introduce scientific language?
- What role, if any, do science notebooks play during this investigation?
- What questions will the teacher ask during each phase of the inquiry? (For example, does the teacher allow for an open response or direct answer?)

A. Exploration
- How does the teacher introduce the investigation?
  - How does the teacher relate the investigation to students' lives outside of school in a meaningful way?
  - How does the teacher solicit students' prior knowledge related to the investigation?
- How does the teacher introduce the materials?
  - How does the teacher make the materials available to students?
  - How does the teacher instruct the students to use the materials?

B. Investigation and data collection
- How does the teacher introduce the experiments?
  - How does the teacher place the experiment(s) in the larger context of the investigation?
  - How does the teacher ask students to make and record predictions based on facts, experience, and/or prior knowledge?
- How does the teacher interact with the groups during the investigation?
  - How does the teacher survey and locate groups that are having problems with equipment or procedures?
  - How does the teacher suggest improvements in procedures (e.g., through explicit directions or by way of leading questions or comparisons to other groups)?

– How does the teacher help students demonstrate standards-based data collection and representation?
  • Is the teacher neutral on the data being collected?
  • Do the students collect similar data across groups?
  • Can students redo their experiments and reproduce their results?

C. Sense making

– How does the teacher have students report their data or observations?
  • Do students display their results for all to see?
  • Does the teacher ensure that all groups present their results?
  • Does the teacher ensure that the students check the data for accuracy?
  • How does the teacher elicit comments from students?
– How does the teacher help students clarify the data or observations?
  • Does the teacher directly question some groups' results or have all students decide on what is valid and useable?
  • How does the teacher deal with discrepant results?
– How does the teacher help students interpret the data?
  • How does the teacher help students isolate patterns or correlations?
  • How does the teacher solicit explanations from students?
– How does the teacher help students clarify explanations and conceptualizations?
  • Do the students accurately represent the information?
  • Does the teacher use student analogies?
  • How does the teacher address students' misconceptions?
  • How does the teacher adapt and build on students' attempted explanations?
  • In what ways does the teacher directly utilize the data collected to introduce formal scientific explanations?

II. Infrastructure

– How are materials organized and managed to provide easy student access?
– How does the teacher manage the class?
  • What routines and procedures are in place to support maximum student learning and safety?
  • What are some strategies the teacher uses to support the smooth, ongoing flow of events in the classroom (e.g., transitions from one event to another, expectations for efficient student work)?
  • How does the teacher interact with students and groups of students?
– What does the teacher do to ensure positive group work outcomes?
  • How does the teacher communicate expectations for group work?

- What strategies does the teacher use to ensure individual accountability in cooperative groups?

III. Assessment

- What should students know, understand, and be able to do?
  - What evidence will show that students understand?
- What assessment methods does the teacher use during each phase of inquiry (e.g., informal checks for understanding, observation/dialogue, quiz/test, open-ended prompt, performance task/project)?
  - How does the assessment match the opportunity to learn?

Appendix B

Resources

Averette, P. 2003. Save the last word for me. National School Reform Faculty Harmony Education Center. Retrieved September 12, 2006, from *www.smallschoolsproject.org/PDFS/save_last_word.pdf*

Boston Area Educators for Social Responsibility. 1995. *Conflict management styles*. Boston: Author.

Boston Area Educators for Social Responsibility. 1995. *Management categories*. Boston: Author.

Boston Area Educators for Social Responsibility. 1996. *Myths of misconceptions about conflict*. Boston: Author.

Boston Area Educators for Social Responsibility. 1996. *Relationships versus issues*. Boston: Author.

Boston Area Educators for Social Responsibility. 1996. *Uses and limitations of six different conflict management styles*. Boston: Author.

California Commission on Teacher Credentialing and California Department of Education. 1997. *California standards for the teaching profession*. Sacramento, CA: Authors.

Costa, A., and B. Garmston. 2002. *Cognitive coaching: A foundation for renaissance schools*. Norwood, MA: Christopher Gordon.

Edelman, M. W. 2000. *Lanterns: A memoir of mentors*. New York: Harper Paperbacks.

Education Development Center, Inc. 2007. *Investigating pond organisms: An exploration of pond life and its environment*. Nashua, NH: Neo/Sci.

Estgeest, J. 1985. The right question at the right time. In *Primary science: Taking the plunge,* ed., W. Harlen. Portsmouth, NH: Heinemann.

Furtak, E. M., and M. A. Ruiz-Primo. 2005. Questioning cycle: Making students' thinking explicit during inquiry. *Science Scope* 28 (5): 22–25.

Gordon, T. 1980. *Leadership effectiveness training*. New York: Bantam Books.

Little, J. W. 1990. The mentor phenomenon and the social organization of teaching. *Review of Research in Education* 16: 297–351.

Marshall, K. 1985. *Teachers helping teachers: A guidebook for the new professional in education.* Kit Marshall.

National Research Council (NRC). 1996. *National Science Education Standards*. Washington, DC: National Academy Press.

Thomas, G. 1980. *Leadership effectiveness training*. New York: Bantam Books.

Troen, V., and K. C. Boles. 2004. *Who's teaching your children?: Why the teacher crisis is worse than you think and what can be done about it.* New Haven, CT: Yale University Press.

Watson, B., and R. Konicek. 1990, May. Teaching for conceptual change: Confronting children's experience. *Phi Delta Kappan 71* (9): 680–684.

Zubrowski, B. 1994. *Ice cream making and cake baking*. White Plains, NY: Cuisenaire Company of America.

Index

National Science Teachers Association

SESSION 1
Handouts and Overheads

Not a Profession Versus a Profession

Not a Profession	A Profession
Egalitarianism—No career ladder	Recognition for achievement—Clearly defined career path
Isolation—Practice is a freelance craft	Practice characterized by teamwork and collaboration
Poor preparation ("Anybody can do it")	Rigorous educational standards and required skills
Little or no mentoring	Mentoring the expectation and the norm
Weak professional development	Professional development integral to the career
Practice not based on research	Research informs practice
Lack of accountability	Everyone accountable
At bottom of power structure	Shared decision making

Source: Mentor Training, Brandeis University, October 2004
Reprinted with permission from Vivian Troen

[Handout 1]

Teaching for Conceptual Change: Confronting Children's Experience

Watson, Bruce and Richard Konicek.
Phi Delta Kappan
May 1990, pp. 680-684

For nine winters, experience had been the children's teacher. Every hat they had worn, every sweater they had donned contained heat. "Put on your warm clothes," parents and teachers had told them. So when they began to study heat one spring day, who could blame them for thinking as they did?

"Sweaters are hot," said Katie.

"If you put a thermometer inside a hat, would it ever get hot! Ninety degrees, maybe," said Neil.

"Leave it there a long tune, and it might get to a hundred. Or 200," Christian added.

If Deb O'Brien had begun her lesson on heat in the usual way, she might never have known how nine long Massachusetts winters had skewed her students' thinking. Her fourth-graders would have learned the major sources of heat, a little bit about friction, and how to read a thermometer. By the end of two weeks, they would have been able to pass a simple test on heat. But their preconceptions, never having been put on the table, would have continued, coexisting in a morass of conflicting ideas about heat and its behavior.

However, like a growing number of educators at all levels, O'Brien periodically teaches science for "conceptual change." Her students, allowed to examine their own experiences, must confront the inconsistencies in their theories. In the process they find the path toward a deeper understanding of heat, have a great time with science, and refine their thinking and writing skills.

O'Brien began with the simple question, "What is heat?" Using journals and the chalkboard to record their ideas, the students, with O'Brien's help, wrote down their "best thinking so-far" on the subject of heat. Heat came from the sun, they wrote. And from our bodies. But when Owen spoke about the heat in sweaters, everyone else agreed. Sweaters were very hot. Hats, too. Even rugs got "wicked hot," the children said. Sensing the first of many naive conceptions, O'Brien stopped them and said the magic words in science, "Let's find out."

For two whole days the testing went on. Experience, that most deceptive of teachers, had to be met head on. With their teacher's help, Christian, Neil, Katie, and the others placed thermometers inside sweaters, hats, and a rolled-up rug. When the temperature inside refused to rise after 15 minutes, Christian suggested that they leave the thermometers overnight. After all, he said, when the doctor takes your temperature, you have to leave the thermometer in your mouth a long time. Folding the sweaters and hats securely, the children predicted three-digit temperatures the next day.

Source: Watson, B., and R. Konicek. 1990, May. "Teaching for conceptual change: Confronting children's experience." *Phi Delta Kappan.*
Reprinted with permission from Bruce Watson and *Phi Delta Kappan*

When they ran to their experiments first thing the next morning, the children were baffled. They ha
wrong. Now they'll change their minds, and we can move on, O'Brien thought.

But experience is an effective, if fallible, teacher. The children refused to give up. "We just didn't le
them in there long enough," Christian said. "Cold air got in there somehow," said Katie. And so the
testing went on.

Conceptual Change And How It Grew

Since the late 1970s, the notion of "conceptual change" has been a pedagogical football among science
educators. Arguing that reading and observing scientific principles will not alone move the mountain of"
alternative frameworks" about science that children bring to the classroom, that even hands-on activities
allow such thinking to go undetected, teachers are beginning from square one, helping children construct
their own models of scientific principles.

If children base their thinking on what they have seen and felt, then their experience must be structured to
challenge their erroneous beliefs. If alternative views of scientific principles are not addressed, they can
coexist with "what the teacher told us" and create a mishmash of fact and fiction. When studying
astronomy, for instance, if one brings up the common belief in astrology, children can learn every
available fact about the planets and still go away thinking that Venus somehow controls their destiny. But
if each child is given a chance to test his or her own model of the universe and find its limits, then a
deeper understanding, without the naive conceptions, can result.

As early as the 1920s John Dewey emphasized science as inquiry, and Gerald Craig in his landmark
dissertation spoke eloquently in favor of teaching science as investigation.[1] Yet the texts and curricula of
the 1950s told a different story. Science texts were reading books, punctuated by predigested
demonstrations of various facts embedded in such obvious questions as, "Does air have weight?"

When the orbiting Sputnik I beeped to the world that the U.S. space program was second best, the golden
age of science education began. Millions of dollars were made available for writing and implementing
new science curricula. The National Defense Education Act (NDEA) of 1958 provided matching federal
dollars for equipment purchased by schools. Probably most important, the new emphasis on science
education gave scientists, psychologists, and educators the opportunity to combine efforts on a single
task: improving science and mathematics education for all children.

Drawing on the world of such psychologists as Jerome Bruner, Robert Gagne and Jean Piaget,[2] the
emphasis in science education finally caught up with what Dewey, Craig, and others had been saying
since the 1920s. Science is an inquiry-oriented subject; subjects should be taught and ultimately learned
according to the structure of the discipline; children and how they learn should be at the center of the
teaching of any subject.

Since the early 1960s science educators have tried to follow these tenets through times of financial feast
and famine. The plethora of programs --- from the 1960s: Science A Process Approach (SAPA), Science
Curriculum Improvement Study (SCIS), Minnesota Mathematics and Science Teaching ProJect
(MINNEMAST), Elementary Science Study (ESS), from the 1970s: Conceptually Oriented Program in
Elementary Science (COPES), Science 5/13, Nuffield; and from the 1980s: Great Explorations in Math
and Science (GEMS), TOPS, Activities in Integrating Math and Science (AIMS) --- all subscribe, with
mild variations, to the basic philosophies described above. Children are the focus, and science is viewed
as a combination of content, process, skills, attitudes, and values.

.nese alphabetic programs, later published by commercial firms, made a modest impression on the market. Their ideas and activities were incorporated into such commercial texts as Space, Time, Energy, and Matter (STEM), but even these books have made no more than a ripple in the ocean of school science. The latest generation of texts once again pays lip service to science as an inquiry-oriented discipline, but the books themselves resemble their ancestors of the 1950s more than they do those produced during that brief "golden age." Today's texts, which have the greatest influence on how science is taught in American schools, have come almost full circle, and teachers who rely primarily on them are little closer to teaching science as inquiry than were their counterparts in the 1920s. In too many classrooms across the U.S., science is skill taught as a cohesive set of facts to be absorbed, and children are viewed as blank slates on which teachers are to write.

But in the last 20 years such people as David Ausubel, Joseph Novak, Rosalind Driver, John Clement, and others have begun to ask different questions about children's learning.[3] Cognitive psychology and neo-Piagetian philosophy agree that knowledge, for both children and adults, grows and changes in very interesting ways. Learners bring their idiosyncratic and personal experiences to most learning situations. These experiences have profound effect on the learners' views of the world and a startling effect on their willingness and ability to accept other, more scientifically grounded explanations of how the world works. Teachers who take a personal, adaptive view of knowledge are known as constructivists because their model of learning posits that all knowledge is constructed by the individual in a scheme of accommodation and assimilation.

Deb O'Brien is such a teacher. Her students, actively constructing their conceptual understanding of heat and its behavior, eagerly tackled their surprising data with yet another experiment.

The Investigation Heats Up

When the shock of the room temperature readings on the bundled-up thermometers wore off, the children went at it again. If, as they insisted, cold air had seeped inside the clothes overnight, what could they do to keep it out? While O'Brien would have preferred to focus on one variable at a time, the children's discussion brought out other naive conceptions. Remembering attics and cars, some of them said that closed spaces were hot. "How could you test that?" O'Brien wondered. Neil decided to seal the hat, with a thermometer inside, in a plastic bag. Katie chose to plug the ends of the rug with hats. Others placed sweaters in closets or in desks, far away from the great gusts of cold air they seemed to think swept through their classroom at night. With their new experiments snugly in place, time-that old heat maker - was left to do its job.

On Wednesday morning the children rushed to examine their experiments. They checked their deeply buried thermometers. From across the room, they shared their bewilderment. All the thermometers were at 68 degrees Farenheit. Confused, they wrote in their journals.

"Hot and cold are sometimes strange," Katie wrote. "Maybe [the thermometer] didn't work because it was used to room temperature.

Owen didn't know what to write, and Christian wrote simply, "I don't know why."

Meanwhile, O'Brien kept her own journal. This was one of her first attempts at teaching through conceptual change, and she wondered how long she should let these naive conceptions linger.

"The kids are holding on to and putting together pieces of what they know of the world. But the time we are taking to explore what kids think is much longer than if I told them the facts." If she told her students that hats didn't make heat, she knew that most would parrot her statement just to please her. Lacking the evidence to prove that fact, however, they would continue to prefer their own conceptions of their teacher's answer.

Surprises await the teacher who expects children to give up their conceptions at the first sign of a discrepancy. Stubbornness, a trait not limited to children, causes students to grasp at straws, O'Brien found. When the temperature inside a sweater rose even one degree, the students cheered and shouted, "Finally!" And if, as was more often the case, the thermometer stayed at room temperature, well, then, perhaps the thermometer was broken. Or perhaps the cold air got in somehow. Or maybe they just hadn't let the sweaters sit long enough. Christian wanted to seal a hat and thermometer in a metal box and leave it for a year. Then the temperature would be sure to rise.

Should she tell them the difference between holding heat and emitting heat, O'Brien wondered. Should she devise her own experiment on insulation? She decided to let the conceptions linger through one more round of testing. And so the sweaters, hats, and even a down sleeping bag brought from home were sealed, plugged, and left to endure the cold.

The Sleep of Reason

While we often assume that reason is the guiding light of science, the history of scientific thought shows otherwise. When confronted with contradictory evidence, scientists are sometimes as puzzled as children. Through further testing, they seek additional evidence. If the results continue to disprove what they once thought, scientists often behave very much like children: they argue among themselves, they cling to their old theories, and they devise experiments that will reinforce the traditional way of thinking. As Thomas Kuhn showed in *The Structure of Scientific Revolutions,*[4] scientists are capable of holding contradictory theories about scientific concepts. Scientific communities, such as O'Brien's classroom, can take this a step further by dividing into camps that simultaneously believe several different explanations of the same event, often for many years' duration. When it comes to confronting the errors in one's thinking, scientists of all ages seem equally susceptible to certain barriers.

In theory, at least, when confronted with evidence that contradicts existing assumptions, rational observers will accommodate their thinking to fit the latest observations. A theory, says the philosopher of science Irme Lakatos, is judged on how well it solves problems.[5] If a theory generates problems that it can't solve or explain, Lakatos says, it is rejected in favor of a new theory that solves those problems and offers promise of further investigation. Even fourth-graders seek answers that can be explained by their theories. But the substitution of one theory for another is not as easy as erasing the chalkboard. Certain preconditions for conceptual change must exist if the barriers in the path to understanding are to be overcome.

We suggest several barriers to conceptual change, barriers strong enough to laugh in the face of discrepant events. Among schoolchildren the strongest of these obstacles is likely to be stubbornness, the refusal to admit that one's theory might be wrong. Children who are not often asked their opinions are especially reluctant to admit the errors in their thinking and will find ways to adjust old ideas before assimilating new ones.

Lakatos cites the varying strengths of scientific concepts as reasons why some beliefs are changed and others are not. "Hard-core ideas" take precedence over "protective-belt ideas," Lakatos posits. In the face of discrepant evidence, believers will change their "protective-belt ideas" in order to protect their hard-core beliefs, much as astronomers devised endless variations on cosmological theories, adding epicycles, altering distances, and so on just to keep the earth at the center of their cosmos. Katie was willing to believe that "hot and cold are sometimes strange," surrendering her belief in the consistency of temperature in order to build walls around the idea of "warm clothes." When children are unable to call on scientific knowledge to explain a piece of contradictory evidence, they will often call the discrepant event "magic." As many teachers know, tenacity in children makes scientists look downright flexible.

Another barrier to conceptual change is language. A teacher seeking conceptual change should be cautious about vocabulary. The difficulty of mastering new terms in addition to a new way of thinking about a concept can cause children to cling even more tenaciously to their old beliefs. Even the vernacular usage of nonscientific terms, such as "warm clothes," can cause confusion. There must be a reason why everyone calls them "warm," O'Brien's students conjectured.

Perception itself can block conceptual change as well. We tell children that "seeing is believing," but in science that often isn't true. Touch is an even more deceptive sense. Though O'Brien's thermometers had stayed at room temperature, each night the children kept warm beneath their blankets, just as each winter they had put on warm hats and sweaters and actually felt the warmth that the thermometers refused to register. A few days of surprising results in the classroom are not likely to change such deeply "felt" thinking. Teachers and students learn firsthand the inadequacy of empiricism as a theory of knowledge. As Eleanor Duckworth so aptly put it, "The critical experiments themselves cannot impose their own meanings. One has to have done a major part of the work already, one has to have developed a network of ideas in which to imbed the experiments." [6]

O'Brien and some of her abler students could have imposed their findings on the class saying, "Look at the thermometer. Room temperature! Now do you believe that sweaters don't make heat?" Textbooks attempt to do just this, presenting events and critical experiments from the history of science up to the present day. But, to paraphrase Louis Pasteur, understanding favors the prepared mind. If the learner has done a major part of the work already and has developed Duckworth's "network of ideas in which to imbed" the new idea, an enlightened view is more likely to evolve. If not, the experience may mean nothing.

While children and adults face many of the same barriers to learning, a few of the obstacles to conceptual change are developmental. Children in the middle elementary grades are only beginning to use concrete operations. As Piaget's research showed, when confronted with new evidence, children in these grades tend to revert to the earlier stage --- in this case the preoperational stage, characterized by an inability to conserve concrete properties, such as size and weight, and by difficulties in measurement and logical reasoning.

Children at this stage of development swear by their feelings in the face of the evidence and, having limited experience with the scientific method, trust their lifelong convictions more than they trust a thermometer. They particularly susceptible to what researcher Judith Tschirigi calls "sensible reasoning" [7] Such reasoning Tschirigi says, often takes precedence over Piaget's "concrete reasaoning in." Children will modify their experiments to accommodate their beliefs long before they will change their beliefs to fit the evidence.

Because children's minds are still "under construction," they must be treated with care where conceptual change is concerned. As O'Brien learned, expecting students to exhibit conceptual change after having observed a few discrepant events is bound to be frustrating for both teacher and students. A teacher who chooses to let students tackle their own misconceptions is well advised to consider Lev Vygotsky's "zone of proximal development," [8] also known as a child's "construction zone." Such developmental factors as memory, skill acquisition, and reasoning ability affect a child's capacity to incorporate new knowledge into existing schemes of thought, Vigotsky said.

The "construction zone" encompasses what a child is developmentally ready to consider. Any new information or skills needed for conceptual change may lie outside the zone if the child is developmentally unprepared to learn them. O'Brien's students who cheered when the temperature inside the "warm" clothes rose a single degree evinced such unpreparedness. They failed to recognize that the single degree was an insignificant rise and may even have resulted from a misreading of the thermometer. Conceptual change can take place only within the "construction zone." Since children's scientific skills are constructed more slowly than many buildings, conceptual change in science will not happen overnight. Unfortunately for teachers, there are no prefabricated units to be assembled in mental constructions , though many science texts would seem to suggest otherwise.

Finally, science itself has "critical barriers" to understanding, which present difficult hurdles to children and adults alike, according to David Hawkins. [9] Along with the seemingly innate problems involved in understanding size, volume, weight, and elementary mechanics, Hawkins identifies the concept of heat as containing some of these critical barriers. The perception of things as "hot" and "cold" conflicts with the scientist's conception of heat as a measurable quantity contained by all objects, Hawkins says. Since scientists held misconceptions about heat for hundreds of years, Hawkins reminds us, understanding heat is a hurdle that will not be cleared by students in a single two-week unit.

Fighting The Good Fight

With so many obstacles standing the way, conceptual change in science might seem not merely difficult to achieve, but impossible, especially based on a few measly discrepant events. Yet certain teaching strategies have been devised that can help teachers overcome these obstacles.

When discrepancies between children's thinking and the evidence are laid on the table, the teacher assumes a crucial role. Far from being a passive observer, the teacher can actively promote new thinking patterns through a variety of methods.

1. Stressing relevance. Because children so frequently assume new information to be "stuff we learned in school," the teacher must connect new concepts to the child's everyday life. In the case of heat, O'Brien asked her students about times when they had felt heat coming from an object. She asked them if they could think of anything that trapped heat, that kept things warm without heating them. She asked them to think about animals that have "warm coats" and to consider whether those coats make heat. She asked them whether a handful of fur would stay warm if removed from the animals. Unless children appreciate the relevance of their experiments to their everyday life, they may just brush off a discrepant event as "some weird thing we saw in science."

2. Making predictions. Children who are asked to predict the results of their experiments are more willing to change their thinking than are children who function as passive observers. This neglected aspect of elementary-science instruction is essential because it asks students to link their new knowledge with what they already know in order to form hypotheses. Through ample writing in journals, O'Brien's students predicted temperatures and gave reasons for their predictions. Even though they were often wrong, they had the chance to incorporate yesterday's thinking into today's task. The use of journals in O'Brien's class also facilitated what Piaget called "reflective abstraction"[10] --- the chance to reflect on one's thinking, without which development does not occur.

3. Stressing consistency. Although nearly everyone lives quite comfortably while embracing a wealth of ideological and political contradictions, a teacher should encourage children facing new patterns of thought to be consistent in their thinking. A child can state categorically that the thickness of a sleeping bag "causes the heat inside and that pressure "causes the heat inside" a rolled-up rug. Yet that same child can maintain that hats, which are neither thick nor compressed, will be hot for no reason at all.
The teacher should tactfully draw attention to the inconsistencies in children's thinking and ask them to consider how two contradictory statements could both be true. While some children will blithely ignore

the illogic of contradictions, many will confront inconsistencies and change their thinking as a result. The development of logical, consistent thought is thus a by-product of teaching aimed at conceptual change, and developing an orderly view of the world can prevent the compartmentalization of knowledge that occurs when students think that nature works one way at home and another way at school. Katie reflected such inconsistency when she wrote that "hot and cold are sometimes weird." If she is encouraged to seek consistency, however, she will not be satisfied until she has seen some order in the world around her.

If one concept is to replace another, then certain conditions must prevail.[11] First, the old way of thinking must be challenged by direct observation, by a discrepant event. Next, a new explanation for the phenomenon in question must arise, an explanation that is understandable (take care with vocabulary) and plausible. Finally, the new explanation must lead to further testing. If these conditions can be created in the classroom, conceptual change can occur.

Bringing It All Back Home

Overcoming resistance to conceptual change in children is clearly an ongoing struggle. Children will not easily surrender their carefully constructed schemes of thought to the onslaught of new evidence, no matter how convincing it seems. Dedicated teachers using a variety of strategies, including infinite patience and the willingness to let children swim upstream toward an elusive understanding, can help their students overcome these barriers. But reluctance to change one's way of thinking is not limited to scientists and students.

Despite massive evidence suggesting that students learn by doing, by manipulating, by experimenting, the great bulk of science teaching is still based on textbooks. Some independent teachers have pursued conceptual change in their science classes, but doing so presents a number of monumental questions to curriculum builders, school administrators, textbook authors, and anyone whose-job description includes monitoring the "coverage" of curriculum in any subject area.

- Is mere "coverage" of curriculum material-a viable or reasonable goal?
- What is "growth. in science, and how will we assess it?
- What content should teachers know in order to be able to recognize and then challenge children's naive conceptions?
- How can teachers adapt texts and curriculum to meet the constructivists' challenge about how children learn?
- Are there appropriate grade levels for various science topics, and what content areas are appropriate at which levels?

Any teacher who has really tested his or her effectiveness by checking students' understanding of concepts faces a startling dilemma. Teaching science in a constructivist mode is slower and involves discussion, debate, and the recreation of ideas. Rather than following previously set steps, the curriculum in a constructivist classroom evolves, depends heavily on materials, and is determined by the children's questions. Less "stuff" will be covered, fewer "facts" will be remembered for the test, and progress will sometimes be exceedingly slow. It is definitely a process of uncovering rather than covering.

The alternative is to cover the prescribed material, knowing full well that the students may be masking their lack of conceptual growth by solving the teacher rather than learning the content. In order to survive, students learn to give teachers what they want, whether memorizing and regurgitating book definitions of terms, completing lab reports in a certain format, or filling in the correct blanks on an exam.

Successful students have always done these things, and we suspect that they always will. It is their path to survival in schools. Nevertheless, their doing so presents teachers with an age-old dilemma: Do we cover the material, knowing full well that what we cover will be understood superficially at best ---

accommodated, but not assimilated? Or do we forget about coverage and work to help children test their untutored conceptions against the real world through challenging questions, predictions, and experiments, knowing that we will be sacrificing breadth for the sake of depth? We suspect that these questions will be central in the coming decade. Moreover, further study is needed to find out more about the social aspects of learning, about how students use their conceptual understanding outside the classroom, and about how their experience grows into scientific models that they find satisfactory.

One thing is certain. We need to study more deeply the views held by children, to learn the purposes they serve, to learn their innate structures, and to learn how they are formed and used. Perhaps then we will be better able to understand role as teachers.

Putting Students In The Hot Seat

For the third day in a row in O'Brien's classroom, the children rushed to their experiments as soon as they arrived. The sweater, the sleeping bag, and the hat were unwrapped. Once again the thermometers uniformly read room temperature. O'Brien led the disappointed children to their journals. But after a few moments of discussion, she realized that her students had reached an impasse. Their old theory was clearly on the ropes, but they had no new theory with which to replace it. She decided to offer them a choice of two possible statements. "Choose statement A or statement B," she told them. The first stated that heat could come from almost anything, hats and sweaters included. In measuring such heat, statement A proclaimed, we are sometimes fooled because we're really measuring cold air that gets inside. This, of course, was what most children had believed at the outset. Statement B, of O'Brien's own devising, posed the alternative that heat comes mostly from the sun and our bodies and is trapped inside winter clothes that keep our body heat in and keep the cold air out.

"Write down what you believe," O'Brien told the class. "Then stand in this corner if you believe A and in that corner if you believe B. If you're not sure, stand here in front."

Pencils went to lips, and eyes studied the ceiling. Finally, after much thought, the statements were recorded in the journals. Students approached the chalkboard, ready to turn right or left. Katie turned left toward the B corner. Owen stood in the center for a moment, then followed Katie. Neil turned right and dung to his "hot hat" theory. Christian stood in the middle. One by one, the students took a stand. And when the cold gusts of approaching recess blasted through the class room, O'Brien counted noses. A few children had joined Neil. Stubborn, perhaps, but O'Brien had to admire the strength of their convictions. Christian and one other child stood undecided in the center, while the rest of the class stood proudly with Katie and Owen, convinced by their own testing that "warm clothes" aren't really warm and that the heat that seems to come from them actually comes from the warm bodies they envelop.

"How can we test this new theory?" O'Brien asked. Immediately, Neil said, "Put the thermometers in our hats when we're wearing them." And so the children went out to recess that day with an experiment under their hats. As Deb O'Brien relaxed during recess, she asked herself about the past three days. Had the children really changed their minds? Or had they simply been following the leader? Could they really change their ideas in the course of a few class periods? Would any of their activities help them pass the standardized science test coming up in May? O'Brien wasn't sure she could answer any of these questions affirmatively. But she had seen the faces of young scientists as they ran to their experiments, wrote about their findings, spoke out, thought, asked questions --- and that was enough for now.

References

1. John Dewey, *How We Think* (Boston: Heath, 1910); and Gerald S. Craig, "Certain Techniques Used In Developing a Course of Study in Science for the Horace Mann Elementary School" (Doctoral dissertation, Columbia University, 1927)

2. Jerome S. Bruner, *The Process of Education* (Cambridge, Mass.: Harvard University Press, 1960), Robert M. Gagne, *The Conditions of Learning* (New York: Holt, Rinehart & Winston, 1977); and Jean Piaget, "Cognitive Development in Children: Development and Learning," *Journal of Research in Science Teaching*, vol. 2, 1964, pp. 176-86.

3. David P. Ausubel, Joseph D. Novak, and Helen Hanesian, *Educational Psychology: A Cognitive View*, 2nd ed. (New York: Holt, Rinehart & Winston, 1978); Rosalind Driver and J. A. Easley, "Pupils and Paradigms: A Review of Literature Related to Concept Development in Adolescent Science, *Studies in Science Education*, vol. 5, 1978, pp. 61-84; and John Clement, Students Alternative Conceptions in Mechanics: A Coherent System of Preconceptions?," in H. Helm and Joseph D. Novak, eds., *Proceedings of the International Seminar: Misconceptions in Science and Mathematics*, N.Y.: Cornell University Press, 1983).

4. Thomas Kuhn, *The Structure of Scientific Revolutions* (Chicago: University of Chicago Press, 1962).

S. Irme Lakatos, *Proofs and Refutations: The Logic of Mathematical Discovery* (Cambridge: Cambridge University Press, 1976).

6. Eleanor Duckworth, *Inventing Density* (Grand Forks, N.D.: Center for teaching and learning, University of North Dakota, 1986), p. 39.

7. Judith E. Tschirigi, "Sensible Reasoning: A Hypothesis About Hypotheses," *Child Development*, vol. 51, 1980, pp. 1-10.

8. Lev S. Vygotsky, *Thought and Language* (Cambridge, Mass.: MIT Press, 1962).

9. David Hawkins, "Critical Barriers to Science Learning," *Outlook*, vol. 29, 1978, pp. 3-23.

10. Jean Piaget, *Structuralism* (New York: Harper & Row, 1968).

I 1. George J. Posner et al., "Accommodation of a Scientific Conception: Toward a Theory of Conceptual Change," *Science Education*, vol. 66, 1982, pp. 211-27.

BRUCE WATSON, a former elementary science teacher, is a freelance writer living in Amherst, Mass. RICHARD KONICEK is a professor of science education at the University of Massachusetts, Amherst.
Funding for the research on which this article is based was awarded to the Five College, Inc., Amherst, Mass., by the National Science Foundation. The Partnership in Elementary Science provided inservice education for 100 teachers from 1987 until 1990.

Venn Diagram—Making Sense of Science

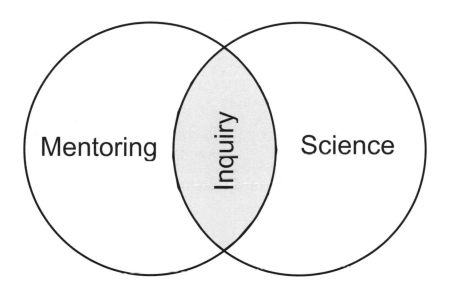

Science Notebook Prompts

- How do you introduce a unit, investigation, or activity in your own classroom?

- How is this similar to or different from the way this investigation was introduced?

Article-Reading Discussion Prompts

- How did the teacher begin her unit on heat?

- How did the teacher use what she learned about her students' prior knowledge about heat?

- What concepts about heat was the teacher trying to develop?

- What might the teacher have done differently?

- What are the implications of everyday language for the development of students' science conceptual understanding?

[Overhead 4, Handout 3]

Inquiry Learning Cycle

Exploration

- Teacher introduces the inquiry.
- Students get acquainted with a problem or phenomenon and decide what kind of experiments they will set up.

Investigation and Data Collection

- Students carry out experiments and make measurements or observations.
- Students collect data on their experiments.
- Students report their measurements or observations.

Sense Making

- Teacher and students analyze the usefulness and meaning of the data.
- Teacher and students develop explanations and conceptualizations.

Elements of infrastructure and assessment are present throughout the whole cycle.

Infrastructure

- Teacher decides how to manage materials.
- Teacher decides when and how students will work with other students.
- Teacher develops routines and procedures.

Assessment

- Teacher determines what students will need to know and be able to do.
- Teacher decides how and when he or she will assess students.

Inquiry Protocol
Exploratory Phase and Infrastructure

I. Phases of Inquiry/Learning Cycle

Across All Phases

- How does each phase promote student learning of concepts, skills, and ideas?
- How are directions given to students? (Does the teacher use multiple modalities?)
- How and when is scientific language introduced?
- What role, if any, do journals play during this investigation?
- What questions will the teacher ask during each phase of the inquiry? (Does the teacher allow for an open response or direct answer?)

Group A: Exploratory Phase

- How is the investigation introduced?
  - ➤ How is it related to students' lives outside of school in a meaningful way?
  - ➤ How does the teacher solicit students' prior knowledge related to the investigation?

- How are the materials introduced?
  - ➤ How are the materials made available to students?
  - ➤ How are students instructed to use the materials?

[Handout 5]

Viewing Tool—DVD Note-Taking Form

Science Classroom: Exploratory Phase/Infrastructure

Teacher	Students	Elements of Exploration/Infrastructure

[Overhead 6, Handout 6]

Journal Prompts

- Why am I interested in science mentoring and what's in it for me?

- What qualities and skills do I bring?

- What skills do I need to develop so I can work more effectively with my colleagues?

- How might I introduce the investigation if I used this ice cream-making unit in my classroom?

- What infrastructure would I need to have in place before I could begin an exploration?

SESSION 2
Handouts and Overheads

Journal Prompts

- Why am I interested in science mentoring and what's in it for me?

- What qualities and skills do I bring?

- What skills do I need to develop so I can work more effectively with my colleagues?

- How might I introduce the investigation if I used this ice cream-making unit in my classroom?

- What infrastructure would I need to have in place before I could begin an exploration?

[Overhead 2, Handout 2]

Why Does Peer Support Work?

- Provides for positive reinforcement

- Encourages continuation of effective practices

- "Nudges" new practices onto the agenda rather than "shoving" them off

- Private sense → Common sense

- Lowers the stress and isolation of teaching

- Alters the experience of teaching → teachers become the managers of their own experience

- Powerlessness and top-down impact of mandates are replaced by inside-out change

Source: Marshall, K. 1985. *Teachers helping teachers: A guidebook for the new professional in education:* Kit Marshall and Associates Reprinted with permission from Action Learning Systems (formerly Kit Marshall and Associates)

[Overhead 3, Handout 3]

Three Mentoring Goals

Trust

Learning

Reflective teaching

Based on Costa, A., & Garmston, B. (2002). *Cognitive coaching: A foundation for renaissance schools*. Christopher Gordon Publishing.

Components of Good Mentoring

Consciousness

Efficacy

Interdependence

Precision

Flexibility

Based on Costa, A., & Garmston, B. (2002). *Cognitive coaching: A foundation for renaissance schools*. Christopher Gordon Publishing.

Components of Observation: Preobservation Prompts

Focus: Investigation, Data Collection, and Infrastructure

- What is or are your goal(s) for the lesson? What is or are the science concept(s)?

- What should students know at the end of the lesson? How does this build on their prior knowledge?

- How will you introduce the experiment?

  o How will you place the experiments in the larger context of the investigation?

  o How will materials be introduced? Are directions needed for use of the materials or will students develop their own approaches and procedures?

- What kind of observations or data do you expect students to report and in what form?

- What is the sequence of activities?

- How will you know when you've reached your goal? What actions with materials and talk might reveal students' level of skills?

- What anticipated problems may occur?

- How will you uncover any misconceptions students may have?

- Based on the investigation and data-collection phase of the inquiry protocol, what kind of data would you like me to collect?

Review agreed-upon plans.

[Overhead 6, Handout 6]

Viewing Tool—DVD Note-Taking Form

Science Classroom: Exploratory Phase/Infrastructure

Teacher	Students	Elements of Exploration/Infrastructure

Activity Card 1: Amount of Metal

Take five 12 x 12 in. sheets of aluminum foil. Stack four sheets of foil, shiny side facing up, on top of one another.

Press down firmly to make sure there are no air bubbles. Put one ice cube on top of the stacked sheets and one on

top of the single sheet at the same time. Carefully observe and time how long it takes the ice to melt. **After you**

have set up the experiment, predict in your science notebook which ice cube will melt first and why. Did all

the ice cubes melt at the same rate? Record the results in your notebook.

Activity Card 2: Amount of Surface Area

Take 4 12 x 12 in. sheets of foil, shiny side facing up. Leave the first sheet as is; fold the second sheet in half, the

third sheet twice, and the fourth sheet four times. Make sure to flatten the layers of each sheet so that no air bubbles

or lumps remain in the final fold. Place one ice cube on each sheet at the same time. Carefully observe and time

how long it takes the ice to melt. **After you have set up the experiment, predict in your science notebook which**

ice cube will melt first and why. Did all the ice cubes melt at the same rate? Record the results in your

notebook.

Activity Card 3: Size of Metal Sheet

Line up four sheets of different sizes, shiny side facing up: 24 x 12 in., 12 x 12 in., 6 x 12 in., and 3 x 3 in. Place an ice cube in the center of each of these sheets at the same time. Carefully observe and time how long it takes the ice to melt. **Predict in what order the ice cubes will melt and record in your notebook. Record the results in your notebook.**

[Overhead 7, Handout 8]

Journal Prompts

1. What are some of the most important things my mentee needs to know about me, my teaching, and my class before we begin our work together?

2. What are my hopes and fears about mentoring?

3. What supports do I need?

Activity Card 4: Shape of Metal

With a partner, design an experiment to melt an ice cube as quickly as possible or as slowly as possible. You have a 12 x 12 in. piece of foil. Decide with your partner what shape would best facilitate or delay the melt rate of the ice cube. **In your science notebook draw the shape and explain why you choose that shape to reach your desired outcome of quickly or slowly melting the ice.** As a control, place an unfolded 12" x 12" inch sheet of foil next to it and place an ice cube on each. Carefully observe and time how long it takes the ice to melt.

Source: Zubrowski, B. (1994). *Ice Cream Making and Cake Baking.* White Plains, NY: Cuisenaire Company of America, Inc. Reprinted with permission from Bernie Zubrowski.

Classroom Connections Prompts

- What opportunities do you currently give your students to design their own investigations? What challenges do students encounter?

- What are some potential challenges for students when they are asked to design their own investigations?

Abilities Necessary To Do Scientific Inquiry, Grades 5–8

- Identify questions that can be answered through scientific investigations.

- Design and conduct a scientific investigation.

- Use appropriate tools and techniques to gather, analyze, and interpret data.

- Develop descriptions, explanations, predictions, and models using evidence.

- Think critically and logically to make the relationships between evidence and explanations.

Source: National Research Council. (1996). *National science education standards.* Washington, DC: National Academy Press.

[Overhead 11, Handout 9]

Evaluation Form

Date: _____

We're very interested in your initial feelings about the workshop. Please take a moment to comment below:

1. Please draw a face to show how you felt about the day.
   Add a speech bubble if you wish!

2. What were the positive aspects of the day?

3. What parts of the day would you change?

4. Any further comments or things we should know for upcoming sessions?

Session 3
Handouts and Overheads

[Overhead 1, Handout 1]

Second Phase of Inquiry Protocol: Investigation and Data Collection

B. Investigation and Data Collection

- How are the experiments introduced?
  - ➤ How does the teacher place the experiment(s) in the larger context of the investigation?
  - ➤ How does the teacher ask students to make and record predictions based on facts, experience, and prior knowledge?

- How does the teacher interact with the groups during the investigation?
  - ➤ How does the teacher survey and locate groups that are having problems with equipment or procedures?
  - ➤ How does the teacher suggest improvements in procedures (e.g., through explicit directions or by way of leading questions or comparisons to other groups)?

- How does the teacher help students demonstrate standards-based data collection and representation? (Is the teacher neutral on the data being collected? Is the data collected similar across groups? Can students redo their experiments and reproduce their results?)

[Overhead 2, Handout 2]

Investigation and Data Collection:
Possible Areas of Focus for Observation

During the lesson:

- How does the teacher interact with the groups during the investigation? Is the teacher neutral on the data being collected?

- How does the teacher suggest improvements in procedures—through explicit directions or by way of leading questions or comparisons to other groups?

- What scientific ideas do you think Cindy Wrobel had hoped to address in this activity?

- What do you think students understand? What are they confused about?

- What is Cindy Wrobel trying to accomplish with her questioning?

[Overhead 3, Handout 3]

Components of Observation:
Doing the Observation . . . Data Collection

Observation	Questions/Evaluations/Comments

SESSION 3

[Overhead 4]

Reflecting on the Observation

- What issues might I raise with this teacher?

- How would I begin the postobservation conference?

SESSION 3

Journal Prompts

- Three observations I have about the peer-coaching process

- Two questions I still have about the process

- One goal I have for improving my science teaching

[Handout 5]

Science Activity Card 1

Using the 8-oz. paper container to measure, pour 16 oz. of hot water into the container you selected. Then pour 32 oz. of cold tap water into the plastic bucket. Place the hot water container in the bucket so that the cold water surrounds it.

Quickly place one thermometer in the bucket of cold tap water and one in the container of hot water. Try to position the thermometers so that they can be read without removing them.

Keeping the thermometers in place, take temperature readings every 30 seconds and record the readings. Keep taking the readings until the temperatures of the two liquids remain the same for three to four readings. Record your results on a data table, and plot the data for the hot water and the data for the cold water on a line graph.

Source: Zubrowski, B. (1994). *Ice Cream Making and Cake Baking*. White Plains, NY: Cuisenaire Company of America, Inc. Reprinted with permission from Bernie Zubrowski

Science Activity Card 2

Using the 8-oz. paper container to measure, pour 16 oz. of hot water into the container you selected. Then pour 32 oz. of cold tap water into the plastic bucket. Fill the bucket half full with ice. Place the hot water container in the bucket so that the ice water surrounds it.

Quickly place one thermometer in the bucket of cold tap water and one in the container of hot water. Try and position the thermometers so that they can be read without removing them.

Keeping the thermometers in place, take temperature readings every 30 seconds and record the readings. Stir the hot water occasionally between readings. Continue to stir and take the readings until the temperatures of the two liquids remain the same for three to four readings. Let the small container sit undisturbed in the ice and water. Do not take any more temperature readings.

Record the hot water temperature data for your container on a graph. (Before you leave for the day, look inside your small container while you slowly pour out the water. Record your observations.)

Science Activity Card 3

Measure 4 oz. of cold tap water and 4 oz. of salt into a plastic bucket. Fill the bucket halfway up with ice and then mix it thoroughly. Place a thermometer into the solution so that the thermometer can be read without removing it and take a reading immediately.

Measure 16 oz. of hot water, and pour it into the container you chose. Place the hot water container into the bucket so that the ice-salt-water solution surrounds the hot water container. Be careful not to get any salt in the hot water.

Place the second thermometer into the container with the hot water. Try to position it so that it can be read without being removed. Take temperature readings every 30 seconds, and record the temperatures in the data table. Stir the hot water occasionally between readings. Continue to stir and take the readings until the temperatures of the two liquids remain the same for three to four readings.

Let the container sit undisturbed in the ice-salt-water solution without taking any further temperature readings. Observe any changes in the container for at least 5 minutes. Before the end of the session, look inside the container while you pour out the water. Record your observations and make a graph of your results.

SESSION 3

[Overhead 6, Handout 6]

Evaluation Form

Please choose from the following as a way of reflecting on our work together today:

- One thing I'm thinking differently about as a result of today's session is....

- One thing I'm struggling with in thinking about today's session is....

SESSION 4
Handouts and Overheads

[Overhead 1]

Reflecting on the Observation

- What issues might I raise with this teacher?

- How would I begin the postobservation conference?

[Overhead 2]

Postobservation Conference Protocol

- Share perceptions of lesson. (Person who was observed begins.)

- Study data the observer gathered.
    - What questions are raised by the data?
    - What do you think students learned and how do you know?
    - What are the implications for your teaching?

- Possible modifications.

- How will you build on today's lesson?

- Next steps
    1. In planning
    2. In teaching
    3. In observing

Postobservation Video Questions

- What are the core issues that are being discussed?

- What was and was not addressed in the postobservation conference?

- What do you think the teacher might have learned as a result of the postobservation conference?

- How does the mentor help the teacher foster student learning in the lesson coached?

Mentoring Journal

MENTOR:_____

MENTEE:_____

DATE:_____

TYPE OF MEETING

planning____

pre-observation conference____

post-observation conference____

other_____

Teaching Growth / Progress	**I. PHASES OF INQUIRY / LEARNING CYCLE** **A. Exploration** • How is this investigation introduced? • How are the materials introduced? • How are directions given? • How and when is scientific language introduced? • How does the teacher interact with the groups? • What role, if any, will science notebooks play?
Teaching Focus	**B. Investigation and Data Collection** • How are investigations/experiments introduced? • How does the teacher interact with the groups? • How do students demonstrate actual, standards-based data collection? • Are students able to reproduce data?
Mentee's Next Steps	**C. Sense-Making Discussions** • How does the teacher have students report their data or observations? • How does the teacher help students clarify the data or observations? • How does the teacher help the students interpret the data? • How does the teacher help students clarify explanations and conceptualizations? **II. INFRASTRUCTURE** • How will materials be organized and managed to provide easy student access? • How does the teacher manage time?
Support from Mentor	**III. ASSESSMENT** • What should students know, understand and be able to do? • What assessment method will the teacher use? • How will the teacher assess student progress during each phase of inquiry?

Procedure for Making Ice Cream

1 1-gal. plastic bucket
ice to fill the bucket halfway
4 oz. cold water
4 oz. rock salt
1 coffee can with cover
1 stirrer
4 oz. cream (milk or half-and-half)

2 tsp. sugar
½ tsp. vanilla flavoring
1 large metal spoon
spoons (1 for each group member)
cups (1 for each group member)
newspaper (to cover the work surface)
handout for making ice cream

Fill the bucket with ice, salt, and water as you did before and mix well. Place the coffee can immediately in the ice-salt-water mixture. Mix the cream with flavorings and sugar and pour it into the can. (The recipe is a guideline and does not need to be rigidly followed.) Position the can so that the ice cream mixture is below the surface of the ice. Cover the can. Turn the can continuously to ensure that the ice cream mixture freezes evenly. Every three to four minutes remove the lid and scrape the sides of the container with a spoon to remove the ice. Continue turning the container and scraping until the mixture forms a slush.

Source: Zubrowski, B. 1994. *Ice Cream Making and Cake Baking.* White Plains, NY: Cuisenaire Company of America, Inc. Reprinted with permission from Bernie Zubrowski

[Overhead 5, Handout 3]

Components of RARE

RARE is an acronym for good communication skills:

- **Reflect** the Facts

- Pay **Attention**

- **Reflect** Feelings

- **Encourage** the Other Person to Talk

Source: Gordon, T. 1980. *Leadership effectiveness training.* New York: Bantam Books. Reprinted with permission from Sobel Weber Associates, Inc.

Communications Potholes

Giving Advice

- Listen —don't you take that from him or her!
- You ought to . . .
- If I were you I'd . . .

Passing Judgment

- I can't believe you let this happen.
- Oh, swell. This is another one of your great jobs.
- It's your own fault.

Avoiding the Issue

- Just ignore it.
- What a pain she is. Do you want to go shopping?
- Read a book for a while; you'll feel better.

Source: Gordon, T. 1980. *Leadership effectiveness training.* New York: Bantam Books. Reprinted with permission from Sobel Weber Associates, Inc.

[Handout 4]

Listener Card 1

As you sit with your partner, demonstrate active listening:

R—**Reflect** the facts
A—Pay **Attention**
R—**Reflect** feelings
E—**Encourage** the other person to talk

After your partner has talked for about a minute, gradually and subtly start to:

Give Advice, telling them what to do, trying to solve the problem for them.

Gradually stop the Active Listening. After about two minutes, make it clear that you're not listening at all…you're just interested in Giving Advice and saying things like:

- "Don't take that from him or her."
- "You ought to ..."
- "If I were you I'd ..."

Source: Gordon, T. 1980. *Leadership effectiveness training.* New York: Bantam Books.
Reprinted with permission from Sobel Weber Associates, Inc.

[Handout 5]
Listener Card 2

As you sit with your partner, demonstrate active listening:

R—**Reflect** the facts
A—Pay **Attention**
R—**Reflect** feelings
E—**Encourage** the other person to talk

After your partner has talked for about a minute, gradually and subtly start:

Passing Judgment. Criticize the speaker, blame him/her for the problem, be sarcastic.

Gradually stop the Active Listening. After about two minutes, make it clear that you're not listening at all … you're just interested in Passing Judgment and saying things like

- "I can't believe you let that happen."
- "It's your own fault."
- "Great job."

Source: Gordon, T. 1980. *Leadership effectiveness training.* New York: Bantam Books.
Reprinted with permission from Sobel Weber Associates, Inc.

Listener Card 3

As you sit with your partner, demonstrate active listening:

R—**Reflect** the facts

A—Pay **Attention**

R—**Reflect** feelings

E—**Encourage** the other person to talk

After your partner has talked for about a minute, gradually and subtly start

Avoiding the Issue. Make jokes, interrupt, change the subject.

Gradually stop the Active Listening. After about two minutes, make it clear that you're not listening at all … you're just interested in Avoiding the Issue and saying things like

- "Just ignore it."
- "Read a book for a while, then you'll feel better."
- "Let's talk about something else."

Source: Gordon, T. 1980. *Leadership effectiveness training.* New York: Bantam Books.
Reprinted with permission from Sobel Weber Associates, Inc.

12 Roadblocks to Communication

1. Ordering, commanding, directing.
   Example: "Stop whining and get back to work."

2. Warning, threatening.
   Example: "You had better get your act together if you want to continue teaching."

3. Moralizing, preaching, giving "shoulds" and "oughts."
   Example: "You should leave your personal problems out of the classroom."

4. Advising, offering solutions or suggestions.
   Example: "I think you need to get a daily planner so you can organize your time better."

5. Teaching, lecturing, giving logical arguments.
   Example: "You better remember you only have four days to complete that project."

6. Judging, criticizing, disagreeing, blaming.
   Example: "You never do what you say you will."

7. Name calling, stereotyping, labeling.
   Example: "You're a disciplinarian."

8. Interpreting, analyzing, diagnosing.
   Example: "You are having this problem because you rushed the directions."

9. Praising, agreeing, giving positive evaluations.
   Example: "You are smart. You can figure out a way to improve this problem."

10. Reassuring, sympathizing, consoling, supporting.
    Example: "I know exactly how you are feeling. If you just begin, it won't seem so bad."

Source: Gordon, T. 1980. *Leadership effectiveness training.* New York: Bantam Books.
Reprinted with permission from Sobel Weber Associates, Inc.

11. Questioning, probing, interrogating, cross-examining.
    "Why did you wait so long to ask for assistance? What was so hard about this problem?"

12. Withdrawing, distracting, being sarcastic, humoring, diverting.
    "Seems like you got up on the wrong side of the bed today."

Many people are unaware that they respond in one of these twelve ways. It is important that we know alternative ways of responding. Many of the above responses have hidden messages when the teacher hears them. They may hear you saying that they are to blame or that they can't do anything right, when your intention for the message was quite different.

Communications Skills Self-Assessment

(1 means "I do it well." 5 means "I really need improvement.")

1.	Speaking clearly and directly	1	2	3	4	5
2.	Listening	1	2	3	4	5
3.	Disagreeing in reasonable ways	1	2	3	4	5
4.	Clarifying	1	2	3	4	5
5.	Confronting	1	2	3	4	5
6.	Saying what you really mean	1	2	3	4	5
7.	Saying how you feel	1	2	3	4	5
8.	Expressing mixed feelings about the same event	1	2	3	4	5
9.	Taking turns	1	2	3	4	5
10.	Expressing empathy for the other person's opinions, ideas, feelings, while not agreeing with them	1	2	3	4	5
11.	Sharing ideas	1	2	3	4	5
12.	Waiting	1	2	3	4	5

Reprinted with permission from Louise Thompson

Communications Skills Self-Assessment

In your group, share

1. Your individual ratings

2. Where you think other teachers are relative to successfully using these skills

3. What the obstacles seem to be to effectively apply these skills when working with other teachers

[Overhead 8]

Journal Prompts

- How will I benefit from my work as a science mentor?

- How might my students benefit from my work as a science mentor?

SESSION 4

[Handout 8]

Mentor-Mentee Handbook

This handbook contains information and forms to support your mentoring work.

Contents

- Mentee Expectations
- Planning Guide
- Middle Grades Science Mentoring Protocol
- Standards-Based Science Teaching Continuum
- Science Mentor Teacher Practice Continuum
- Creating and Maintaining an Effective Environment for Student Learning Continuum
- Components of a Classroom Visit
- Mentoring Journal
- Cartoon—"Last Page"
- Marian Wright Edelman Quote

Expectations for Mentees

❖ Commitment to meet with mentor at least twice a month, follow the "Planning Guide for Mentors and Mentees" and maintain a conference log.

❖ Commitment to reflect critically on his or her inquiry science teaching and be open to new ideas.

❖ Commitment to collaborate with mentor to continuously improve inquiry science instruction, assessment and student achievement. Use the inquiry protocol.

❖ Willingness to become a coinvestigator with mentor—share information and bring ideas, questions, and concerns to meetings

❖ Maintaining a confidential and honest relationship; in case of concerns, speaking to mentor

❖ Setting reasonable expectations for growth, remembering that to become a skillful teacher is challenging.

Planning Guide

To Be Completed by Mentor with Mentee

In an effort to stage and support the Mentee's learning over time, we offer the following framework for developing an individualized plan that fits the needs of the mentor, mentee and the classrooms.

Activity	Date
Before teaching begins for the mentee, if possible. Otherwise within first two weeks of teaching.	
With New Mentees:	
1. Meet, welcome your mentee, explain expectations for year.	
2. Share your teaching philosophy with your mentee.	
3. Share school-wide policies and schedules.	
4. Explain the roles of various support staff and structures within the school.	
5. Help mentee set up classroom.	
6. Introduce mentee to faculty, staff, parents.	
7. Explain procedures for signing out AV equipment, supply ordering procedures, tech facilities in building.	
8. Other:	
With All Mentees	
1. Meet with principal to clarify program expectations for mentor and mentee and discuss introduction of mentors and mentees at opening day meeting.	
2. Set schedule for meeting times for next two months (at least twice a month).	
3. Review mentoring orientation materials.	
4. With your mentee, set up e-mail communication procedures.	
5. Discuss general mentoring goals for the year.	
1st Month	
1. Share classroom management strategies (e.g., materials management, group work, etc.). Use protocol (infrastructure elements).	
2. Co-plan (mentor/mentee)—use protocol.	

Planning Guide

Activity	Date
3. Have mentee observe in your classroom, focusing on one element from protocol as a guide to pre-conference and post observation discussion. Protocol element_____	
4. Review procedures for grading, marking periods, interim reports.	
5. Review evaluation procedures with mentee.	
6. Plan for Back-to-School Night.	
7. With mentee, meet with principal to talk about benefits of program.	
2nd Month	
1. With mentee, co-teach in both of your classrooms. Protocol element:_____	
2. Co-plan, observe, and discuss a lesson in mentee's classroom.	
3. With mentee, videotape class and use for discussion about inquiry teaching and learning.	
4. Discuss communication with families—parent conferences.	
3rd/4th Months	
1. Continue observation and feedback cycle (video a conference and lesson).	
2. With mentee, continue to co-teach in both of your classrooms. Element of protocol:_____	
3. Focus on a different phase of inquiry for observation or planning. Element of protocol:_____	
4. Revisit management strategy from infrastructure of protocol, reflect on effectiveness, discuss modifications.	
5. Report cards.	
6. Help the mentee choose some aspect of her/his teaching (e.g., discussion questions, student sharing of data) to work on in depth.	
7. With mentee, meet with principal to inform him/her about mentoring activities.	

Planning Guide

Activity	Date
5th/6th Months	
1. With mentee, continue to co-teach in both of your classrooms. Element of protocol:_____	
2. Co-plan, observe, and discuss a lesson in mentee's classroom.	
3. Have mentee observe in your classroom.	
7th/8th Months	
1. Review procedures for standardized tests with mentee.	
2. With mentee, continue to co-teach in both of your classrooms.	
3. Help the mentee choose **another** aspect of her/his teaching (e.g., discussion questions, student sharing of data) to work on in depth.	
4. Continue to conference, observe, and have conversations about teaching and learning with mentee.	
5. Other:	
9th/10th Months	
1. Continue to plan, observe, co-teach, and have conversations about teaching and learning with mentee.	
2. Report cards/student files.	
3. Close down the classroom/storing materials.	

Middle Grades Science Mentoring Protocol

I. Phases of Inquiry/Learning Cycle:

The observer (mentor) can use SOME of these questions as a way of co-planning, focusing observations during the post-observation discussions.

A. Exploratory Phase
- How is the investigation introduced?
  - ➤ How is it related to students' life outside of school in a meaningful way?
  - ➤ How does the teacher solicit students' prior knowledge related to the investigation?

- How are the materials introduced?
  - ➤ How are the students instructed to use the materials?
  - ➤ How are the materials made available to the students?

- How are directions given to students? Think about using multiple modalities.
- How and when is scientific language introduced?
- How does the teacher interact with the groups during the exploration?
- What role, if any, will journals play during this investigation?

B. Conducting Experiments and Data Collection
- How are the experiments introduced?
  - ➤ How does the teacher place the experiment or experiments in the larger context of the investigation?
  - ➤ How does the teacher ask the students to make and record predictions based on facts, experience, and prior knowledge?

- How does the teacher interact with the groups during the investigation?
  - ➤ How does the teacher survey and locate groups that are having problems with equipment or procedures?
  - ➤ Is the teacher neutral on the data being collected?
  - ➤ How does the teacher suggest improvements in procedures through explicit directions or by way of leading questions or comparisons to other groups?

- Are the students able to demonstrate actual, standards-based data collection? Are they able to reproduce data?

C. Sense Making Discussions
- How does the teacher have students report their data or observations?
  - ➤ Are the results displayed for all to see?
  - ➤ Are all groups' results presented?
  - ➤ Is the data accurate?
  - ➤ How does the teacher elicit comments from the students?

- How does the teacher help students clarify the data or observations?
  - How does the teacher directly question some groups' results or have all the students decide on what is valid and useable?
  - How does the teacher deal with discrepant results?

- How does the teacher help the students interpret the data?
  - How does the teacher help the students isolate patterns or correlation?
  - How does the teacher solicit explanations from students?
  - What type of questions does the teacher asked in this phase? Do they allow for an open response or direct answer?

- How does the teacher help students clarify explanations and conceptualizations?
  - In what ways does the teacher directly utilize the data collected to introduce formal scientific explanations?
  - How does the teacher adapt and build on students' attempted explanations?
  - How does the teacher address students' "misconceptions"?
  - Is the information represented accurately? Is it factual?

II. Infrastructure
- How will materials be organized and managed to provide easy student access?

- How does the teacher interact with groups?
  - How are expectations for group work communicated?
  - What strategies does the teacher use to ensure individual accountability in cooperative groups?

- Time management
  - What routines are in place to support maximum student learning?
  - What are some strategies the teacher uses to support the smooth ongoing flow of events in the classroom, such as transitions from one event to another and expectations for efficient student work?

III. Assessment
- What should students know, understand, and be able to do?
  - What evidence will show that students understand?
  - Does the teacher use multiple forms of assessment?
  - How does the assessment match the opportunity to learn?

- What assessment method will you use?
  - Informal checks for understanding
  - Observation/Dialogue
  - Quiz/Test
  - Open ended prompt
  - Performance task/project

- How will student progress be determined during each phase of inquiry?

Standards-Based Science Teaching Continuum

	Working Toward →		
DEVELOPMENT OF TOPIC	Frequent users of one-shot activities.	Investigations go beyond one shot, and activities have some connecting theme.	Extended investigations continue as long as 6–8 weeks on topic.
CONCEPTUAL COHERENCE	Activities jump from concept to concept with vague connections between activities.	Activities are deliberately connected in an explicit manner and are related by a common theme but unrelated concepts.	Extended investigation focus on a few basic concepts and center around one basic phenomena or technological artifact.
STUDENT INVOLVEMENT DURING EXPLORATION AND EXPERIMENTATION	All questions for exploration and all activities are teacher generated. Very little student input.	Some input by students in directing the investigation. Teacher still dominates in what activities are done and the kind of questions considered.	High involvement on part of students. Students generate some questions for exploration, procedures for experimentation. Balance of teacher-student input.
DEVELOPMENTAL APPROPRIATENESS	Some questions and experimental procedures require conceptual understanding that students have not acquired. Skills in manipulating materials too challenging for students.	Some questions and experiments are allowed to proceed that are beyond student understanding and/or current capabilities.	Teacher modifies questions and experiments of students through dialogue to fit with current background and abilities of students. Constantly keeps in mind the practice of manageable complexity.
DATA COLLECTION AND EVIDENCE	Student-collected data is not used and discussion of evidence by teacher is absent. Data is not posted for student groups to compare.	Student-collected data is accepted as is. Teacher rejects or accepts data without involving students in discussing its reliability. Data is used as illustrative and conclusive.	Teacher and students review the reliability and appropriateness of data. Data is used to support student hypothesis. Role of evidence in scientific process is explicitly emphasized.

	Working Toward →		
FOLLOW-UP OR SENSE MAKING	Very limited discussion about the significance of data. Students are told what activities are supposed to illustrate in terms of targeted concepts. Emphasis is on backing up vocabulary or facts.	Follow-up discussions are used frequently. Teacher introduces terms and concepts without much attention to students' prior knowledge.	Frequent use and thorough discussions about observations and data are carefully related to targeted concepts. Scientific terms are introduced after clarification of observation. Process is dialectical, not didactic.
ASSESSMENT	Heavy reliance on formal tests, worksheets, and written reports. Formal tests are more about recall than conceptual understanding	Teacher uses mix of assessment techniques but still relies mostly on formal assessment. Limited use of embedded assessment.	Teacher uses mix of assessment techniques, giving special attention to the type of investigation. Teacher views embedded assessment as continuous and ongoing.

Science Mentor Teacher Practice Continuum

	Working Toward →		
RELATIONSHIP	Mentor usually maintains confidentiality with peers and administrators.	Mentor maintains confidentiality at all times.	Mentor respects the confidentiality of the mentor/mentee relationship at all times and reinforces trust.
	Advocacy is peripheral to the mentor/mentee relationship	Mentor advocates for mentee when asked by mentee.	Mentor and mentee strategize together how and when the mentor can advocate for mentee.
MECHANICS	Mentor/mentee contact is irregular and generally precipitated by a need for information or assistance.	Mentor and mentee maintain regular contact.	Contact between mentor and mentee is scheduled frequently, protected from competing demands, meets the needs of both partners, and advances the goals of the school district.
	Mentor rarely uses data during conversations after observations.	Mentor sometimes uses data to support conversations after observations.	Data is consistently the basis for conversations after observations.
	The mentor provides suggestions and advice as requested.	Focus of meetings is mentor presenting information to mentee.	Mentor engages mentee as fellow student of teaching and learning.
INQUIRY PROCESS	Inquiry protocol is not part of mentor-mentee conversations	Inquiry protocol is used in a limited way.	Inquiry protocol is used as a guide during mentor-mentee conversations about teaching and learning.
	The greatest learnings are within the management domain.	Mentor/mentee conversations touch on "fixing" problems of implementation of inquiry science. The focus is on "quick" solutions.	Conversations focus on implementation of the phases of inquiry science, using the protocol for planning and observations.

	Working Toward →		
INQUIRY PROCESS (CONT')	Survival strategies are the emphasis of mentee's learning.	Mentor/mentee discussions center on specific episodes and situations.	Mentor/mentee interactions promote collaboration through co-planning, co-teaching, problem solving, and decision making regarding inquiry science.
	Textbook and its ancillaries are the sole references for discussion during planning.	In addition to textbook, mentor gives mentee materials he/she has used successfully.	Mentor models reflective practice and an openness to new ideas, new materials.
	Mentor's stance is predominantly one of "telling" and answering specific mentee questions.	Mentor's stance is one of giving suggestions and advice.	Mentor has a repertoire of mentoring strategies to draw upon and selects appropriate ones to meet the needs of specific situations.
	Mentor makes suggestions for improving discipline used in the class.	Mentor focuses on giving mentee additional activities to help keep students more engaged.	Mentor/mentee conversations promote making connections between instructional practice and student results.
	Mentee questions are used as focus for discussion.	Mentee questions dominate; mentor attempts to introduce inquiry.	Mentor integrates mentee issues with inquiry phases.
ASSESSMENT	Mentee uses textbook assessments or other pre-made testing procedures.	Mentor introduces mentee to teacher-created tests and other forms of assessment.	Mentor engages mentee in assessment discussions that promote embedded assessments and that introduce the mentee to a variety of assessment strategies to support an investigation.

Creating and Maintaining Effective Environments for Student Learning

Teachers create physical environments that engage all students in purposeful learning activities and encourage constructive interactions among students. Teachers maintain safe learning environments in which all students are treated fairly and respectfully as they assume responsibility for themselves and one another. Teachers encourage all students to participate in making decisions and in working independently and collaboratively. Expectations for student behavior are established early, clearly understood, and consistently maintained. Teachers make effective use of instructional time as they implement class procedures and routines.

Creating a physical environment that engages all students.
As teachers develop, they may ask, "How do I …" or "Why do I …"
- arrange the room to facilitate positive classroom interactions?
- arrange and adapt classroom seating to accommodate individual and group-learning needs?
- manage student and teacher access to materials, technology, and resources to promote learning?
- create a classroom environment that reflects and promotes student learning?
- make the classroom environment safe and accessible for all students?

Establishing a climate that promotes fairness and respect.
As teachers develop, they may ask, "How do I …" or "Why do I …"
- help all students become respectful of others who may be different from them?
- model and promote fairness, equity, and respect in the classroom?
- encourage, support, and recognize the achievements and contributions of all students?
- encourage students to take risks and be creative?
- understand and respond to inappropriate behaviors in a fair, equitable way?

Promoting social development and group responsibility.
As teachers develop, they may ask, "How do I …" or "Why do I …"
- help all students accept and respect different experiences, ideas, backgrounds, feelings, and points of view?
- group students to promote social development and learning?
- facilitate the development of each student's self esteem?
- create opportunities for all students to communicate and work with one another?
- teach leadership skills and provide opportunities for all students to use them?
- use classroom rules to support all students in assuming responsibility for themselves and one another?
- create opportunities for all students to become self-directed learners?

Establishing and maintaining standards for student behavior.
As teachers develop, they may ask, "How do I …" or "Why do I …"
- understand the reasons for student behavior?
- establish and consistently maintain standards for behavior that reflect my students' developmental and personal needs?
- intervene when student behavior does not meet agreed-upon classroom standards?
- facilitate student participation in classroom decision making?
- help all students learn to solve problems and resolve conflicts?

- support all students as they develop responsibility for their own behavior?
- work collaboratively with families to maintain standards for student behavior?

Planning and implementing classroom procedures and routines that support student learning.
As teachers develop, they may ask, "How do I ..." or "Why do I ..."
- develop a daily schedule, timelines, classroom routines, and classroom rules?
- involve all students in the development of classroom procedures and routines?
- support students to internalize classroom rules, routines, and procedures and to become self-directed learners?
- develop classroom procedures and routines that promote and maintain a climate of fairness and respect?
- make decisions about modifying procedures and rules to support student learning?

Using instructional time effectively.
As teachers develop, they may ask, "How do I ..." or "Why do I ..."
- structure time with students to support their learning?
- help students move from one instructional activity to the next?
- pace and adjust instructional time so that all students remain engaged?
- redirect student behavior in the most productive and time-effective way?
- ensure that adequate time is provided for all students to complete learning activities?
- provide time for all students to reflect on their learning and process of instruction?
- structure time for day-to-day managerial and administrative tasks?

Source: California Commission on Teacher Credentialing and California Department of Education. 1997. *California standards for the teaching profession*. Sacramento, CA: Authors. Reprinted with permission from the California Commission on Teacher Credentialing

Components of a Classroom Visit

Preparing for the Observation…(Exploratory)

* 1. What are students supposed to be learning? What critical-thinking skills will be addressed?

2. How does this lesson or activity fit into the larger curriculum framework? How does it connect to previous lessons? Which standards are you addressing?

* 3. Which phase of the inquiry cycle will be used in this lesson?

4. What is the sequence of activities? Which of these activities promote inquiry?

5. What aspect of the infrastructure would you like to focus on for this lesson?

* 6. How do the teaching and learning activities promote the desired learning outcomes?

* 7. How will you check for student understanding during the lesson?

8. Does the teacher have any concerns about the lesson?

* 9. What kind of data would the teacher like the observer to collect?
    - inquiry
    - infrastructure
    - assessment

* These questions are the basis for all observations.

Doing the Observation…(Data Collection)

Observer records (based on agreed upon focus) what he or she sees and hears, avoiding generalizations or judgments.

Observation	Questions / reflections / comments

Discussing the Observation... (Sense Making)

(Recommended structure for conversation. Try to have discussion within a day or two after observation.)

Teacher and observer analyze the lesson using data gathered by the observer, probing for specificity.

1. Share perceptions of lesson (person who was observed begins).

2. Study data that the observer gathered.

   - What questions does the data raise?
   - What stands out in the data?
   - What does the data say about the focus of the observation?
   - What does the data say about student learning?
   - What are the implications for your teaching?

3. Possible modifications

4. How will you build on today's lesson?

5. Next steps:

   - In planning
   - In teaching
   - In observing

Mentoring Journal

MENTOR:_____

MENTEE:_____

DATE:_____

TYPE OF MEETING

planning____

pre-observation conference____

post-observation conference____

other_____

Teaching Growth / Progress	**I. PHASES OF INQUIRY / LEARNING CYCLE** ***A. Exploration*** • How is this investigation introduced? • How are the materials introduced? • How are directions given? • How and when is scientific language introduced? • How does the teacher interact with the groups? • What role, if any, will science notebooks play?
Teaching Focus	***B. Investigation and Data Collection*** • How are investigations/experiments introduced? • How does the teacher interact with the groups? • How do students demonstrate actual, standards-based data collection? • Are students able to reproduce data?
Mentee's Next Steps	***C. Sense-Making Discussions*** • How does the teacher have students report their data or observations? • How does the teacher help students clarify the data or observations? • How does the teacher help the students interpret the data? • How does the teacher help students clarify explanations and conceptualizations? **II. INFRASTRUCTURE** • How will materials be organized and managed to provide easy student access? • How does the teacher manage time?
Support from Mentor	**III. ASSESSMENT** • What should students know, understand and be able to do? • What assessment method will the teacher use? • How will the teacher assess student progress during each phase of inquiry?

ANTHONY TABER

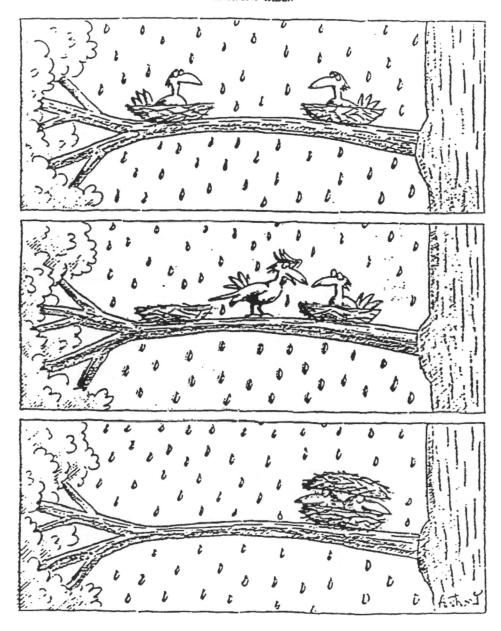

Source: *Audubon Magazine*, May 1990
Reprinted with permission from Anthony Taber

All of my mentors, men and women of different faiths and colors, in their own way personified excellence and courage, shared and instilled a vision and hope of what could be, not what was, in our racially, gender, class and caste constricted country; kept America's promise of becoming a country free of discrimination, poverty and ignorance ever before me; (and) put the foundations of education, discipline, hard work, and perseverance needed to help build it beneath me.

What they all had in common was their respectful treatment of me as an important, thinking individual human being. They expressed no sense of limits on my potential or on who they thought I could become, and they engaged me as a fellow wayfarer and struggler. They saw me inside and not just outside and affirmed the strengths I had.

From Lanterns, A Memoir of Mentors
By Marian Wright Edelman,
President, Children's Defense Fund

Source: Edelman, M. W. 2000. *Lanterns: A memoir of mentors.* New York: Harper Paperbacks

Planning Guide

To Be Completed by Mentor with Mentee

In an effort to stage and support the Mentee's learning over time, we offer the following framework for developing an individualized plan that fits the needs of the mentor, mentee and the classrooms.

Activity	Date
Before teaching begins for the mentee, if possible. Otherwise within first two weeks of teaching.	
With New Mentees:	
1. Meet, welcome your mentee, explain expectations for year.	
2. Share your teaching philosophy with your mentee.	
3. Share school-wide policies and schedules.	
4. Explain the roles of various support staff and structures within the school.	
5. Help mentee set up classroom.	
6. Introduce mentee to faculty, staff, parents.	
7. Explain procedures for signing out AV equipment, supply ordering procedures, tech facilities in building.	
8. Other:	
With All Mentees	
1. Meet with principal to clarify program expectations for mentor and mentee and discuss introduction of mentors and mentees at opening day meeting.	
2. Set schedule for meeting times for next two months (at least twice a month).	
3. Review mentoring orientation materials.	
4. With your mentee, set up e-mail communication procedures.	
5. Discuss general mentoring goals for the year.	
1st Month	
1. Share classroom management strategies (e.g., materials management, group work, etc.). Use protocol (infrastructure elements).	
2. Co-plan (mentor/mentee)—use protocol.	

Planning Guide

Activity	Date
3. Have mentee observe in your classroom, focusing on one element from protocol as a guide to pre-conference and post observation discussion. Protocol element_____	
4. Review procedures for grading, marking periods, interim reports.	
5. Review evaluation procedures with mentee.	
6. Plan for Back-to-School Night.	
7. With mentee, meet with principal to talk about benefits of program.	
2nd Month	
1. With mentee, co-teach in both of your classrooms. Protocol element:_____	
2. Co-plan, observe, and discuss a lesson in mentee's classroom.	
3. With mentee, videotape class and use for discussion about inquiry teaching and learning.	
4. Discuss communication with families—parent conferences.	
3rd/4th Months	
1. Continue observation and feedback cycle (video a conference and lesson).	
2. With mentee, continue to co-teach in both of your classrooms. Element of protocol:_____	
3. Focus on a different phase of inquiry for observation or planning. Element of protocol:_____	
4. Revisit management strategy from infrastructure of protocol, reflect on effectiveness, discuss modifications.	
5. Report cards.	
6. Help the mentee choose some aspect of her/his teaching (e.g., discussion questions, student sharing of data) to work on in depth.	
7. With mentee, meet with principal to inform him/her about mentoring activities.	

Planning Guide

Activity	Date
5th/6th Months	
1. With mentee, continue to co-teach in both of your classrooms. Element of protocol:_____	
2. Co-plan, observe, and discuss a lesson in mentee's classroom.	
3. Have mentee observe in your classroom.	
7th/8th Months	
1. Review procedures for standardized tests with mentee.	
2. With mentee, continue to co-teach in both of your classrooms.	
3. Help the mentee choose **another** aspect of her/his teaching (e.g., discussion questions, student sharing of data) to work on in depth.	
4. Continue to conference, observe, and have conversations about teaching and learning with mentee.	
5. Other:	
9th/10th Months	
1. Continue to plan, observe, co-teach, and have conversations about teaching and learning with mentee.	
2. Report cards/student files.	
3. Close down the classroom/storing materials.	

SESSION 4

[Overhead 9]

"All of my mentors, men and women of different faiths and colors, in their own way personified excellence and courage, shared and instilled a vision and hope of what could be, not what was, in our racially, gender, class and caste constricted country; kept America's promise of becoming a country free of discrimination, poverty and ignorance ever before me; (and) put the foundations of education, discipline, hard work, and perseverance needed to help build beneath me.

What they all had in common was their respectful treatment of me as an important, thinking individual human being. They expressed no sense of limits on my potential or on whom they thought I would become, and they engaged me as a fellow wayfarer and struggler. They saw me inside and not just outside and affirmed the strengths I had."

Source: Edelman, M. W. 2000. *Lanterns: A memoir of mentors.* New York: Harper Paperbacks

Evaluation Form

Three things I have learned

     1 _____

     2 _____

     3 _____

Two questions I have

     1 _____

     2 _____

One action I will take

     1 _____

SESSION 5
Handouts and Overheads

[Handout 1]

Mentor Update Prompts

1. What is something you have learned about being a mentor that has surprised, pleased, or annoyed you?

2. Have you managed to set up a regular meeting time? If so, when? If not, what's getting in the way?

3. Do you have some burning issues that you'd like to discuss today?

Mentoring Journal

MENTOR:_____

MENTEE:_____

DATE:_____

TYPE OF MEETING

planning___

pre-observation conference___

post-observation conference___

other_____

Teaching Growth / Progress	**I. PHASES OF INQUIRY / LEARNING CYCLE** **A. Exploration** • How is this investigation introduced? • How are the materials introduced? • How are directions given? • How and when is scientific language introduced? • How does the teacher interact with the groups? • What role, if any, will science notebooks play?
Teaching Focus	**B. Investigation and Data Collection** • How are investigations/experiments introduced? • How does the teacher interact with the groups? • How do students demonstrate actual, standards-based data collection? • Are students able to reproduce data?
Mentee's Next Steps	**C. Sense-Making Discussions** • How does the teacher have students report their data or observations? • How does the teacher help students clarify the data or observations? • How does the teacher help the students interpret the data? • How does the teacher help students clarify explanations and conceptualizations? **II. INFRASTRUCTURE** • How will materials be organized and managed to provide easy student access? • How does the teacher manage time?
Support from Mentor	**III. ASSESSMENT** • What should students know, understand and be able to do? • What assessment method will the teacher use? • How will the teacher assess student progress during each phase of inquiry?

Inquiry Protocol, Sense-Making Phase

C. Sense Making

- How does the teacher have students report their data or observations? (Are the results displayed for all to see? Are all groups' results presented? Is the data checked for accuracy?)
  - ➤ How does the teacher elicit comments from students?

- How does the teacher help students clarify the data or observations? (Does the teacher directly question some groups' results or have all students decide on what is valid and useable?)
  - ➤ How does the teacher deal with discrepant results?

- How does the teacher help students interpret the data?
  - ➤ How does the teacher help students isolate patterns or correlation?
  - ➤ How does the teacher solicit explanations from students?

- How does the teacher help students clarify explanations and conceptualizations? (Is the information represented accurately? Does the teacher use student analogies?)
  - ➤ How does the teacher address students' "misconceptions"?
  - ➤ How does the teacher adapt and build on students' attempted explanations?
  - ➤ In what ways does the teacher directly utilize the data collected to introduce formal scientific explanations?

Inquiry Protocol

OVERVIEW

I. Phases of Inquiry/Learning Cycle

Teacher decides how to develop and implement units, lessons, and activities within the inquiry framework.

A. Exploration
Teacher introduces the inquiry.
Students get acquainted with a problem or phenomenon and decide what kind of experiments they will set up.

B. Investigation and Data Collection
Students carry out experiments and make measurements and observations.
Students collect data on their experiments.
Students report their measurements or observations.

C. Sense Making
Teacher and students analyze the usefulness and meaning of the data.
Teacher and students develop explanations and conceptualizations.

II. Infrastructure

Teacher decides how to manage materials.
Teacher decides when and how students will work with other students.
Teacher develops routines and procedures.

III. Assessment

Teacher determines what students will need to know and be able to do.
Teacher decides how and when he or she will assess students.

PROTOCOL

Teachers may choose some of these questions to use as a guide during coplanning or pre- and postobservation discussions, or to help focus observations.

I. Phases of Inquiry/Learning Cycle

Across All Phases
- How does each phase promote student learning of concepts, skills, and ideas?
- How are directions given to students? (Does the teacher use multiple modalities?)
- How and when is scientific language introduced?
- What role, if any, do journals play during this investigation?
- What questions will the teacher ask during each phase of the inquiry? (Does the teacher allow for an open response or direct answer?)

A. Exploration
- How is the investigation introduced?
  - ➤ How is it related to students' lives outside of school in a meaningful way?
  - ➤ How does the teacher solicit students' prior knowledge related to the investigation?

- How are the materials introduced?
  - ➤ How are the materials made available to students?
  - ➤ How are students instructed to use the materials?

B. Investigation and Data Collection
- How are the experiments introduced?
  - ➤ How does the teacher place the experiment(s) in the larger context of the investigation?
  - ➤ How does the teacher ask students to make and record predictions based on facts, experience, and prior knowledge?

- How does the teacher interact with the groups during the investigation?
  - ➤ How does the teacher survey and locate groups that are having problems with equipment or procedures?
  - ➤ How does the teacher suggest improvements in procedures (e.g., through explicit directions or by way of leading questions or comparisons to other groups)?

- How does the teacher help students demonstrate standards-based data collection and representation? (Is the teacher neutral on the data being collected? Is the data collected similar across groups? Can students redo their experiments and reproduce their results?)

C. Sense Making

- How does the teacher have students report their data or observations? (Are the results displayed for all to see? Are all groups' results presented? Is the data checked for accuracy?)
  - ➤ How does the teacher elicit comments from students?

- How does the teacher help students clarify the data or observations? (Does the teacher directly question some groups' results or have all students decide on what is valid and useable?)
  - ➤ How does the teacher deal with discrepant results?

- How does the teacher help students interpret the data?
  - ➤ How does the teacher help students isolate patterns or correlation?
  - ➤ How does the teacher solicit explanations from students?

- How does the teacher help students clarify explanations and conceptualizations? (Is the information represented accurately? Does the teacher use student analogies?)
  - ➤ How does the teacher address students' "misconceptions"?
  - ➤ How does the teacher adapt and build on students' attempted explanations?
  - ➤ In what ways does the teacher directly utilize the data collected to introduce formal scientific explanations?

II. Infrastructure

- How will materials be organized and managed to provide easy student access?

- How does the teacher manage the class?
  - ➤ What routines and procedures are in place to support maximum student learning and safety?
  - ➤ What are some strategies the teacher uses to support the smooth, ongoing flow of events in the classroom (e.g., transitions from one event to another, expectations for efficient student work)?
  - ➤ How does the teacher interact with students and groups of students?

- What does the teacher do to ensure positive group work outcomes?
  - ➤ How are expectations for group work communicated?
  - ➤ What strategies does the teacher use to ensure individual accountability in cooperative groups?

III. Assessment

- What should students know, understand, and be able to do?
  - ➤ What evidence will show that students understand?

- What assessment methods does the teacher use during each phase of inquiry (e.g., informal checks for understanding, observation or dialogue, quiz or test, open-ended prompt, performance task or project)?
  - ➤ How does the assessment match the opportunity to learn?

Studying the Inquiry Protocol

- Both partners silently read Phase 1 —exploration.

- Partner A summarizes description.

- Partner B gives examples of what that phase might look like in a classroom or instances of how the phase was exemplified during the science components of the training sessions.

- Process is repeated for Phase 2, and roles are reversed

- Repeat switching roles back and forth for Phase 3 —sense making

- Repeat switching roles back and forth for infrastructure and assessment.

Video Note-Taking Organizer

Phase of Inquiry: (Your viewing focus) _____	Infrastructure	Assessment

Stages of New Teacher Development

Anticipation and Excitement (Visions of Success): Before experiencing a new challenge, teachers have many concerns about what the change will entail. They may anticipate the potential to be successful. New teachers come in the beginning of the school year with many ideas of what they can accomplish.

Adjustment: Teachers adjust their initial perceptions of a situation as they experience it and learn about the reality of it.

Frustration and Struggle (Feelings of Failure): Change is hard. Teachers need to learn new skills, try new strategies, gain knowledge and resources—or at least apply them differently—and often change attitudes to succeed. Teachers experiencing change may feel as though, no matter how hard they are working, they are not experiencing the success they would like. Depending on the degree of challenge and the internal or external resources and interventions that are available, they may move through this period more or less quickly before starting to feel some success.

Survival and Renewal: Teachers have survived the lowest point on the cycle and have begun to experience success in coping and making changes. They have been able to take a rest from the frenetic daily struggle they have been experiencing and step back to plan beyond that day-to-day struggle.

Anticipation and Excitement (Visions of Success) revisited: Armed with the skills, strategies, knowledge, and resources, teachers have now gained and, with the success they have experienced, they again have a sense of excitement about upcoming challenges. For first-time teachers, this phase of anticipation is more reality based. They have reflected on the past year and begun to plan how to do things differently in the next year. For any teacher experiencing change, these high points represent the teachers' success in moving toward a greater focus on student learning.

Viewing Tool—DVD Note-Taking Form

Science Classroom: Sense-Making Phase/Infrastructure

Teacher	Students	Element of Sense Making

[Handout 5]

Stage of New Teacher Development _____

Need of teacher/mentee	Support strategy for mentor
1.	1.
2.	2.
3.	3.

Possible Areas of Focus for Observation: Sense Making

- What science concepts does this investigation develop?

- What kinds of questions might the teacher ask to elicit these understandings from her students?

- How does the teacher begin the sense-making session?

- What kinds of questions does the teacher ask?

- How does the teacher incorporate artifacts from their investigations in this sense-making session? Is the teacher neutral on the data being collected?

- What do you think students understand about these concepts? What are they confused about?

- Why do you think the teacher has students repeat the investigations?

Journal Prompts

1. As you think about implementing inquiry science in your own classroom, what areas will be good entry points for you and your students?

2. Which areas of the inquiry protocol will be most challenging to implement in your particular context? Why?

3. What is one thing you would like your mentee to work on?

4. How can you help him or her learn that?

5. What will progress look like?

Evaluation Form

Please choose from the following as a way of reflecting on our work together today:

1. One thing I'm thinking about differently as a result of today's session is …

2. One thing I am struggling with in thinking about today's session is …

Mentoring Journal

MENTOR: John

MENTEE: Mike

DATE:_____

TYPE OF MEETING
planning____
pre-observation conference____
post-observation conference_X_
other_____

Teaching Growth / Progress	Students have developed skills of questioning and observation.	**I. PHASES OF INQUIRY / LEARNING CYCLE** **A. Exploration** • How is this investigation introduced? • How are the materials introduced? • How are directions given? • How and when is scientific language introduced? • How does the teacher interact with the groups? • What role, if any, will science notebooks play?
Teaching Focus	To have students probe deeper with their questions Practice with inquiry	**B. Investigation and Data Collection** • How are investigations/experiments introduced? • How does the teacher interact with the groups? • How do students demonstrate actual, standards-based data collection? • Are students able to reproduce data?
Mentee's Next Steps	Take a look at different organisms Students compare and contrast Look at the timing of how and when to introduce vocabulary	**C. Sense-Making Discussions** • How does the teacher have students report their data or observations? • How does the teacher help students clarify the data or observations? • How does the teacher help the students interpret the data? • How does the teacher help students clarify explanations and conceptualizations?
Support from Mentor	Have a planning conference about introducing vocabulary Help Mike with guiding students from activity to activity and when to introduce vocabulary	**II. INFRASTRUCTURE** • How will materials be organized and managed to provide easy student access? • How does the teacher manage time? **III. ASSESSMENT** • What should students know, understand and be able to do? • What assessment method will the teacher use? • How will the teacher assess student progress during each phase of inquiry?

Mentoring Journal

MENTOR: Marian

MENTEE: Brenda

DATE:_____

TYPE OF MEETING
planning___
pre-observation conference___
post-observation conference_X_
other_____

Teaching Growth / Progress	Students are doing well with procedures and process skills
Teaching Focus	Questioning: Do my questions open up student thinking? Do I ask more directed or open-ended questions?
Mentee's Next Steps	Work on students' graphing skills Continue to work on questioning skills to focus students' thinking Focus questions on making ice cream vs. storing ice cream
Support from Mentor	Review potential questions for the next lesson with Brenda

I. PHASES OF INQUIRY / LEARNING CYCLE

A. Exploration
- How is this investigation introduced?
- How are the materials introduced?
- How are directions given?
- How and when is scientific language introduced?
- How does the teacher interact with the groups?
- What role, if any, will science notebooks play?

B. Investigation and Data Collection
- How are investigations/experiments introduced?
- How does the teacher interact with the groups?
- How do students demonstrate actual, standards-based data collection?
- Are students able to reproduce data?

C. Sense-Making Discussions
- How does the teacher have students report their data or observations?
- How does the teacher help students clarify the data or observations?
- How does the teacher help the students interpret the data?
- How does the teacher help students clarify explanations and conceptualizations?

II. INFRASTRUCTURE
- How will materials be organized and managed to provide easy student access?
- How does the teacher manage time?

III. ASSESSMENT
- What should students know, understand and be able to do?
- What assessment method will the teacher use?
- How will the teacher assess student progress during each phase of inquiry?

Mentoring Journal

MENTOR: Marian

MENTEE: Cindy

DATE:_____

TYPE OF MEETING
planning____
pre-observation conference____
post-observation conference_X_
other_____

Teaching Growth / Progress	Students are doing well with: • Graphing the data • Analyzing the data • In-depth thinking about their data
Teaching Focus	Questioning: Are the questions too leading? Am I inhibiting the inquiry by giving the students too much information?
Mentee's Next Steps	Review molecule motion Talk to colleagues for resources/ideas Focus on having students lead the discussion Look at the data again
Support from Mentor	Resources for teaching about molecular motion Help with planning

I. PHASES OF INQUIRY / LEARNING CYCLE

A. Exploration
- How is this investigation introduced?
- How are the materials introduced?
- How are directions given?
- How and when is scientific language introduced?
- How does the teacher interact with the groups?
- What role, if any, will science notebooks play?

B. Investigation and Data Collection
- How are investigations/experiments introduced?
- How does the teacher interact with the groups?
- How do students demonstrate actual, standards-based data collection?
- Are students able to reproduce data?

C. Sense-Making Discussions
- How does the teacher have students report their data or observations?
- How does the teacher help students clarify the data or observations?
- How does the teacher help the students interpret the data?
- How does the teacher help students clarify explanations and conceptualizations?

II. INFRASTRUCTURE
- How will materials be organized and managed to provide easy student access?
- How does the teacher manage time?

III. ASSESSMENT
- What should students know, understand and be able to do?
- What assessment method will the teacher use?
- How will the teacher assess student progress during each phase of inquiry?

SESSION 6
Handouts and Overheads

Reflections

- Share and discuss mentoring journals.

- What was the science concept taught? What phase of the inquiry cycle was taught?

- What is difficult about teaching this concept?

- What might we do differently to improve the next round of observations?

What?   What have I learned about science and observing or being observed?

So what?   What difference might this make to my teaching?

Now what?   What steps can I take to make the most of what I have learned?

[Overhead 2, Handout 2]

Observation Form

Time	Descriptive data	Questions, thoughts, interpretations

Sample Observation Form

Time	Descriptive data	Questions, thoughts, interpretations
9:00	T: Draw 3 critters of organism. Why 3? 3 students respond with ideas. T: Let me give you a hint. Draw them from different perspectives. Record all the details you can. #2. In writing explain what you observe. 3. Ask 5 good questions. Good questions—things you may not have the answer to; things that will help us learn. (Mike talking to a small group) Notice what you did…take what you think you know and turn it into a question. Has a conversation with students about playing dead. Ends with: Think about the conversation we had and turn it into a question.	I wonder why Mike didn't have this also in writing on a chart in the room. What are the criteria for a good question? If they've done this already, it might benefit the kids to have this posted so they can build on prior knowledge. Will this be an investigable question? Is it possible for these students to find out if this particular critter plays dead as a defense and why it might do this?

CST Triangle

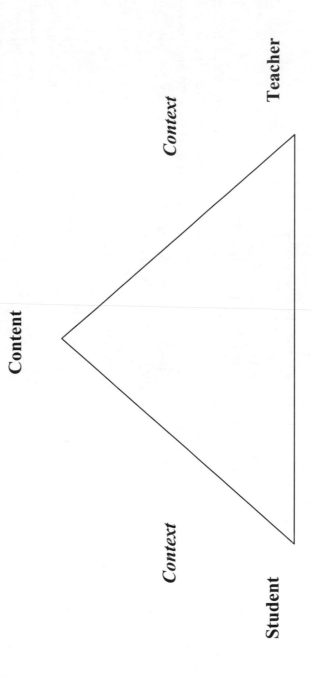

Content

Context

Context

Teacher

Student

Based on the work of Joseph Schwab (1909-1988), University of Chicago

[Overhead 4, Handout 4]

A Framework for Interpreting Observation

Using your observation notes, answer the following questions about the lesson. Provide evidence to support your answers.

- Did the lesson have a clear **purpose(s)**? What was the science being taught?

- How well did the **learning activities** support the purpose?

- How well did the teacher **understand the science** to be taught? What is your evidence?

- How did the lesson build on **students' prior knowledge**?

- How did the lesson **accommodate individual differences**?

- Did the opening of the lesson **motivate** students and **focus their attention** on the content or task?

- How did the **management** of materials, time, space, and behavior support the learning?

- Was there evidence of **student learning**?

- Which parts of the **inquiry protocol** do you think were used in the planning of this lesson?

- Based on your analysis of the lesson and what you know about the teacher and context, what would be an appropriate focus or goal for the teacher's development? Why? How would you go about helping him/her learn?

Feedback Focus

What?	How?	Why?

SESSION 6

[Overhead 6, Handout 6]

Evaluation Form

We're very interested in your initial feelings about the workshop. Please take a moment to comment below:

1. Please draw a face to show how you felt about the day. Add a speech bubble if you wish!

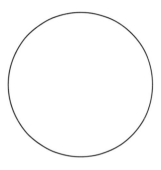

2. What were the positive aspects of the day?

3. What parts of the day would you change?

4. Any further comments or things we should know for upcoming sessions?

SESSION 7
Handouts and Overheads

[Overhead 1, Handout 1]

Developing Minicurricula for Learning to Teach

What	How	Success

Source: Book Tour presentation of Troen, V., & Boles, K. C. 2004. *Who's teaching your children?: Why the teacher crisis is worse than you think and what can be done about it.* New Haven, CT: Yale University Press. Reprinted with permission from Vivian Troen

[Overhead 2, Handout 2]

Issues Around Helping – 1

Think of an occasion when you:

1. Asked for help and received it

2. Gave help and it was accepted

3. Received help, but it was not requested

4. Offered help, and it was rejected

Source: Based on Little, J. W. 1990. The mentor phenomenon and the social organization of teaching. *Review of Research in Education*, 16, 297-351
Reprinted with permission from Judith Warren Little

[Overhead 3, Handout 3]

Issues Around Helping – 2

1. Was there an opportunity for reciprocity?

2. Did the offer of help limit the way the recipient could or should act?

3. Did the request for help show lack of ability or did it simply demonstrate the complexity of the task?

4. Did the acceptance of help threaten self-esteem?

Source: Based on Little, J.W. (1990). The mentor phenomenon and the social organization of teaching. *Review of Research in Education*, 16, 297-351
Reprinted with permission from Judith Warren Little

Protocol for Presenting Student Work

It would be best to bring samples of student work from the ice cream-making unit, if you are using it with your students. If not, be sure to select your student work samples from an inquiry-based lesson that represents the kinds of principles emphasized in that unit. Select three student work samples that represent a range of student understanding: one that shows a student struggling with the concepts, one that represents a student whose ideas are developing, and one that shows a student who has developed the targeted concepts and skills.

- Begin by describing the class in terms such as grade level, number of students, if there is inclusion, and English language learners.

- Give a brief summary of the lesson and where the lesson falls within the unit. Be sure to specify the part(s) of the inquiry learning cycle the lesson represents.

- Tell participants the science concepts and skills the lesson targets.

- Describe the students' task.

- Indicate whether students worked individually or in groups and the amount of time they had to complete the task.

- Share how you evaluated the work—for instance, by criteria or rubric.

[Overhead 4, Handout 5]

Reflective Journal Summary

Three things I learned today

Two questions I have

One new learning I will implement this month either in my teaching or my mentoring

[Overhead 5, Handout 6]

Evaluation Form

1. Which aspects of today's session were most beneficial for you?

2. Which aspects of today's session would you like to be changed? Please explain.

3. Please list other feedback you would like to share.

SESSION 8
Handouts and Overheads

[Overhead 1, Handout 1]

Reflections on Your Experience

1. What focus did you try with your mentee this month?

2. What happened?

3. What have you learned?

4. What questions do you have?

5. What are next steps?

[Overhead 2, Handout 2]

Fishbowl Exercise

Questions for observers

Observers in the outer circle sit opposite their partners in order to easily hear and see them. The observers should take notes about specific instances that illustrate their partners' skills in discussion. Some suggested questions are:

How often did your partner:

- State his or her opinion clearly so that others could picture it in their own minds?

- Offer assumptions on which her or his opinions and ideas are built?

- Provide observable data (facts, not opinions or anecdotes) to support a line of reasoning?

- Invite others in the group to add to his or her ideas?

- Ask questions about others' assumptions without invoking defensiveness?

- Ask questions that increased the group's understanding of someone's opinions?

- Listen without judgment (attentively and without interruptions) as others spoke?

Tuning Protocol

1. Introduction (5 minutes)

2. Presentation (15 minutes)

Presenter has an opportunity to share the context for the student work:

⇧ Information about students and class. How does this lesson fit into the unit?

⇧ Assignment that generated the student work, context for the assignment. What are some approaches you anticipated students would take?

⇧ Student learning goals: What are the underlying science ideas? Which phase of inquiry is the focus?

⇧ Samples of student work (one strong, one average, one weak)

⇧ Evaluation format—scoring rubric and/or assessment criteria

⇧ Focusing question for feedback

⇧ Participants are silent; no questions are entertained at this time

3. Clarifying questions (5 minutes)

⇧ Participants have an opportunity to ask "clarifying" questions (clarifying questions are matters of fact)

4. Examination of student work samples (15 minutes)

(Participants should use the "Student Work Analysis Recording Sheet," Handout 4)

⇧ Participants look closely at the work, taking notes where it seems to be in tune with the stated goals and where there might be a problem. Participants focus particularly on the presenter's focusing question

⇧ Presenter is silent; participants examine work silently

5. **Warm and cool feedback (15 minutes)**
   ⇧ Participants share feedback while the presenter is silent
   Warm feedback—how the lesson meets desired goals; cool feedback—may include disconnects, gaps, or problems. Participants offer ideas or suggestions for strengthening the work presented
   ⇧ Comments are primarily focused on the questions of the presenter
   ⇧ Presenter is silent and takes notes

6. **Reflection (10 minutes)**
   ⇧ Presenter speaks to those comments and questions he or she chooses while participants are silent
   ⇧ Presenter reflects aloud on ideas and questions that seemed interesting

7. **Debrief (5 minutes)**
   ⇧ Comments on the experience—how did the structure help achieve the goals?

Source: McDonald, J., Mohr, N., Dichter, A., & McDonald, E. 2003. *The power of protocols, An educator's guide to better practice*. New York: Teachers College Press
Reprinted with permission from the National School Reform Faculty Harmony Education Center

[Overhead 4, Handout 4]

Student Work Analysis Recording Sheet

Student	Evidence	Interpretation

[Overhead 5, Handout 5]

Implications for Classroom Practice

- What issues, insights, and questions did the discussion raise?

- What steps might the teacher take next with these students? What teaching strategies might be most effective?

- What other information would you like to see in the student work? What kinds of assignments or assessments could provide that information?

- How could teaching and assessment be better aligned with your picture of how this student learns?

- For presenting teacher: specific next steps

Reflective Journal Prompts

1. What are some of the benefits of examining student work with your mentee or with other teachers in your science department?

2. What will be most challenging about examining student work in your particular context? Why?

3. What kinds of support would you like from the facilitators?

SESSION 8

[Overhead 7, Handout 7]

Evaluation Form

1. Which aspects of today's session were most beneficial for you?

2. Which aspects of today's session would you like to be changed? Please explain.

3. Please list other feedback you would like to share.

SESSION 9
Handouts and Overheads

Inquiry Protocol

OVERVIEW

I. Phases of Inquiry/Learning Cycle

Teacher decides how to develop and implement units, lessons, and activities within the inquiry framework.

A. Exploration

Teacher introduces the inquiry.
Students get acquainted with a problem or phenomenon and decide what kind of experiments they will set up.

B. Investigation and Data Collection

Students carry out experiments and make measurements and observations.
Students collect data on their experiments.
Students report their measurements or observations.

C. Sense Making

Teacher and students analyze the usefulness and meaning of the data.
Teacher and students develop explanations and conceptualizations.

II. Infrastructure

Teacher decides how to manage materials.
Teacher decides when and how students will work with other students.
Teacher develops routines and procedures.

III. Assessment

Teacher determines what students will need to know and be able to do.
Teacher decides how and when he or she will assess students.

Teachers may choose some of these questions to use as a guide during coplanning or pre- and postobservation discussions, or to help focus observations.

I. Phases of Inquiry/Learning Cycle

Across All Phases
- How does each phase promote student learning of concepts, skills, and ideas?
- How are directions given to students? (Does the teacher use multiple modalities?)
- How and when is scientific language introduced?
- What role, if any, do journals play during this investigation?
- What questions will the teacher ask during each phase of the inquiry? (Does the teacher allow for an open response or direct answer?)

A. Exploration
- How is the investigation introduced?
  - ➤ How is it related to students' lives outside of school in a meaningful way?
  - ➤ How does the teacher solicit students' prior knowledge related to the investigation?

- How are the materials introduced?
  - ➤ How are the materials made available to students?
  - ➤ How are students instructed to use the materials?

B. Investigation and Data Collection
- How are the experiments introduced?
  - ➤ How does the teacher place the experiment(s) in the larger context of the investigation?
  - ➤ How does the teacher ask students to make and record predictions based on facts, experience, and prior knowledge?

- How does the teacher interact with the groups during the investigation?
  - ➤ How does the teacher survey and locate groups that are having problems with equipment or procedures?
  - ➤ How does the teacher suggest improvements in procedures (e.g., through explicit directions or by way of leading questions or comparisons to other groups)?

- How does the teacher help students demonstrate standards-based data collection and representation? (Is the teacher neutral on the data being collected? Is the data collected similar across groups? Can students redo their experiments and reproduce their results?)

C. Sense Making

- How does the teacher have students report their data or observations? (Are the results displayed for all to see? Are all groups' results presented? Is the data checked for accuracy?)
  - ➢ How does the teacher elicit comments from students?

- How does the teacher help students clarify the data or observations? (Does the teacher directly question some groups' results or have all students decide on what is valid and useable?)
  - ➢ How does the teacher deal with discrepant results?

- How does the teacher help students interpret the data?
  - ➢ How does the teacher help students isolate patterns or correlation?
  - ➢ How does the teacher solicit explanations from students?

- How does the teacher help students clarify explanations and conceptualizations? (Is the information represented accurately? Does the teacher use student analogies?)
  - ➢ How does the teacher address students' "misconceptions"?
  - ➢ How does the teacher adapt and build on students' attempted explanations?
  - ➢ In what ways does the teacher directly utilize the data collected to introduce formal scientific explanations?

II. Infrastructure

- How will materials be organized and managed to provide easy student access?

- How does the teacher manage the class?
  - ➢ What routines/procedures are in place to support maximum student learning and safety?
  - ➢ What are some strategies the teacher uses to support the smooth, ongoing flow of events in the classroom (e.g., transitions from one event to another, expectations for efficient student work)?
  - ➢ How does the teacher interact with students and groups of students?

- What does the teacher do to ensure positive group work outcomes?
  - ➢ How are expectations for group work communicated?
  - ➢ What strategies does the teacher use to ensure individual accountability in cooperative groups?

III. Assessment

- What should students know, understand, and be able to do?
  - ➢ What evidence will show that students understand?

- What assessment methods does the teacher use during each phase of inquiry (e.g., informal checks for understanding, observation/dialogue, quiz/test, open-ended prompt, performance task/project)?
  - ➢ How does the assessment match the opportunity to learn?

Trio Activity—Directions

1. Discuss what could be the reasons for the given behavior.

2. Using the language of the inquiry protocol—identify an area of practice that could be contributing to the problem.

3. Draft some questions or prompts that could help the new teacher understand the issue or its causes.

4. Determine what data you might be ready to collect to bring your mentee to a new place.

5. How will you collect this data?

6. Be prepared to share your group's discussion and coaching strategies with others at your table and the whole group.

[Overhead 3, Handout 3]

Mentoring Worksheet

1. Issue:

2. Possible causes
   -
   -
   -
   -

3. Questions to encourage mentee to recognize this as an important issue to consider:

4. Data to collect:

5. How will I collect the data?

[Overhead 4, Handout 4]

Myths or Misconceptions About Conflict

Harmony is normal and conflict is abnormal

FALSE. Conflict is natural, normal, and inevitable whenever people interact together.

Conflict is the result of personality differences

FALSE. Personalities do not conflict—people's behaviors conflict. Too often, we use "personality conflict" as an excuse to do nothing about the conflict.

[Overhead 5, Handout 5]

Conflict Management Styles

Read each of the techniques listed and decide whether you use that technique frequently, occasionally, or rarely during conflicts. If it describes a frequent response, write "3" next to the technique. If it is an occasional response, write "2." Write "1" if you rarely make the response described.

How do you usually handle conflict?

1. Use all your resources to win
2. Try to deal with the other person's point of view
3. Look for a middle ground
4. Look for ways to let the other person win
5. Avoid the person
6. Look for someone with more expertise
7. Insist that the other person do it your way
8. Investigate the problem from many angles
9. Try to reach a compromise
10. Give in
11. Change the subject
12. Bring in stronger authorities to back you up
13. Persevere until you get your way
14. Try to get all concerns out in the open
15. Give in a little; encourage the other party to do the same
16. Make quick agreements if only to keep the peace
17. Joke your way out
18. Get help from someone who can make a decision

19. Decide what must be done and do it yourself
20. Present alternatives to consider
21. Settle for a partial victory
22. Aim to be liked
23. Wait for the conflict to recede
24. Appeal to the people in charge

	I	II	III	IV	V	VI
	1	2	3	4	5	6
	7	8	9	10	11	12
	13	14	15	16	17	18
	19	20	21	22	23	24
Total for each column						

[Overhead 6, Handout 6]

Management Categories

I = Directing

II = Collaborating

III = Compromising

IV = Accommodating

V = Avoiding

VI = Appealing to Greater Authorities

Uses and Limitations
of Six Different Conflict Management Styles

I. **Directing**—When we do not, cannot, or will not bargain or give in. At times we are standing up for our rights and deeply held beliefs; we may also be caught in a power struggle and not see a way to negotiate to get our needs met.

    Potential Uses: when immediate action is needed; when safety is a concern; when you believe you are right.

    Potential Limitations: intimidates people, doesn't allow for others to participate in problem solving or to own the solution.

II. **Collaborating**—When we work with others to find mutually satisfying ways to get all of our needs met. We are interested in finding solutions and in building the relationships; the others are seen as partners, not opposition.

    Potential Uses: when there is time to develop satisfactory solutions; when the two parties see their needs as compatible.

    Potential Limitations: requires time, skill, and commitment from everyone to go through the process of building solutions.

III. **Compromising**—When we must give in on some concerns to get something else that we want.

    Potential Uses: when parties are of equal strength; when there doesn't seem to be a better solution; when the goals of each do not seem compatible.

    Potential Limitations: everyone leaves with some disappointment; significant issues may remain unresolved.

IV. **Accommodating**—When we yield to another person's point of view or needs.
Potential Uses: when the relationship is more important than the current issue; when we want to demonstrate a willingness to be flexible; when the issue can be postponed.
Potential Limitations: one begins to feel like a "doormat"; significant needs are never addressed; one loses moral authority.

V. **Avoiding**—When we withdraw from the situation or take steps to never confront it; behaving as though the situation were not happening; leaving it to others.
Potential Uses: when confronting is too dangerous or damaging; when the situation may resolve of its own accord; when we want to buy time and observe; when the issue is not very important.
Potential Limitations: important issues are never addressed; conflict may escalate or resurface later.

VI. **Appealing to Greater Authorities**—When we turn to those who we perceive as having more power and/or wisdom to solve our conflicts.
Potential Uses: when the parties are unable to reach any agreement; when appropriate laws and rules are already established; when we cannot adequately defend our own interests.
Potential Limitations: we lose control of the decision-making process; our issues get lost in bureaucracies; our issues are misconstrued; the authorities have prejudices.

Relationships Versus Issues

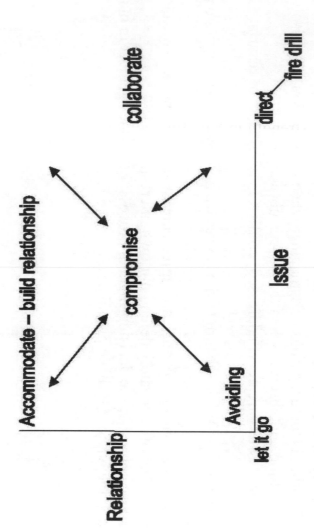

Reflective Journal Prompts

1. I feel most vulnerable during conflict when …

2. My greatest strength in handling conflict is …

3. Another conflict management style I want to develop is …

ASSESSMENT

QUESTIONING CYCLE:
Making students' thinking explicit during scientific inquiry

by Erin Marie Furtak and Maria Araceli Ruiz-Primo

Inquiry learning is an excellent way for students to get actively involved in science. It is essential that while inquiry learning is in progress, teachers continuously elicit students' conceptions and take action to move students toward learning goals (Black and Wiliam 1998; Bell and Cowie 2001; Duschl 2003).

The informative questioning cycle

During inquiry activities, teachers need to ensure their students are making progress toward learning goals. The informative questioning cycle can help teachers and students achieve these goals through simple techniques that can redirect and improve the quality of students' learning while it is in progress. The informative questioning cycle assists the teacher in making students' thinking explicit so the teacher can help students develop deeper understanding. The teacher begins by *eliciting* a response

from students that reveals the state of the students' understanding. Next, the teacher *recognizes* the response by reflecting it back to the student or asking another follow-up question. The third step involves taking some form of *action* to help the student move toward the essence of the activity or concept. The process can be thought of as a cycle to reflect the ongoing nature of informative questioning throughout inquiry activities.

Setting and aligning learning goals

Science inquiry units, like all other instruction, should have an ultimate goal to focus daily activities. Conversely, each daily activity should contribute in some way to reaching the

*Erin Marie Furtak is a research assistant in the School of Education at Stanford University in Stanford, California. **Maria Araceli Ruiz-Primo** is a senior research scholar in the School of Education at Stanford University in Stanford, California.*

Source: Furtak, E. M., and M. Araceli Ruiz-Primo. 2005.
Questioning cycle: Making students' thinking explicit during scientific inquiry. *Science Scope* 28 (5): 22–25

ultimate goal. The goals for an activity can consist of learning about a concept, such as density, or developing a process skill, such as using a balance or constructing a graph properly.

A useful analogy for thinking about daily activity goals is the preparation of food. Different ingredients are combined together because of their individual flavors, and the flavors of these ingredients together create the taste of the dish. Similarly, each activity in an inquiry unit must have an essence that, when combined with those from other activities, contributes to the ultimate instructional goal.

To determine what the essence of an activity might be, a teacher may ask: *What will students need to know and be able to do at the end of the unit? What are the concepts and skills students need to acquire during each of the activities to reach the goal?* If a certain activity does not contribute to the ultimate goal, the teacher should question why it is being included. While competencies that satisfy the criteria for the ultimate goal are not developed in a single activity, the contribution of each activity toward the ultimate goal should be clearly understood for each classroom activity.

Eliciting student responses
Eliciting questions serve the purpose of drawing out what students know and are able to do, and to help them learn how to share this information in an inquiry activity. Although teachers already use questions of this style, we suggest their purpose be changed to increase their informative potential. Asking students to provide evidence for an explanation, to share

FIGURE 1 Suggested questions for the eliciting stage of the informative questioning cycle

Types of eliciting questions Ask students to:	Examples
Provide evidence	What evidence do you have for your statement?
Formulate explanations	How do you explain the trend you see in the data?
Evaluate the quality of evidence	Based upon the methods you used, tell me what you think about the evidence you collected.
Interpret data or patterns	What does this pattern mean about the question you were asking?
Compare/contrast others' ideas	How is your idea different from Joe's idea?
Share observations	What did you observe as you were completing the activity?
Elaborate	What do you mean when you say that?
Take votes on ideas	How many of you agree with this idea?
Share everyday experiences	Have any of you encountered a similar phenomenon at home?
Use/apply known procedures	How do you draw a best-fit line?
Share predictions	What do you think will happen to the depth of sinking if I add more mass to this carton?
Define concept(s)	What do you think this word means?

FIGURE 2 Suggested responses for the recognizing stage of the informative questioning cycle

Type of recognizing question or statement Teacher:	Examples
Incorporates student's comments into the ongoing classroom conversation	Carlos is referring back to our discussion a few days ago, when we talked about how things sink when their density is greater than the medium.
Explores student's ideas	Alice, you suggested that the liquid looks very thick, so I'm going to pour it into this container so you can all see what she means.
Captures/displays student's responses	[Writes down students' responses on the board or easel for future discussion, comparing explanations, etc.]
Clarifies/elaborates based upon student's responses	You said things sink because they are heavy, but what are some heavy things that do not sink?
Takes vote to acknowledge student's ideas	How many of the rest of you agree with Blake?
Repeats or paraphrases student's words	You said the rock will sink because it has a greater density than the water?

FIGURE 3 — Suggested strategies for the acting stage of the informative questioning cycle

Type of acting question or statement Teacher:	Examples
Promotes argumentation	[Providing counter-examples, encouraging students to address each other and to cite evidence for their claims.]
Helps relate evidence to explanations	The evidence in the graph shows us that as mass increases, depth of sinking increases. It looks like mass is at least one factor that contributes to why things sink and float.
Provides descriptive or helpful feedback	We're trying to develop a universal explanation for why things sink and float. Right now, you're just telling me why things sink. The next step for you is to learn about the variables that control why things float, to put that together as we develop our explanation.
Promotes making sense	This object is sinking because it has a density of 1.2, whereas this object floats because it has a density of 0.9. The difference is in the density of water, which is 1.0. Things with a density greater than 1.0 sink, and things with a density less than 1.0 float.

predictions based upon previous experiences, and to describe patterns in their data are all ways that the teacher can elicit students' thinking. Figure 1 includes a list of eliciting questions. Teachers should use the list as a source of suggestions, tailoring the questions to fit their own activities.

Eliciting questions may be used at any point in a lesson. For example, the teacher may use eliciting questions to determine students' prior knowledge when introducing a new activity, or to focus class discussion around an important concept at the conclusion of an investigation. In some cases the teacher may choose to develop eliciting questions in advance by writing them into a lesson plan. At other times, such as when the students are collecting data, the eliciting questions may be more spontaneous and responsive to what the students are doing at a given time.

Recognizing student responses

Once teachers have successfully elicited students' responses, they can acknowledge what the student has said in some way. Recognizing students' responses makes clear the students' contribution during whole class conversations or small group work and allows students to agree or disagree with what the teacher or other students have said. It should go beyond repeating students' words verbatim; rather, teachers should incorporate the student's comment into the ongoing classroom discussion (O'Connor and Michaels 1993), or rephrase the comment so that the student can acknowl-

edge or take credit for their response (van Zee and Minstrell 1997). Note that this step in the cycle involves not only questions, but also statements the teacher can make in response to a student comment. Figure 2 lists these and several other types of recognizing responses.

In some cases, the student's response will be unclear or incomplete. After recognizing the response, the teacher should return to the first step in the cycle and ask the student another question to elicit further information, such as asking the student to elaborate on a previous response, which will allow the teacher to continue the cycle in a more informed manner to help the student progress toward the ultimate learning goal of the activity.

Acting on student responses

Because one of the goals of informative questioning is to continually move students toward ultimate learning goals, the third part of the cycle, acting, involves using students' responses as an opportunity to advance student learning based upon information attained in the previous two steps. In our research, it is this final step that we found to be most powerful in terms of student performance on different types of assessments because it leads students to learn the essence of the activity, which is necessary for them to reach the ultimate goal.

For example, if conflicting responses have been elicited from students, the teacher can encourage students to discuss their conceptions with each other by providing counter-examples or explanations, allowing students to argue their sides, *always based on evidence*. This process will help students evaluate for themselves what might be the best explanation and come to an agreement based upon the quality of the evidence provided to support the explanation.

The teacher can also act more directly in the form of providing meaningful feedback to the students. High-quality feedback consists of three steps: explaining the goal, explaining to the student where they are with respect to the goal, and suggesting steps the student might make to achieve that

| FIGURE 4 | Sample learning conversation that demonstrates informative questioning during small group work. |

Ms. Yin's example	Role of question
Ms. Yin: Can you predict the displaced volume of this floating object now that its mass is known?	Making a prediction *(eliciting)*
Rich: I think that displaced volume will be about the same.	
Ms. Yin: How do you know? Can you show me some evidence from your graph that supports your prediction?	Asking Rich to provide evidence *(eliciting)*
Rich: I'm not sure. I don't see anything.	
Ms. Yin: Can you give me an example from your data table?	Asking Rich to provide an example *(eliciting)*
Rich: Well, I have this container of sand, and it floated. Its mass is 11.84 grams, and it displaced 12 ml of water.	
Ms. Yin: So Rich, you're telling me that the volume of displaced water is equal to the mass in this container of sand, based upon the data you collected in the activity?	Revoicing Rich's statement, noticing that Rich seems to understand the essence of the activity, but does not generalize from one object to the trend on the graph *(recognizing)*
Rich: Yeah.	
Ms. Yin: Okay Rich, you're telling me the relationship for this one object. Ayita over here is saying something else—I heard her say a few minutes ago that the graph shows that mass and displaced volume are equal for all objects. Rich, why don't you use your graph to see whether you agree or disagree?	Promoting argumentation *(acting)*

goal (Sadler 1989). There are a number of strategies teachers can employ in this final step (Figure 3).

Informative questioning as assessment for learning
In the context of inquiry, telling students whether their responses are right or wrong focuses them on whether they have the correct answer, rather than allowing them to explore how they are coming to know what they know (Duschl 2003). Teachers should avoid the pattern of asking a question, receiving a response from a student, evaluating the answer, and moving quickly to the next question. The targeted actions possible in the informative questioning cycle can help students to understand more clearly how they are thinking about concepts and processes and to lead them to reach inquiry learning goals. A sample conversation incorporating the entire cycle is provided in Figure 4. The sample is based upon the investigation "Sinking and Floating Objects" from the Foundational Approaches to Science Teaching curriculum (Pottenger and Young 1992), in which students are provided with a collection of sinking and floating objects and are asked to determine if it is possible to predict the volume of water a floating object will displace if its mass is known.

Informative questioning helps the teacher become aware of the students' thinking and provides a basis for action. Practicing informative questioning is practicing high quality informal formative assessment, which improves student learning. We have evidence that teachers using informative questioning had students who performed better on several types of formative embedded assessments (e.g., predict-observe-explain, open-ended questions) and summative assessments (e.g., performance assessments, predict-observe-explain, open-ended questions) aligned with the learning goals of their curriculum (Ruiz-Primo and Furtak 2004). ∎

References
Bell, B., and B. Cowie. 2001. *Formative assessment and science education*. Dordrecht, Netherlands: Kluwer Academic Publishers.
Black, P., and D. Wiliam. 1998. Assessment and classroom learning. *Assessment in Education* 5 (1): 7–74.
Duschl, R. A. 2003. Assessment of inquiry. In *Everyday assessment in the science classroom*, eds. J. M. Atkin and J. E. Coffey, 41–59. Arlington, VA: NSTA Press.
O'Connor, M. C., and S. Michaels. 1993. Aligning academic task and participation status through revoicing: Analysis of a classroom discourse strategy. *Anthropology and Education Quarterly* 24 (4): 318–335.
Pottenger, F. M., and D. B. Young. 1992. *The local environment: FAST 1. Foundational approaches to science teaching.* 2nd ed. Honolulu: Curriculum Research and Development Group.
Ruiz-Primo, M. A., and E. M. Furtak. 2004. *Informal formative assessment of students' understanding of scientific inquiry.* In *Assessment for reform-based science teaching and learning*, ed. A. C. Alonzo (Chair). Symposium conducted at the American Educational Research Association annual meeting, San Diego.
Sadler, D. R. 1989. Formative assessment and the design of instructional systems. *Instructional Science* 18 (2): 119–144.
van Zee, E., and J. Minstrell. 1997. Using questioning to guide student thinking. *The Journal of Learning Sciences* 6 (2): 227–269.

[Overhead 10, Handout 11]

Evaluation Form

1. Which aspects of today's session were most beneficial for you?

2. Which aspects of today's session would you like to be changed? Please explain.

3. Please list other feedback you would like to share.

Session 10
Handouts and Overheads

Read and React

Appoint a timekeeper/facilitator who keeps the process moving. This protocol is designed to build on each other's thinking, rather than to enter into a conversation. Timing is important. Each round should last about seven minutes

1. Create groups of four participants. Choose a timekeeper.

2. Each participant silently identifies what he or she considers to be the most significant idea addressed in the article.

3. When the group is ready, a member of the group identifies the point in the article he or she thinks is most significant and reads it out loud to the group. This person does not explain why he or she chose this point.

4. The other three participants have one minute each to respond to that idea.

5. The first participant then has three minutes to explain why he or she chose that point and to respond to his or her colleagues.

6. The same pattern is followed until all four members have had a chance to have the last word.

Source: Averette, P. (2003). *Save the last word for me.*
Reprinted with permission from the National School Reform Faculty Harmony Education Center

[Overhead 2, Handout 2]

Mentoring Reflections

- Share and discuss conference logs.

- Did you focus on a particular phase of the questioning cycle? If so, which one?

- What are some challenges involved with making students' thinking explicit?

- What might you do differently to improve the next round of observations with your mentee?

What?   What have I learned about the questioning cycle and mentoring?

So what?   What difference might this make to my teaching or the teaching of my mentee?

Now what?   What steps can I take to make the most of what I have learned?

Mentor Roles

1. What are the three mentor roles that took up most of your time?

2. What are some specific tasks you performed in this role?

3. Choose one role you would like to use more of next year.

4. Identify some of the things you might do in that role.

[Handout 3]

Mentoring Practice Growth Plan

- Think about what you can (are able to, willing to) change to go to the next level in at least one area of your mentor practice.

- Think about what support (resources, skills, knowledge) you need to achieve that level. How can you get that support?

SESSION 10

[Overhead 4]

Benefits of Mentoring

- Retention goes up

- Attitudes improve

- Feelings of efficacy and control increase

- Wider range of instructional strategies is demonstrated

[Handout 4]

Evaluation Form

Science Mentoring Check-in

1. What did you like best about the science mentoring sessions?

2. What did you learn that you can apply to your science teaching and mentoring?

3. Indicate one thing that would have most improved these sessions.

4. Any other comments?